Bomber Command Pilot

Bomber Command Pilot

From the Battle of Britain to the Augsburg Raid

Gerald Sherwood

First published in Great Britain in 2021 by
Pen & Sword Air World
An imprint of
Pen & Sword Books Ltd
Yorkshire – Philadelphia

Copyright © Gerald Sherwood 2021

ISBN 978 1 39901 249 2

The right of Gerald Sherwood to be identified as Author of this work has been asserted by him in accordance with the Copyright, Designs and Patents Act 1988.

A CIP catalogue record for this book is available from the British Library.

All rights reserved. No part of this book may be reproduced or transmitted in any form or by any means, electronic or mechanical including photocopying, recording or by any information storage and retrieval system, without permission from the Publisher in writing.

Typeset by Mac Style
Printed and bound in the UK by CPI Group (UK) Ltd, Croydon, CR0 4YY.

Pen & Sword Books Limited incorporates the imprints of Atlas, Archaeology, Aviation, Discovery, Family History, Fiction, History, Maritime, Military, Military Classics, Politics, Select, Transport, True Crime, Air World, Frontline Publishing, Leo Cooper, Remember When, Seaforth Publishing, The Praetorian Press, Wharncliffe Local History, Wharncliffe Transport, Wharncliffe True Crime and White Owl.

For a complete list of Pen & Sword titles please contact

PEN & SWORD BOOKS LIMITED
47 Church Street, Barnsley, South Yorkshire, S70 2AS, England
E-mail: enquiries@pen-and-sword.co.uk
Website: www.pen-and-sword.co.uk

Or

PEN AND SWORD BOOKS
1950 Lawrence Rd, Havertown, PA 19083, USA
E-mail: Uspen-and-sword@casematepublishers.com
Website: www.penandswordbooks.com

This book is dedicated to the memory of:

Wing Commander John Seymour Sherwood DSO DFC*
aka Flap
15.3.18 to 8.2.73
and
Bernice Sherwood, nee Gain
8.1.21 to 12.3.83

Love and grateful thanks must go to:

My wife Hilary for so much encouragement, and countless hours spent seeking out information during online searches through National Archive records.

My son Simon for searching out items of useful information and contacts, as well as proofreading an early draft version.

My daughter Katie for her stated belief that I would have a way of finding the right words to tell Flap's story.

My two grandsons, Aaron and Travis for their interest, help, and words of encouragement.

Contents

Author's Foreword		ix
Chapter 1	Early Days	1
Chapter 2	How to Fly and Fight	8
Chapter 3	Flying with 76 Squadron RAF	12
Chapter 4	The Trained Become Trainers	17
Chapter 5	During the Phoney War	21
Chapter 6	Preparing for Action	28
Chapter 7	Into the War with 144	33
Chapter 8	Meeting the Manchesters	47
Chapter 9	Manchesters Go to War	54
Chapter 10	Daylight Raid on German Cruisers	67
Chapter 11	New Year, New Babies, New Ideas	76
Chapter 12	The Most Daring Raid So Far	88
Chapter 13	The Cost of the Daring	97
Chapter 14	Into Enemy Hands	105
Chapter 15	Home Life Continues	115
Chapter 16	Settling in to Kriegie Life	119
Chapter 17	To The North Compound	125
Chapter 18	Over the Wooden Horse	134

Chapter 19	Kriegie Life Continues	137
Chapter 20	Kriegie Winter of 1943/44	141
Chapter 21	The Great Escape	146
Chapter 22	Unexpected Aftermath	150
Chapter 23	Then Life Went On	157
Chapter 24	The Long March	162
Chapter 25	Train Terminus Tarmstedt	171
Chapter 26	To the End of the Road	177
Chapter 27	Kriegie Exodus	184
Chapter 28	Making a Family Home	189
Chapter 29	Into the Air Again	196
Chapter 30	Off to Civvy Street	203

Last Words — 212
Famous Raids — 213
Bibliography — 214
Index — 215

Author's Foreword

I was born on 16 January 1942; bang in the middle of the Second World War! More specifically, I was born a son to Squadron Leader John Seymour Sherwood DFC*, and his wife Bernice Sherwood, at Lingfield, Tor-o-Moor Road, Woodhall Spa, Lincolnshire; bang in the middle of the territory of Bomber Command of the Royal Air Force.

At the time of my birth, my father was an already twice decorated bomber pilot, serving with 97 Squadron of Bomber Command, where amongst the squadron personnel he was affectionately known as "Flap". At that time, stationed at nearby RAF Coningsby, Flap and the crews of 97 Squadron had just been informed that they would be the second of only two RAF squadrons, so far appointed, to each receive delivery of one of the very first two brand spanking new, Rolls-Royce Merlin powered, four engine Avro Lancaster Bombers to familiarise themselves with.

Then, almost exactly three months after my birth, on 17 April 1942, Flap, my father, disappeared! I did not miss him of course, for I was obviously far too young to know that he had been there in the first place.

Now fast forward seventy years to the year 2012. Until then, there had been a prolonged reluctance to erect a memorial acknowledging the brave deeds of the 55,573 RAF Bomber Command aircrew members who had lost their lives during the Second World War, and whose number included many drawn from the countries and dominions of the Commonwealth and the British Empire, as well as early volunteers from the USA and escapees from the German occupied countries of Europe.

In the four-year run up to the Queen's 2012 Diamond Jubilee, there was a long overdue resurgence of interest in Bomber Command, all prompted by the determined campaigning of surviving Bomber Command aircrew veterans, backed up by fund raising celebrities, journalists, and industrialists. That campaign finally culminated in a fully funded decision to build a Bomber Command Memorial.

Accordingly, the spectacular Bomber Command Memorial, depicting the larger than life figures of a bomber crew in their full flying gear, was erected on its covered plinth in London's Green Park, in time for its unveiling by Her Majesty the Queen as part of her Diamond Jubilee celebrations.

For me, the general resurgence of interest in Bomber Command, in the run-up to 2012, was further prolonged by the later announcement that a Bomber Command clasp was being made available for Bomber Command veterans, or their descendants, to attach to their relevant 1939–45 war medals. I promptly applied for Flap's Bomber Command clasp and, soon thereafter realising that I could also relatively simply secure a copy of his RAF Service Record, I eventually completed an application for that also.

I have always collected anything available to me from relatives and friends pertaining to Flap and our family history in general, inclusive of books, documents, photos and news cuttings. Subsequent receipt of Flap's Service Record in 2014 immediately enhanced the information value of my collection, by ensuring that all events of which I already had knowledge could then be placed into their correctly dated context and location. The Service Record also provided sufficient dates and information to enable me to draw very specific additional information from the various RAF squadron records held in the National Archives.

When I wrote this in 2019, after approximately five years of on/off writing and research, the 100th Anniversary of the formation of the Royal Air Force had passed during March 2018, and the 75th Anniversary of the Victory in Europe (VE Day) was fast approaching in May 2020. It therefore seemed apt that I am now in a position to relate the circumstances in which Flap, my father, having already witnessed and partaken in many well-known events during his earlier war service, then took part in a very early major Lancaster daylight bombing raid, which is coincidentally also the earliest raid shown on the Royal Air Force's list of the twelve most famous Second World War bombing raids. That early Lancaster raid, now commonly regarded, on a scale of daring do, to be on a par with the later Dam Busters raid.

So, for those that have previously asked me – "What did happen to Flap?" – I have chosen to relate his story within the biography that follows herewith…

Chapter 1

Early Days

Flap, my father, was born on 15 March 1918 in Suez, Egypt, on the southern end of the Suez Canal. He was not Egyptian! He was not called Flap either; that came much later! However, it is most convenient for me to call him Flap from the outset, being the nickname that would in later life be bestowed upon him.

In 1918, Egypt was a British Protectorate, and Flap's birth was soon registered with the British Vice Consulate, Suez, in the name of John Seymour Sherwood; the British son of British subjects, who were both working for British interests abroad.

Flap's father, Captain Charles Alexander Sherwood, who preferred to be called Alec as a shortened version of his second forename, was Chief Officer of the Eastern Telegraph Company's Cable Ship (CS) *Cambria* when he first met Flap's mother and was leading a very adventurous life in that occupation. In 1914, the CS *Cambria* was busy laying and repairing telegraphic cables in the depths of the oceans around the world, that work being necessary in order to create, preserve, and extend the undersea electronic communications network between Great Britain and the rest of the world in general, but most particularly between the countries of what was then the British Empire.

Flap's mother, Violet Anna Rose Sherwood, was a daughter of Captain Roger Edward Pertwee, a marine pilot of the Suez Canal Company, who was responsible for ensuring the safe passage of ships through the Suez Canal. Violet, for some reason, also preferred to be called by her second forename. She was therefore known to all as Anna on and around the Suez Base, where she was working as a nurse prior to and during the First World War. Anna had caught the eye of Captain Sherwood as his ship frequently passed through the Suez Canal on its way to the East Coast of Africa, India and the Far East. On such trips, the cable ship would pause mid-passage at Suez, whilst taking on supplies and giving the crew some well-earned leave between their undertakings. During such stopovers, it was the custom for the ship's officers to socialise with the officers of the Suez Canal Company and their families; amongst whom of course was Captain Pertwee and his family, who lived at Port Tawfik at the southern end of the Suez Canal.

Romance soon followed the friendship between Alec and Anna. A Marriage Certificate issued in the Registration District of the British Consul, Port Said, and signed by the British Consul, shows that on the 6 October 1915, at the British Consulate, Port Said, the marriage of Alec and Anna was solemnised by special permission of the Secretary of State. A church wedding followed the next day at St. Saviour's Church, Suez.

Following her marriage, and whilst Flap's father Alec continued to roam the high seas laying and maintaining those important telegraphic cables, Anna remained living near to her family at Port Tawfik, until sometime well after the arrival of her first born son, who was, of course, Flap.

It is commonly believed that the date of one's birth, and various planetary alignments at that time, can inexplicably define one's life destiny and the degree of good fortune, or otherwise, that might arise therein. In that respect, 1918, the year of Flap's birth was to prove itself to be a very influential year, the collective events of which would converge and conspire to fatefully determine many of Flap's future adventures for him. For on the 20 March 1918, a mere five days after Flap's birth, 144 Squadron was also born in Egypt, at Port Said, on the northern end of the Suez Canal; that birth being in preparation for the imminent formation of the Royal Air Force, by a merger of the old Royal Flying Corps and the old Royal Naval Air Service, that soon followed on 1 April 1918. Further, before the end of that same year, on 11 November 1918, the First World War ended with a commitment to commence the negotiations that would eventually lead to the signing of the Treaty of Versailles. However, the most detrimental and punitive of terms that were forced upon Germany by the Treaty of Versailles were such that Germany was then left in a state of festering resentment. That German resentment was destined to then determinedly fester for the first twenty-one years of Flap's life, until it would eventually lead directly to the outbreak of the Second World War.

During his early childhood, Flap with his mother Anna, and from 1920 a younger brother Tony (Anthony), were lucky enough to live in several exotic locations around the world. Such locations were usually close to whatever area father Alec's ship was based in at any one time, and included Port Said, Malta and Cape Town, South Africa.

Exotic locations ensured an early start to many exciting childhood adventures for Anna's children, and I can recall Anna, who was of course later to become my grandmother, relating to me how Flap, together with his younger brother and friends, had watched the local children of Cape Town make improvised canoes out of discarded metal roof sheets. Anna's boys and their friends had then scrounged some discarded roof sheets for themselves and copied the process that they had previously seen. That process involved forcibly shaping each roof sheet around a tree trunk, or similar shape, before hammering, shaping, and folding the ends together to form the pointed bows and stern of the canoe. The middle sides of the folded sheet would then be forced open and held apart by rough wooden planks that then formed the seats, as well as serving as stretchers to maintain the required open-topped shape of the canoe. The end joints were then sealed and waterproofed with hot pitch, as it was poured from a tin can that had been heated over a campfire.

Flap developed an ever-increasing lust for adventure, mainly fired by the reported deeds that appeared to be incidental to his father's maritime occupation. For whilst Captain Alec Sherwood was a Master Mariner, whose opinion was often sought on maritime matters, and was frequently requested to sit on boards of enquiry following maritime disasters, he had, on several occasions during his career, taken various ships in his own charge into precarious situations, usually in order to successfully rescue the crews of other vessels that had been wrecked or stranded.

Thus, when Alec was home on leave, he was able to inspire his sons and their friends with true stories of exciting and dramatic real-life adventures upon the high seas.

In March 1928, with Flap then aged ten, preparations for some serious schooling had to be considered. Mother Anna and her two boys therefore moved back to England to seek an English education for the boys, and a home was established at Kingston upon Thames. In the meantime, father Alec continued with his seafaring adventures, steaming the seven seas whilst continuing to lay and maintain the all-important telegraphic cables.

During the school holidays of December 1932, Flap and the family at home were amazed to read a *Daily Express* newspaper headline on 27 December that carried an account of how Captain Alec Sherwood, at that time master of the cable ship *Norseman*, had on Christmas day, believe it or not, just masterminded the rescue of the whole thirty-one man crew of the British steamer *Newborough*.

In extremely stormy conditions, the *Newborough* had been holed and driven on to a reef near Morant Cay, sixty miles from Kingston, Jamaica. The rescue, under Captain Alec's direction, and in very difficult conditions, lasted over several hours involving small boats and his crewmen in some rather unorthodox but successful manoeuvres, before the *Newborough*'s crew were all safely aboard the *Norseman*. The rescued crewmen were then landed safely at Kingston, Jamaica, on Boxing Day.

The first that Anna and her boys knew of the *Norseman* crew rescue was when they saw a headline in the *Daily Express* newspaper that had been delivered through their front door. It would appear that the news had quickly reached the *Daily Express* in England, via the various press agencies that were directly linked to the worldwide news through the very cables that Captain Alec had been busy laying around the world. The newspaper had simply arrived long before the news later reached the Sherwood family home at Kingston upon Thames, in the form of a more personal hand delivered message.

Sometime later, the *Lloyds Gazette* of 21 September 1933 reported that the rescue by the *Norseman* had resulted in a Board of Trade Award for Captain Sherwood in respect of his ingenuity and seamanship, with gallantry awards going to two of his own crew for their particularly brave acts that had secured the absolute success of the rescue.

Flap had just left school in December 1935, and was living at Woodbines Avenue, Kingston upon Thames, when there were further reports of his father's adventures. A *Daily Sketch* headline on 5 February 1936 shouted out "Cable Ship Saves Nine Lives". At that time, Alec Sherwood was Captain of the Cable Ship *Lady Denison Pender*, and Commodore Captain of Cable and Wireless Limited, then with a total of over thirty-five years loyal and distinguished service on cable ships under his belt.

The all white painted *Lady Denison Pender*, which apparently was able to carry one hundred and sixty miles of undersea telegraphic cable, had been en route to Singapore when this rescue occurred. The cable ship, whilst on the high seas, had come across an open boat containing nine emaciated souls who had survived from a party of twelve. Those survivors, it seems, were apparently from a shipwrecked dhow, and had been in the hot sun without food or water for several days. The report stated that the survivors were taken aboard for revival and medical treatment from the *Lady Denison Pender*'s own doctor, before they were later landed ashore on the ship's arrival at Singapore.

The *Daily Sketch* report concluded with remarks from Mrs Anna Sherwood, at home in Kingston upon Thames, who on being told of the successful rescue supposedly exclaimed: "I am delighted to hear of it, and so pleased that someone has managed to have contact with my husband. For I have not seen or spoken to him for at least two years, and that was when he had just carried out a similar rescue".

The Kingston upon Thames home situation suited Flap well, and he had always been able to find plenty of adventures of his own in the various Thames riverside surroundings. He had enjoyed his school holidays on or about the river Thames, where there was always plenty to do and something to watch. Summertime was the best, when nature on the river and the river traffic were both at their busiest. He could fish and explore from his very own proper canoe, non-corrugated, and follow his general interest in bird life and nature, whilst just generally messing about on the river.

However, as Flap grew on into his teens, it was his own natural feelings that led him to become very conscious of other interesting occurrences on the river. Those feelings prompted him to keep an eye at all times on the privately owned motor yachts and cruisers that continuously plied up and down the river Thames. Those boats were usually on pleasure joyrides, aimlessly to anywhere and back, at any time from Easter until the late autumn during a fine weather season. His naturally occurring interest was not so much the motor yachts themselves, but rather the daughters associated with such family-owned craft. For if girls were aboard a cruising boat, they were usually posing on the fore deck in the sunshine. Sometimes, the girls would even wave to him, as they motored leisurely by from one mooring place to another.

One particular boat that had caught Flap's attention was the motor cruiser *Bernice*. That boat was owned by a Lieutenant Commander Kenneth E. Gain, retired First World War Royal Navy veteran, who was at that time a controlling director of a chain of London butchery shops, but also a Royal Navy Volunteer Reserve officer. During the boating season, the Gains' boat could appear moored up anywhere on the navigable stretches of the Thames and, through familiarity over a period of time, Flap had struck up a friendship with the Gain family aboard that boat. The family consisted of the skipper and his wife, plus three children, of which the eldest was a daughter, Bernice, after whom the boat would also appear to have been named, and it was Bernice that had caught Flap's interest!

During his senior school years, spurred on by his father's tales of his adventures, Flap gradually developed a lust for some adventures of his own. He had harboured thoughts of following his father, Alec, into an exciting maritime career. However, during his schooldays he found that he had been heavily influenced by reading the many published tales of the daring exploits of the First World War pilots of the Royal Flying Corps, and very early on the thought of flying had appealed to him. He had therefore joined his school's Officer Training Corps (OTC). By the time he left school in December 1935, he had, through the school's Officer Training Corps, obtained sufficient educational and basic Royal Air Force (RAF) Proficiency Certificates as to enable him to apply for a short service commission, as an officer in the Royal Air Force.

Fortuitously, during 1935 and onward, the RAF had developed a government sponsored rapid expansion plan in response to the already perceived threat of a coming war with Germany. That threat being generated by Germany's continued seething discontent over the settlement terms that had been imposed on that country by the conditions set out in the Treaty of Versailles, as signed at the end of the First World War. Therefore, having grown up with and followed the progress of the RAF in existence for the whole of his life and, as pilots might soon be urgently required in the event of war, Flap had decided that he would apply to fly with the RAF.

Following Air Ministry interviews and medical examinations, within days of his eighteenth birthday in March 1936, Flap's application to the RAF was accepted in principle, subject to his ability to first successfully obtain a private pilot's licence, by learning to fly with Air Service Training Ltd (AST), at the Civil Flying School, Walsgrave on Sowe, Ansty, Coventry, before his commission could take effect.

On returning home from his Air Ministry medical examination, Flap related the following risqué anecdote to some of his young friends concerning the doctor that had conducted his medical examination. The bizarre behaviour of the examining doctor had been drawn to Flap's attention by other medical attendees as they queued for attention. It would appear that the doctor in question, instead of keeping a pencil in the customary position behind the ear, preferred to keep the blunt end of his own very special pencil stuck firmly in his mouth. Apparently, the special pencil was first used for poking each candidates' various body parts, sores, moles and other mysteries, before then being used for the parting of buttocks and, as a finale, the raising of male members and their under adornments for inspection of their respective parts. Finally, when the necessary comments and reports had been written on a form with the sharp end of the pencil, the blunt end of the pencil was then returned once more to the corner of the doctor's mouth. The boys had shown great delight in expressing their pity for the doctor's wife, especially if she was used to greeting her husband with a welcoming kiss on his arrival home each evening.

Following receipt of an Air Ministry letter of confirmation dated 3 June 1936, Flap's flying training commenced at Air Services Training (AST), Ansty on 6 July 1936. The school was situated on the site of what is now Coventry airport.

That particular flying school was a commercial operation of international repute and was actively training men drawn from countries of the whole world to be pilots. In retrospect, it now seems more than likely that Flap would, at that time, have been training to fly amongst foreign contemporaries, any of whom might well have, unknowingly to Flap, later become his enemies during the European hostilities that would soon follow.

By the end of the month, Flap had successfully obtained his Pilot's Licence and a Certificate of Competency to fly private flying machines of all types. Licence number 10095 was signed and issued on 30 July 1936.

Having satisfied the Air Ministry's conditions of appointment, a notice in the *London Gazette* of 22 September 1936 noted the granting of a four-year Short Service Commission, as Acting Pilot Officer on probation, to J.S. Sherwood, effective 31 August 1936.

Correspondence already received had:

- Allocated Flap's further training to No.11 Flying Training School, RAF Wittering, Peterborough, with effect from 12 September 1936, for the purpose of learning aerial warfare flying techniques.
- Notified him of the amount of his first month's pay to be credited to his new bank account.

Chapter 2

How to Fly and Fight

On arrival at No.11 Flying Training School, RAF Wittering near Peterborough, Flap was billeted in the officers' mess. There, he was sure that his adventures would begin. There, he found like-minded trainee RAF pilots to socialise with. And most of all, there, he found much more businesslike aircraft to tangle with, and all very much more exciting than the very sedate machines at the civilian flying school.

Photographs in Flap's old 1936/37 photo album illustrate the types of fixed undercarriage open cockpit biplanes then in use by the Royal Air Force, and consequently in use at the RAF Flying Training School. Those were nearly all made by the Hawker Aeroplane Company and based on designs from the 1920s, mainly single engine Hawker Harts and Hinds, in service as light bombers; but also similarly styled Hawker Furys, in service as fighters. In fact, the Fury was then listed as the fastest fighter of its day with a top speed of 200mph.

The design and construction method of the tubular metal airframes of those early Hawker aircraft was considered revolutionary at the time, especially when compared to the flimsy airframes of previous generations of biplanes that had relied on canvas covered wooden spars and stringers that were held rigid by stressed cables. By contrast, the Hawker tubular metal airframe design was so light and strong that it went on to form the basis of the airframe for the Hawker Hurricane fighters of the coming war.

The Hawker aircraft airframe design must have been extremely tough overall, for further pages of Flap's photo album reveal all manner of what his notes simply describe as "crack-ups". Most pictures are of upside down crashed aircraft that still have solidly complete wings and airframes, whilst only the undercarriages or propellers are missing or broken.

One of Flap's action photos is of a Hawker biplane coming in to land, still airborne, but with the wheels of its broken undercarriage trailing along the ground some feet below the aircraft; all left dangling on the ends of broken undercarriage struts and brake cables that are shown to be still loosely attached beneath the plane. That particular plane must have hit an obstruction that ripped its undercarriage right off its mountings, to leave it suspended beneath. Further photo shots reveal that this particular aircraft was flipped over on to its back by the drag of the trailing undercarriage as it landed; yet it had still managed to remain otherwise intact, and the pilot had survived.

Handwritten notes under the pictures of "crack-ups" explain the nature of the event, being predominantly "collision with a ground target"; such events probably caused by over exuberant flying in the keenness of the pilot to hit the relevant ground target with gunfire. Night landing exercises also made considerable contributions to the "crack-up" score sheet.

There is one particular crack-up photo in Flap's collection that must have caused him and his contemporaries to pause for some considerable thought, for the aircraft concerned had hit the ground with such mighty force that, in the utterly trashed small parts tangle of smashed up crew and aircraft, it must have been extremely difficult to separate the mortal remains from the mangled mechanical and structural remains.

It could then have occurred to Flap that he might possibly experience even worse sights during the expected hostilities that he and his contemporaries were endeavouring to train for.

To train pilots in the skill of live aerial bombing and live gunnery, without endangering the local civilian populations of the Wittering and greater Peterborough area, the training aircraft and their pilots were relocated to a remote target range. To this end, and to avoid the further threat that would be associated with trainee crews having to continually fly over the countryside from their home base to a distant bombing range with live practice bombs and live ammunition aboard, the RAF had refurbished, expanded, and developed the fairly remote old First World War RAF station known as North Coates. Situated south-east of Grimsby and Cleethorpes, the North Coates development provided ample accommodation for both the visiting flying men and their flying machines. Whilst the actual airfield was known as North Coates, the firing and bombing range was situated on the coast at North Coates Fitties. "Fitties" apparently being the local old Lincolnshire dialect name for the nearby extensive and deserted sand dunes, sand flats and salt marshes, all situated on the Lincolnshire coast at the mouth of the river Humber. There could not have been a more suitable location than those

Fitties for confining the processes of practice bombing, live firing, and the incidental wrecking of expensive aircraft, all within the one remote and isolated locality.

Social life at the Flying Training School was good. Much time seems to have been spent on the competitive modelling of miniatures of the aircraft that the trainees were gaining their flying experiences on. In those days, all such modelling was by the scratch modelling method. Whereby, in the absence of the pre-designed off the shelf modelling kits of today, that enclose all the necessary plans and materials, all scratch models had to be self-designed, before then building them from whatever raw materials and scrap that could be found lying around available to be fashioned into shape for any particular improvisational purpose.

Additionally, when on training detachment to North Coates and the coast with their aircraft, the trainee aircrew could let off some steam by generating a seaside holiday atmosphere in their spare time. On one such occasion a mob of the trainee pilots built what might possibly have been the biggest sandcastle ever to appear on the Lincolnshire coast, using the coal shovels and coal buckets scrounged from their accommodation to shovel up and carry the sand. It was suggested that the resultant castle would have been suitable for use as a ground target for the following day's bombing practice. However, the trainees had not thought about the tide, and the castle did not of course survive for the following day's activity.

The trainees' competitive spirits were cultivated by frequent arrangements for teams of trainee pilots to play friendly rugby matches against local teams from Cleethorpes, Grimsby and the surrounding areas. As well as assisting physical fitness of the trainees, these activities provided a post-match social life and some valuable integration with the local inhabitants of the surrounding Lincolnshire countryside. Such events usually entailed much after match banter in the saloon bar of a local pub; for whilst the locals regarded the trainee pilot officers as "acting and talking a bit posh", the trainees for their part were fascinated by the local accents, rural slang words and phrases. Sometimes after a few pints, members of the opposing teams would attempt to mimic each other's mannerisms, accents and catch phrases. At the end of one such post-match pub session, when the trainees had apologised that they were to leave early in order to be up at dawn next day for an exercise, one of the local lads shouted, "you mean at sparrow fart old boy"! On seeking an explanation for the shouted terminology, the trainees soon realised that "sparrow fart" was the local countryside slang for dawn, based on the assumption that, like most warm-blooded creatures when they first awake, the little sparrows must surely let loose a little wind! Now most young men appreciate a good farting joke, so thereafter, the new phrase was adopted by the trainees for every early start to their daily training programme. Many other amusing local Lincolnshire slang words were also deliberately incorporated into the trainees' own vocabulary.

On 7 January 1937, having completed his initial military flying training, Flap was awarded his wings (the double winged flying badge worn on the left breast of RAF pilots' uniforms). By 22 May 1937, Flap, then designated a probationer as Acting Pilot Officer J.S. Sherwood, was posted out to 76(B) Squadron, RAF.

Chapter 3

Flying with 76 Squadron RAF

No. 76 Squadron was stationed at RAF Finningley, south-east of Doncaster (later becoming Robin Hood Airport, serving Doncaster and Sheffield, but having no other Sherwood family connection).

The squadron had been disbanded following the First World War, but re-formed on 12 April 1937 under a planned RAF expansion scheme. That squadron then needed pilots and aircrew to fly their newly arrived Vickers Wellesley long-range medium bombers, and the prospect of flying those new aeroplanes initially instilled some great excitement amongst the newly trained pilots.

By today's eye, the Wellesley was a strange looking aircraft, and even in 1937 it was very different to any other aircraft that the new crews had previously flown in. It looked rather odd, being larger than the Hawker aircraft that the crews were used to, with a very wide wingspan and two separate cockpits. However, it was a design progression, being a monoplane with only one pair of wings instead of two, and it actually had a retractable undercarriage that reduced the drag of the airflow on the aeroplane when flying. This plane also utilised a new confidence boosting metal basketwork airframe design that supposedly improved its overall constructional strength. The overall design was from the drawing board of Barnes Wallace, who would, in the coming war years, achieve great prominence for his further inventive technical innovations, such as development of the bouncing bomb used on the famous Dambusters Raid.

However, after the early euphoria of flying the new machines, it soon became apparent to the crews of 76 Squadron that the Wellesley was not really going to be up to the job of being a serious medium bomber: or even a light bomber for that matter. There were multiple reasons for the craft's failure to impress. Namely, a lack of speed in spite of retractable wheels; a bomb carrying capacity limited to a 2000lb total payload in the minute bomb carriers situated beneath its wings; a lack of defensive weaponry, with only one fixed forward firing gun and one rear facing swivelling gun of limited firing arc. The Wellesley was therefore soon labelled as obsolete, but for the time being continued to be flown in order to keep the crews occupied with their disciplines of formation flying, cross-country navigation and honing of their bombing skills on the available ranges.

In the meantime, Flap's probationary period expired on 6 July 1937, and he immediately received confirmation of his appointment as a fully commissioned Pilot Officer.

Following confirmation of his appointment, Flap decided that he could afford to celebrate his progress by spending some of the money he had managed to save from his first year's pay on a car. Having enjoyed the thrill of the open cockpits of the training aircraft that he had been previously flying, he decided that he really wanted an open top sports car. However, the limited amount of cash that he could actually afford forced him to compromise with the purchase of a second-hand 1932 Standard Nine Avon Coupe soft-top, Reg. No. GX 3765. With this more lowly purchase he still expected to feel the wind in his hair when driving.

Life for Flap was generally progressing well. For during 1936 the Gain family's Thames cruiser *Bernice* had been replaced by a much larger 50ft twin screw motor yacht called *Matoya* and, from the 1937 boating season, photos of the eldest Gain daughter, Bernice, appeared in Flap's photo album pages, together with photos of Flap himself relaxing aboard the *Matoya*. Good all-round progress in 1937 then!

With the 1937 August Bank Holiday fast approaching, on the first Monday of the month as it was then, and being on 2 August in that particular year, Flap sent a hastily written postcard home to the Little House, Kingston upon Thames to announce:

"See you all Friday night – Bank Holiday – till Tuesday morning. I hope this is O.K. by you. 'Am keeping fine, no more crack-ups yet.
Love to all:- John
(P.S. 10 to 11 o'c. Can't tell yet)."

Come Friday, 29 July, the Standard Nine Avon behaved well, and Flap enjoyed the long carefree drive down from Finningley, out to the A1 Great North Road, straight down to the great metropolis, and then on to the Sherwood family home at The Little House, Kingston upon Thames.

Following an enjoyable break of three full days, spent with family and all the friends that mattered to him, Flap and the Avon had then confidently set out on a return journey to Finningley that turned out to be somewhat less relaxing than the downward trip. Herewith is the story in Flap's own words, as subsequently related to his pilot friends:

> "I was belting up the A1 at a fair old rate of knots when, as I was rounding a shallow left-hand bend, I was faced with another car coming towards me, also at a fair old rate of knots, but on its wrong side of the road whilst itself trying to overtake a third car. My right of way was therefore completely blocked! Then, by sheer luck, I spotted a garage forecourt on my left-hand side, and my reflexes automatically prompted me to swerve my car into it. However, I was going far too fast to attempt a halt on the loose gravel and cinder covered surface of the forecourt, for fear of skidding away out of control. Luckily, the forecourt was empty, so I just kept the car going at full tilt in a cloud of dust, gravel and cinders, straight over the garage forecourt and back onto the road once more. Meanwhile, the offending car shot past me still on its wrong side of the parallel road. Following the event, I did not look back! If the garage attendant had eventually appeared on the forecourt in the expectation of serving a customer with petrol, there would merely have been a lot of scattered gravel and a large dust cloud hovering in the air. I reckon my flying reflexes really paid off, for my little car had absolutely flown over the forecourt; and of course, I avoided what could have been a fatal crack-up!"
>
> "Bloody hell," piped up one of Flap's associates.
>
> "What if your overtaking opponent had decided to seek refuge from you by swerving into the other end of that same garage forecourt? The attendant would then have had a bigger mess than dust and disturbed gravel to worry about!"

Flap was left to ponder over the thought that perhaps he should not have tempted providence by mentioning crack-ups at all on his post card home.

Confirmation of Flap's permanent commission was announced to the rest of the world during that same bank holiday week, with the customary notice appearing in the *London Gazette* of 3 August 1937.

Once back at Finningley, the practice flying of the Wellesleys continued in earnest. However, in the expectation that any future war might be fought in a similar fashion to the previous war, the crews from 76(B) Squadron were soon sent in small groups on Gas Defence courses at RAF Uxbridge. Flap's course took place from 30 August to 9 September 1937.

Then back to the flying disciplines of being a pilot again. Those disciplines then included tight formation flying practice to suit the theory of the day that, in the event of attack by enemy fighter aircraft, bombers in tight formation would be able to cover each other by collectively putting up a greater barrage of defensive gunfire than any isolated and easily picked off solitary aircraft.

During November of 1937, Flap found himself going back to North Coates and the Fitties again. This time for bombing practice with the Wellesleys and looking forward to a reunion with some of his Lincolnshire rugby pals and being able to introduce them to his 76 Squadron pals. The North Coates hangars were not large enough to offer shelter to the much larger Wellesleys. Therefore, when not flying, those aircraft had to endure all sorts of winter weather, simply picketed out under basic tie-on canvas covers for the duration of their stay.

Returning from North Coates, the squadron fell into a winter routine that reduced flying dramatically during bad weather. The next significant event to cause any excitement for the aircrew came in early March 1938. *Flight Magazine* visited RAF Finningley with the express purpose of composing an article for the magazine on the history of 76(B) Squadron, from its original creation during the First World War as part of a defensive line against bombing attacks by the marauding German Zeppelins of that war.

The lead page of the magazine article carried a photograph of the sixteen pilots of the squadron lined up against the broadside of a Wellesley. Flap is noted as P/O J.S. Sherwood who, in this photo, looks so young that the magazine reader might wonder whether he should be there at all. He would, however, have been just short of his twentieth birthday when that photo was taken.

The strange thing about the *Flight Magazine* article was that it attempted to talk up the attributes of the Wellesley aircraft and 76(B) Squadron equally, in spite of the fact that the aircraft had been declared obsolete almost from the outset. The magazine article comments that, "No. 76(B) Squadron impresses the visitor as a very good unit with a very good aeroplane. What is the Wellesley going to do in the future? It is a machine of promise, and we await with great interest to see that promise fulfilled." An even stranger comment when the Wellesley's successor, the twin engine Vickers-Armstrong Wellington, which it was planned would be capable of carrying twice the bomb load as the Wellesley over a far greater distance, was due for first delivery to the RAF by the end of October of that same year. However, the Wellesleys did allow the squadron to continue honing their flying and navigational skills in the meantime.

During 1938, with the threat of war already looming large, it would appear that the Vickers Wellesleys were maybe not quite so antiquated looking as some of the aeronautical behemoths that Flap discovered still lurking around inside the hangars of many of the RAF bomber squadrons based around the English countryside. It appeared that the development and manufacture of modern defensive fighter aeroplanes had for some time deliberately been taking preference over the development and manufacture of the more offensive bomber aeroplanes. Or so it seemed to Flap, for the modern, fast and agile Supermarine Spitfire and Hawker Hurricane low wing monoplane fighters had already entered service with RAF Fighter Command during mid-1938; probably at the expense of starving the bomber squadrons of more suitably designed modern aircraft.

Chapter 4

The Trained Become Trainers

The daily routine of 76(B) Squadron was next broken for Flap on 25 May 1938, when he was temporarily detached onto a ten-week Air Navigation Course at Martin's School of Navigation, Shoreham. It was obviously no good being a bomber pilot if you could not, in any condition of light or weather, find your way out from your base to the specified target to be bombed, and then back to your base again. There were no navigational aids for 1937/38 bomber aircraft, only maps, compasses, sextants, and unreliable weather forecasts. Navigation therefore had to be carried out by observational map-reading and the principles of dead reckoning, aided by knowledge of, and familiarity with, the major landmarks and the coastal features of your own home territory, in addition to as much comprehensive knowledge of the geography and distinguishing features of the territory likely to be held by your potential enemy, wherever possible.

Martin's Navigation had a fleet of de Havilland Dragon Rapide aircraft. Those were the ideal form of observational platforms and flying classrooms in which to fly the trainees on practical navigational and observational exercises, in parties of five, including the Rapide pilot and navigational instructors. The navigation course lasted just short of three months, to mid-August, and Flap passed out with a 67.9 per cent pass rate, and the qualification to then instruct others on navigational techniques.

Flap's 1938 periods of leave appear to have been spent near home, on and around the river Thames again! Some further romantic progress must have been made, for more pictures of the Gain family and their boat *Matoya* appear in the photo album, together with pictures taken of the village of Sonning on Thames, and of the Gain family home, Turpins, situated in that same village.

Somewhere towards the end of 1938, Flap and one of his fellow junior officers acquired a German Shepherd puppy each.

Flap named his puppy Simba, and his associate named his Roger. Both dogs lived on station, and soon became more or less part of the staff and much in demand by those stationed at Finningley, especially when required to pose beside the squadron's aircraft for some interesting pictures to be sent home.

The Vickers Wellesleys closed the year of 1938 with a surprise for the RAF pilots who were flying them on a daily basis. On 5 November 1938, three specially modified Wellesleys with a position created for an extra crew member and some additional fuel capacity built in, had set out on a long-distance flight from Ismailia, Egypt. Two of the Wellesleys had then flown 7,158 miles non-stop to Darwin, Australia, within forty-eight hours, thus setting a non-stop long distance flying endurance world record. Unbelievably, this non-stop endurance record remains to this year (2020) in respect of a single engine aircraft.

In Flap's photo album, the end of 1938 was celebrated by a large picture of the Middlesex Yacht Club's Annual Dinner Dance. That photo, featuring those seated at the Gain family's table, included Flap seated next to Bernice Gain. Much better progress being made, with Flap's feet then well under the dining table!

Following Christmas celebrations and on into the new year of 1939, 76(B) Squadron's routine flying duties continued with navigational exercises, formation flying practice and bombing practice. However, for Flap, there were some further celebrations during January. He found himself promoted to the rank of Flying Officer, coincidentally with his short service commission being extended to a period of six years. Both the promotion and the short service period extension were declared effective from 31 January 1939 and were then listed in a later edition of the *London Gazette*, on 28 February 1939.

By March 1939, following Germany's annexation of Czechoslovakia, it was becoming patently obvious that an eventual outbreak of war with Germany was going to be unavoidable. At the same time, it was equally obvious that RAF Bomber Command would be short of the trained crews and machines that would be required in the event of war. Rapid expansion of the RAF bomber force was therefore required. In those circumstances, the Air Ministry soon decided that such trained and experienced RAF bomber crews that did exist would have to act as instructors, for the purpose of rapidly training the additional pilots and crews that would soon be required.

Accordingly, it was announced that, from early April 1939, 76(B) Squadron and its crews should prepare themselves to be transformed into No. 16 Operational Training Unit (OTU) of No. 5 Group Bomber Command; one of several Operational Training Units then being created to cater for the rapid RAF expansion required.

Great relief then followed for the pilots and crews, with the announcement that their Vickers Wellesley aircraft were to be replaced with immediate effect by new and more modern aircraft. Then, as fast as the Wellesleys could be ferried away from Finningley, sixteen of the latest brand-new Handley Page Hampden twin engine bombers, numbered L4137 to L4152, were flown in.

The first of the Hampdens to arrive at Finningley was numbered L4149. The Hampdens were of an all-metal construction, based on a 1936 design specification for a fighter bomber, but later classed as medium bombers on delivery to the squadron. They were designed for a four-man crew, and capable of carrying a bomb load of 4000 pounds. Twice the crew size and twice the bomb load of the Wellesleys.

There was a pleasing and more businesslike shape to the Hampden's front end, although appearing to be of a very narrow profile; whilst the rear end of the plane had a rather fragile appearance about its long thin tail boom. These unusual shapes would soon lead to the Hampden being called "the flying tadpole", on account of the long thin tail boom; or alternatively called "the flying suitcase", on account of the tall slim front section of the fuselage that was supposedly designed to reduce drag. However, the Hampdens were a definite improvement on the outgoing Wellesleys and were soon proved to be strong and rugged aircraft that were basically very manoeuvrable and easy to fly; possibly too easy to fly, for the Hampden did have a weakness that some pilots discovered too late! For reputedly, and as I understand it, if insufficient care was exercised when putting a Hampden into a climbing turn to the right, it had a habit of skidding sideways away from the direction of turn, which immediately caused a loss of lift from the wings that were not designed to fly sideways in the first place. The greatest loss of lift from the right side then caused the nose and right wing of the aircraft to fall away sufficiently far enough as to flip the aircraft over into an uncontrollable spin that could prove fatal for pilot and crew if not corrected before the aircraft reached the ground. This phenomenon was arguably attributed to the unusual shape of this aircraft's long slim tail boom and small rudders, which led to a lack of keelage (resistance to sideways movement through the air when turning).

Some Avro Anson twin engine trainers were also flown into the squadron. Those aircraft were useful to provide flying classrooms suitable for navigational and observational training, whilst also serving as a more sedate aircraft for the initial stages of converting some incoming single engine trained pilots to fly twin engine aircraft.

At roughly the same time as 76(B) Squadron were being re-equipped with their Hampdens, the squadrons of other Bomber Groups had also received, or were in the act of receiving, a steady supply of new twin engine medium bombers, such as Vickers Wellingtons, Armstrong Whitworth Whitleys and Hampdens. All of which were based on design specifications that had been formulated in 1936.

The exceptions to the above twin engine developments were some Bomber Command squadrons that had already been flying Bristol Blenheim twin engine bombers since a very early first delivery to the RAF in late 1936. This aeroplane having arisen from a privately commissioned design for a civilian aircraft that, on first flight in 1935, was immediately of such impressive performance that the Air Ministry became interested in its further development and order for military use as a fast light bomber.

No sooner were 76(B) Squadron's Hampden aircraft settled in, than Flap was sent out on attachment to No.1 Air Observation School (Navigational School) from 24 May 1939. There was an urgent need to devise and finalise a standard navigation course for all the operational training units then being created in response to the urgent need for bomber crew expansion; and to that end, as well as developing the course, it was necessary to create a force of navigational trainers capable of implementing the standard course across all of the new operational training units.

Flap was still attached to No.1 Air Observation School in the autumn of 1939, when as a direct result of the invasion of Poland by Hitler's German forces on 1 September 1939, Britain and France immediately declared war on Germany on 3 September.

Meanwhile, the outgoing 76(B) Squadron Wellesleys were not simply scrapped. They were eventually transferred to the Middle East Royal Air Force, where their long-range capabilities would come to the fore during the East Africa and North East Africa campaigns of 1940/42, against the Italian occupation of Abyssinia.

Chapter 5

During the Phoney War

From the September 1939 declaration of war and onwards, Flap continued with his duties at the Air Observation School, whilst watching the alarming events that were unfolding across Europe.

With Britain and France having declared war on Germany, there then followed a protracted period of time when very little seemed to happen. During this period, quickly dubbed "the Phoney War", German forces regrouped and adjusted to some of the strategic lessons that they had learned in Poland. At the same time their forces replenished their expended stocks of munitions and armoured equipment, and also found uses for the armour and equipment that had been captured from both Czechoslovakia, and, most recently, Poland.

Following the end of the First World War, the French and most of Europe had been left acutely aware of Germany's festering discontent over the restrictive conditions imposed on them by the Treaty of Versailles that had ended that war. Subsequently, the French, in order to defend themselves against any future invasion threat from Germany, had built the strongly fortified defensive Maginot Line along their border with Germany. However, the Maginot Line did not extend along the French borders with Luxembourg and Belgium to meet the English Channel. It was considered by the French that the mountainous and forested Ardennes regions of that border area would, in any case, be impenetrable to any form of mechanised invasion.

On Britain and France's Declaration of War on Germany, Britain had put arrangements in hand for the immediate transport of an initial 158,000-man British Expeditionary Force (BEF) and all its equipment to France. Dispatch of this Force was specifically designed to reinforce the French forces with their defence against the German invasion that was imminently expected to thrust itself against France's border with Germany.

To further bolster Allied forces, Britain had also dispatched ten squadrons of RAF Bomber Command's Fairey Battle single engine light bombers to France; a total of 160 aircraft if all ten squadrons were then at full strength. Those aircraft were provided in the expectation that they would be able to support French and British ground forces by harassing the expected German advance and its supporting supply lines from Germany.

The Fairey Battle had been built as a single engine, all metal monoplane, light day bomber. Based on a 1936 design destined to replace the Hawker Hart biplanes that Flap had encountered and flown at No.11 Flying Training School at RAF Wittering in 1936/37. The Battle carried a crew of three, comprising pilot, bomb aimer/observer, and a radio operator/rear gunner, with a thousand-pound bomb load beneath. Defensive armament consisted of one fixed forward firing .303 machine gun in a wing, and one swivel-mounted machine gun in the rear gunner's cockpit.

Meanwhile, throughout the Phoney War and the inactive stand-off in France that followed, the British Government had ordered RAF Bomber Command to bomb German military targets and shipping only, and to strictly avoid bombing the German mainland. Conversely, the Germans avoided bombing the British mainland. This state of détente was maintained on the basis that both sides were in fear of provoking a bombing backlash that neither side was really ready for. Britain as yet lacking aircraft and equipment good enough to match the rearmed Germany and its modern air force; and Germany needing to regroup and replenish its forces following the massive expenditure of arms and equipment during their invasion of Poland.

At the outbreak of the war, Bomber Command had consisted of some fifty-three bomber squadrons. Of those, the ten Battle squadrons had now been sent to France and twenty squadrons set aside to become the Operational Training Units that would be needed to train the extra crews required for the rapid expansion of the RAF bomber force. This left only twenty-three home-based squadrons available for active bombing operations; totalling approximately 350 bombers only, again depending on the actual aircraft strength of the individual squadrons and whether each was then at full strength.

The aircraft of the RAF home based operational bomber squadrons at this time consisted of the previously mentioned twin engined heavy bombers, such as the Handley Page Hampden, Vickers Wellington, Armstrong Whitworth Whitley, together with the Bristol Blenheim light bombers – all of pre 1936 design, and first flown during 1936 or immediately before. For the foreseeable future, there was little chance of obtaining more modern, heavier, or more powerful bomber aircraft. Government and Air Ministry policy during the mid-thirties had previously decided that the greater bulk of British aircraft manufacturing effort should be directed towards the production of a defensive fighter force, in anticipation of a desperate fight to defend Britain against the massive bombing onslaught that was expected to precede any German invasion attempt against Great Britain.

The RAF were well aware that the German Air Force was already well battle hardened, following practice obtained during Germany's actions to support Franco during the earlier Spanish Civil War, and more latterly from supporting the German blitzkrieg driven occupation of Poland that had prompted Britain and France's declaration of war in the first place.

Meanwhile, Britain's Royal Air Force was as yet un-bloodied!

Because of the lack of electronic or radio navigational aids in the 1930s, it was assumed that Britain's bomber force would fly by day to assist the process of navigation to targets and back by map-reading and dead reckoning navigation. Accordingly, the bombers were supposedly designed to defend themselves by flying in a tight formation in the belief that they would, when attacked, be able to protect each other against enemy fighter aircraft by putting up a massive impenetrable hail of fire from their collective multiple .303 machine gun arrays.

From his safe educational position at the Air Observation School, Flap watched with incredulity as Bomber Command confidently set out on their early daylight bombing operations against German shipping, only for the RAF bombers to be well and truly bloodied by the shocking events that occurred during their early anti-shipping bombing sorties around the North Sea and the Baltic Sea.

On 29 September 1939, 144 Squadron were ordered to send eleven Hampdens on an armed reconnaissance over the Heligoland Bight in order to search out and act against targets in the form of German shipping. Of the eleven aircraft, five under the squadron's commanding officer were detailed to search for shipping to within sight of the German coast. However, having left their base at Hemswell, this whole section of five aircraft and the twenty crew members aboard them disappeared; never to be heard from again. It was assumed that all five aircraft had been shot down into the sea by German fighter aircraft.

It later transpired that the Germans had quickly discovered that the RAF Hampden's gun installations, as well as being limited in number, also had very limited arcs of fire. This limitation created an unreachable blind fire area beside and very slightly ahead of the Hampden's wings, that none of the Hampden's guns could train on. Also, and unfortunately for the Hampden crews, some types of German fighter planes had a side firing gun installation, that assisted the German fighter pilots with their discovery that they only had to fly in formation with a Hampden, right in its blind firing spot, to then be able to shoot the Hampden down using the side firing gun; and all at no risk to themselves!

Then on 14 December 1939, out of twelve Wellington bombers sent on a daylight raid against German warships, five were shot down by enemy fighter aircraft.

And then again on 18 December 1939, out of twenty-four Wellington bombers on a daylight bombing raid against the German Navy, twelve Wellington aircraft, and all their crews aboard, were lost to enemy fighters.

The RAF could ill afford that loss rate of men and machines!

By comparison, and having been banned from bombing the German mainland during the Phoney War, the only early raids permitted over the German mainland during that period were all night time propaganda raids, designed to surprise the sleeping population of Germany by dropping leaflets only. The leaflets were designed to remind the population of Germany of the folly of war and suggested that the citizens of Germany could terminate the war by simply rising up to overthrow Hitler. Seemingly plainly ridiculous to Flap that the citizens of Germany would have ever had a cat's chance in hell of influencing Nazi policy, it was soon decided that the leaflet drops were a complete waste of paper, for logic would have indicated that during the hours of darkness over Germany, most of the leaflets would have been dropped over the fields and forests of the open German countryside where nobody would find them anyway. However, the leaflet raids did establish that there were very few losses or interceptions of British bomber aircraft whilst flying over enemy territory during the hours of darkness.

To avoid continuation of the unacceptable daytime bomber losses, it was immediately ordered that future bombing raids by heavy bombers over enemy territory would have to be carried out under the cover of darkness whenever possible.

Work was also put in hand to urgently develop night-time navigational aids capable of assisting night-time target finding, followed by navigation of a safe return to base.

As previously noted, it had been agreed even before the outbreak of war that there would be an obvious need to massively expand Royal Air Force Bomber Command. Hence the creation of the Operational Training Units (OTUs). Now most urgently, the British Government, in conjunction with the Air Ministry, put forward a blueprint for a British Commonwealth Air Training Plan, designed to recruit and train the additional aircrews that would be required for this expansion. The resultant British Empire Air Training Agreement was finally signed in late December 1939, to allow the plan to commence operations.

Thereafter, the British Commonwealth Air Training Plan enabled trainee aircrew, drawn from Great Britain, the Commonwealth and the British Empire in general, to all undergo their flying and aircrew training for the RAF, without interference, in the enemy free skies over the Dominions of the Commonwealth, namely Canada, Australia, New Zealand and South Africa. Rhodesia, although not a dominion, also joined the scheme.

Under the Commonwealth Air Training Plan, some of the Dominions even pre-formed their own complete air force commands and/or squadrons. Those would then eventually fly with the RAF; e.g. the Royal Canadian Air Force, with forty-eight squadrons attached to the Royal Air Force by the end of the war. This arrangement brought a hugely welcome boost to RAF manpower. Many individual citizens of the British Empire and the United States, together with escapees from German occupied countries, also found their own way direct to Great Britain or Canada, before volunteering for training and service under the scheme.

As for operational training at home, it was confirmed that existing well trained pre-war pilots and aircrew, such as Flap and his contemporaries, would, for the time being, have to remain serving as trainer/tutors to cater for the expected massive expansion of incoming trainee pilots and aircrew yet to come forward, both from Great Britain and those arriving part trained under the Empire Training scheme.

Accordingly, on 2 March 1940, Flap was promoted to the rank of Acting Flight Lieutenant. Then, on 4 April 1940, he was returned to 76(B) Squadron, which by then had been fully converted into 16 Operational Training Unit, Bomber Command, and re-located to a different base at Upper Heyford.

It was generally accepted that it was at 16 Operational Training Unit that Flap's nickname was first bestowed upon him, most likely by fellow officers and men on the training team, who had noticed the student crews referring to him as "Flap" during their conversations among themselves. Then, on seeking an explanation for the nickname from students, it became obvious that the name came about as a result of Flap's habit of treating every task as urgent and referring to the matter as "a flap": e.g. "There is a flap on to train more aircrews in order to man the increasing number of new bombers coming into service, etc".

Also, to give the trainee bomber crews a real sense of belonging within Five Group of the Bomber Command force that they were about to serve with, and also to be sure of holding their attention, Flap found it most useful to make his practical instructional sessions and lectures as memorably entertaining and humorous as possible. This was achieved by Flap's development of an act that, without ignoring the potential seriousness of any failure to observe standard orders or procedures as explained to trainees, included plenty of RAF slang terminology and buzz words to make them feel at home.

Some joke standing orders worked into Flap's lecture routine included: "The avoidance of Newton at all times when flying"; on the basis that it would always be Newton's laws of gravity that could bring you down to earth with a bang. Also: "The avoidance of going for a Burton (Burton's ale, drink)"; a euphemism for being dead, especially if brought down in the drink (sea).

As the trainee crews that passed through Flap's hands were exclusively destined for the squadrons of 5 Group of Bomber Command, all to be stationed in Lincolnshire, Flap found it was popular among the trainees to also include some instruction specifically on Lincolnshire dialect and slang. Recalling his own days at North Coates, when rugby was regularly played against the Lincolnshire lads of Cleethorpes and Grimsby, most of the following local slang had been learned from after match pub visits. The immediate favourite slang words among the trainees were of course "sparrow fart" (dawn), which was always a well-received joke. This was closely followed by the fact that whilst they would be "frim folk" (strangers) in Lincolnshire to start with, after some considerable "chattle" (talk) with the locals over a few beers, they would probably end up as the best of friends before they were all "well slewed and weltered" (drunk). If they then all got "wetchered" (wet) on the way home, it would have been because it was absolutely "siling down" (raining hard).

Temporarily parked at Upper Heyford, Flap and the other training teams around him devoted their time, knowledge and expertise to familiarising incoming pilots and their new crews with the foibles of the Hampden Bombers, which those new pilots would soon be expected to captain and fly into action; for some Hampden foibles did indeed exist, as have previously been mentioned.

A similar familiarity process was also applied to incoming navigators, gunners, wireless operators and bomb aimers, with the aim of then allowing each newly appointed pilot captain to assemble himself a mentally equipped, compatible and cohesive crew, all in readiness for eventual operational duties on the increasing numbers of twin engined Hampden bombers then being made available. Each Hampden required a crew of four; a pilot, navigator/bomb aimer, radio operator/rear gunner, and rear under gunner. Flap and his fellow trainers were therefore destined to be busy.

In the meantime, and within five days of Flap taking up his new duties at Upper Heyford, German forces went on to the offensive again as they turned north to invade Denmark and Norway from 9 April 1940.

By then, it had become very apparent that after approximately seven months of Phoney War, the stand-off between Great Britain and Germany would soon have to come to an end!

Chapter 6

Preparing for Action

On 10 April 1940, at 16 Operational Training Unit, and prompted by the renewed German activity in Denmark and Norway, Flap could feel the pressure of the "massive flap" that was developing to train and assemble a continuous supply of additional bomber crews as quickly as possible.

In the meantime, the war planners were still considering what Germany's next move might be, and on what timescale, when just over a month later on 10 May 1940, Germany commenced its invasion of France. The same day, the British Prime Minister Chamberlain resigned, and Winston Churchill took over. The gloves were now off! Churchill immediately permitted the first British bombs to fall on German soil, and within days had authorised bombing east of the river Rhine.

Then, within only a few further days, there followed disaster for the French forces, disaster for the poorly equipped and outclassed British Expeditionary Force, and disaster for Bomber Command!

Instead of thrusting their forces directly against the fortified French Maginot Line as expected, the Germans directed a powerful armour-led advance around the northern end of the Maginot Line, through Holland, neutral Belgium and the Ardennes Region to then burst out behind France's very own defensive line.

To the dismay of Flap, and Bomber Command in general, within the first four days of the German invasion, three-quarters of the Fairey Battle light bombers, that had been sent out to support the British Expeditionary Forces on the ground, were destroyed by the German Air Force. The Battles were thoroughly outclassed by the fast and heavily armed German fighter aircraft that were pitched against them. Although by repute, the inexperienced pilots of some of those German fighter aircraft were shot down by the Battles as those German pilots had at first mistakenly thought that the Battles were RAF Hurricane fighters with forward facing guns. Consequently, when attacking the Battles from the rear in the traditional manner, the German pilots found that they were confronted by a fatal blast of machine-gun fire from the Battles' rear facing defensive machine gunners.

The German advance swiftly encircled huge swathes of the French Army, and then sandwiched them back against the French side of France's own Maginot Defensive Line. In just over a fortnight, the British Expeditionary Force and the remnants of our French allies had been defeated. Whilst the remnants of the RAF Battles were hurriedly flown back across the Channel, before their French bases were overrun by the Germans, the bulk of the British and French armies were forced back to Dunkirk on the French coast.

On 27 May 1940 there began the evacuation by sea of the British Expeditionary Force and the remaining French forces trapped at Dunkirk, whilst huge quantities of British and French arms and equipment were abandoned to the Germans!

However, due to the heavy damage caused by enemy action, there was a lack of docking facilities for the larger ships at Dunkirk port. An urgent call had therefore gone out over Southern England for all available small shallow-drafted seagoing craft of any size to join escorted flotillas on passage to France to assist with the massive task of evacuating troops from the shallows of the French beaches to the deeper drafted ships offshore.

The previous day, Flap had learned from a telephone conversation with Bernice that she had been requested to urgently remove all her family's personal property from her parents' motor yacht *Matoya*, which had remained on her moorings at the Middlesex Yacht Club, Sonning. The boat had been requisitioned by the government! Then, having been smartly stripped of all the unnecessary fancy upholstery, trappings and furnishings to maximise passenger space, *Matoya* had been motored down to the tidal reaches of the Thames, before then making passage on down the estuary and around to Dover.

By the time of Bernice's phone call to Flap, *Matoya* was well on her way over to France, to assist with the evacuation of forces personnel from Dunkirk.

In many cases, it would later emerge that the more capable of small craft transported small loads of troops all the way back to Britain's southern ports themselves; and then, having dropped off their small loads of evacuated troops, many of those small vessels then left on another voyage to Dunkirk and back.

Meanwhile in Kent, the railways had urgently implemented a massive logistical plan to remove the huge number of incoming troops from the southern ports, and immediately disperse them inland and away from the risk of coming under further attack from air or sea whilst concentrated around their home channel ports.

Immediately after Dunkirk, Britain's war planners could only visualise the situation for Great Britain continuing to worsen. By 22 June 1940, France had signed an Armistice with Germany. All the Allied land forces had been driven out of France or taken prisoner. Hitler's next objective was therefore assumed to be the suppression of Great Britain by invasion. The greater Battle for Britain was about to begin.

As the British Army was now largely impotent, due to the massive loss of men and equipment in France, it now left only the Royal Navy and the Royal Air Force capable of mounting any form of defence against the possible arrival of a German invasion force upon Britain's shores.

It was assumed that Hitler would insist on attempting to clear the Royal Air Force from the skies before attempting any invasion. But thankfully, there had been pre-war foresight on the part of the British Government and Air Ministry that, in the event of a new war with Germany, Great Britain might have to defend itself against a far greater and more capable bombing onslaught than that previously attempted by Germany during the First World War. There had therefore been a pre-war determination to ensure that the bulk of British aircraft production was devoted to the mass production of Spitfire and Hurricane fighter aircraft, designed specifically to defend the skies of Great Britain against German bombers.

In the meantime, however, with the urgent need to disrupt Germany's industrial production of war materials and the build-up of forces towards an invasion of Great Britain, it looked as if Royal Air Force Bomber Command might be the only force left in any immediate condition to carry the fight into the German homelands and occupied territories of Europe.

At this early stage, planning consideration was also given towards the possibility that Germany might succeed in building up an invasion force, in which case RAF Bomber Command would then need to be ready and able at short notice to switch their attentions away from the bombing of

German industry to the bombing of any build-up of German invasion forces in the Continental ports of the English Channel.

Further emergency plans and precautions had also been put in hand to ensure that the normally non-operational training aircraft of all of the RAF Training Schools and Operational Training Units were armed and modified in such a way that would enable them to carry bombs of some sort or another for dropping onto any invasion fleet that the Germans might manage to launch against Britain. Those assorted aircraft, which were then expected to number some five hundred or so, included the surviving Battles that had managed to return from France, the Hawker biplanes that Flap had first flown in 1936, and the training schools and units own training aircraft, with all training aircraft expected to be crewed by the pilot training instructors and their most competent pupils drawn from the training schools and training units; all to be supported by trained spare gunners drawn from wherever they could be spared.

It was also generally rumoured that, in the event of a German invasion force setting out across the Channel, the Royal Navy intended to power their heaviest ships through the middle of the fleets of invading smaller craft at the highest possible speeds, such actions being with the intention of running down the smaller German boats and troop-carrying barges, or at least overwhelming and swamping them with the most ferocious washes that could be so created.

In the meantime, as normal OTU training activities ground to a halt, Flap found himself urgently called up for operational flying duties against the immediately building invasion threats from Germany.

Flap remained as an operational instructor with 16 Operational Training Unit until immediately after the signing of the German/French Armistice on 22 June 1940.

Then, on 26 June 1940, having just been advised that his short term four-year commission was being extended to ten years, Flap was posted to 106 Squadron, which was also acting as an Operational Training Unit (OTU) back at Finningley at that time, this unit having been urgently set up to enable newly appointed bomber pilots/captains to personally select their own Hampden bomber crews, consisting of three compatible additional members, all in preparation for then flying a tour of thirty operations against the enemy.

On arrival at Finningley, Flap was pleasantly surprised to discover that a fellow flight lieutenant pilot, also recently arrived at the OTU, was his friend George, a contemporary from his school days. George was surprised and delighted to see Flap again.

A fortnight with 106 Squadron was sufficient time for Flap and George to organise their respective crews before, on 7 July 1940, both men, and Simba the dog, were posted out to 144 Squadron of Bomber Command, with the express purpose of operating that squadron's Hampden bombers from Hemswell, Lincolnshire, directly against the enemy.

So, into action flying an operational Hampden, as Flap's personal Phoney War came to an end, and the greater battle for Britain was about to begin!

Chapter 7

Into the War with 144

Flap duly arrived on station with 144 Squadron, RAF Hemswell, on 7 July 1940, with the purpose of commencing his designated tour of operational duty. A tour of bombing operations was detailed to consist of thirty missions against the enemy, before the crew members would then be rested from operations, back into a training role or similar.

On his arrival, Flap was surprised to find George already on station at Hemswell ahead of him, and that George had already flown his first missions for the squadron.

Flap's photo album contains a July 1940 photo of the 144 Squadron personnel seated in tiers across the front of a Hampden aircraft. Flap is seated off centre in the front row next to George, with Simba the dog posing dead centre nearby. The dog, now separated from his sibling, appears of his own accord to have filled the vacancy for a 144 Squadron mascot.

Flap might have felt some pre-affiliation with 144 Squadron on his arrival at Hemswell, for it may be recalled that Flap and 144 Squadron were both born in Egypt, during March of 1918. The squadron was later disbanded in February 1919, at the end of the First World War, but was reformed again in January 1937, in response to the same RAF rapid expansion scheme that had prompted Flap to join up and fly with the RAF in the first place.

No. 144 Squadron has of course also been mentioned earlier in a previous chapter, as being the squadron that had lost five out of eleven Hampdens during its very first daylight engagement of the war, on 29 September 1939. Now with some trepidation, Flap and George were expected to fly the same vulnerable Hampdens into action. However, after the debacles of the horrific early daylight bomber losses, all Hampdens had since been banned from operating on daylight raids. Consequently, from the end of 1939, they were only permitted to fly on operations over enemy territory under the protection of darkness.

Additionally, by January 1940, some serious modifications had been made to the operational Hampdens. Whereas previously there were three manually aimed defensive gun positions, each with only a single .303 machine gun, two of those positions had soon been converted to .303 twin machine gun positions. Those two positions, each then with a much wider field of fire than previously, were designated for the use of a gunner/wireless operator in the upper rear position and a gunner in the lower rear position, respectively. The modified Hampdens still carried a crew of four, with the pilot controlling the one offensive fixed position machine gun firing straight ahead for his own use, and a navigator/bomb aimer in the nose with a single manually aimed machine gun. A quantity of strategically placed armour plating had also been introduced around the aircraft for enhanced crew protection, and the fuel tanks were now coated with a self-sealing anti-leak compound to reduce the fire risk in the event of damage from anti-aircraft fire.

Since the phoney war had ended, the restriction on bombing the German mainland had been removed. The gloves were now off as Hitler was soon expected to order the seaborne invasion of Great Britain. The country was going to have to fight hard for survival and the aircrews that were new to operations were keen to set about the enemy.

For a mission to count as a successful operation, the aircraft's bomb load had to be dropped on an enemy target. Missions abandoned because of technical problems or bad weather en route, or just simple failure to find a target, did not count towards the required total of an operational tour. However, because as previously mentioned, bomber missions had been restricted to the hours of darkness, it was extremely difficult to obtain confirmation as to whether a target had been hit or not.

In the opening twelve months of the war, British medium bombers carried various and sometimes mixed loads, selected from the following items listed here under the slang or code words that were assigned to each. The codes being intended to confuse the enemy if they intercepted British radio signals:

Nickels: Bundles of propaganda leaflets, dropped on cities. Intended to dismay and dishearten the German population. Also known as white bombs. Probably a complete waste of paper, although defying German propaganda that had told the population that enemy aircraft would never fly over them. As the Germans had watched their forces sweep through France, they probably did think that they were indeed going to be impregnable.

Razzles: Small incendiary devices, comprising of phosphorous coated wooden strips transported in water to keep them inert, and designed to be dropped to the ground in the act of razzling, where they would ignite as they dried out, to supposedly destroy crops and forests. Also probably rather ineffective.

Vegetables: Various types of sea mines that could be sown into enemy sea lanes, channels, and ports during the coded act of gardening; usually by night. Their presence designed to cause disruption, whilst destroying enemy shipping that might come into contact with them. The mines were very effective, and they destroyed a good tally of German shipping.

Bombs: Of sorts too numerous to mention individually. Most rather feeble at this stage of the war, but soon to gradually improve with fresh innovations that led to more potent chemical compositions and destructive power.

As well as the rather feeble early munitions available to Bomber Command, it should also be borne in mind that there were still no electronic navigation or target finding aids in mid-1940. The earliest of these aids would not really emerge in prototype form until December 1941. The only electronic aid that was available to the early bombers was the Lorenz; a short-range radio beam-assisted blind landing aid, capable of guiding an aircraft to the end of the runway in the event of a lack of visibility due to bad weather or darkness, but effective only within a range of about 30 kilometres from the end of the runway.

Flying navigation still had to be by map-reading and dead reckoning calculations. However, navigation by dead reckoning required accurate additional first-hand information to enable accurate calculation of a course from one known fixed point to another. The navigator would need to know where he was to start with; where he then needed to go, and at what speed; the mileage between the two points; the wind direction and speed thereof at the same height as the aircraft. In the latter respect, accessible weather forecasting was vague, especially for enemy territory where Britain did not have the benefit of information from enemy weather stations. The available home forecast estimates of wind strength, wind direction and visibility between home airfield and a target in enemy territory were often very wrong. Erroneous forecasts of wind speed and direction would then throw the best of calculations out of sync with reality, mainly because of the effect of the wind either moving or resisting the aircraft from a different direction and at a different speed than that forecast or assumed. Therefore, a crosswind unknowingly moving a flying aircraft sideways in a fifty mile per hour gale would move that plane fifty miles away from its intended position within one hour. Unlike the captain of a sailing boat, the pilot of an aircraft cannot simply heave to in order to take readings of wind speed and direction. Aeroplane navigators could of course resort to some navigation by the stars, but that was only possible if they could actually see the stars in the first place through the often murky weather conditions common over Germany, the North Sea and the English Channel. Whichever system of navigation was employed, it was never easy to successfully place yourself exactly where you later wished to be, especially in the darkness above a small, designated target. The absolute flying ceiling for a Hampden was nineteen thousand feet, which in poor weather made it difficult to see the ground or the stars if the aircraft could not fall below, or rise above, the bad weather.

Bomber Command's brief in early July was to cause Germany sufficient damage as to reduce the volume of air attacks falling on Britain by destroying existing German aircraft and the factories producing them. It fell to those squadrons possessing the Blenheim light bombers to reduce the numbers of existing German aircraft by flying continual daylight attacks on the German airfields in France whilst under RAF fighter protection. The likes of the Hampden, Wellington and Whitley heavier bombers were required to attack the airfields, rail communications, waterways and factories of the German homelands by night, if they could find them.

Having only just arrived at RAF Hemswell on 7 July 1940, Flap undertook his first operation for 144 Squadron on 11 July.

Five Hampdens set out into the late evening gloom. The planes did not attempt to fly in formation in the dark, for the obvious fear of collision. Each therefore made its own way independently to the allocated targets.

Of the five Hampdens that set out, only Flap and his crew successfully located and bombed the target. Unfortunately, one Hampden and crew were totally lost somewhere along the way; fate and whereabouts forever unknown.

Flap's first thoughts on returning to base had convinced him that stooging a Hampden around in the home skies of Great Britain for short durations, whilst training or instructing others, was an absolute doddle when compared to the seven hours or more of the body cramping, leg aching, backside numbing discomfort that had been endured during the first completed mission. The narrow, cramped fuselage of the Hampden did not allow for much sideways body movement and, in the event that they might need to, it was very difficult for crew members to swap positions. It was known to be extremely difficult, if not sometimes impossible, to forcibly extricate a pilot from his position in the very narrow Hampden cockpit in order to replace him if he had been killed or injured.

Operational records for 144 Squadron show that in order for Flap to achieve his required thirty successful missions, he actually had to fly out on more than thirty-five separate sorties. Some of those sorties had to be abandoned for various reasons, such as engine problems, heavy icing on flying surfaces and windscreen, or quite simply just getting lost in foul weather and thus being unable to find the target before turning back for home base on a roughly calculated course.

Flap's target of thirty successful missions did not get off to a very good start. Having achieved one successful mission on 11 July, the mid-July weather conditions became so atrocious that only intermittent operations over enemy territory were possible in that period. However, some local flying was possible in spite of the rain and murk.

On the evening of 15 July, Flap and his crew took Hampden aircraft numbered P4391 up for a nighttime cross-country training flight. On returning to base at 00.45 a.m. on 16 July, the grass airfield had become so wet that, on landing, the aircraft's brakes were totally ineffective. When the brakes were applied, the wheels just locked up and the Hampden skidded helplessly along the muddy drizzle lubricated grass runway. As the out of control Hampden was then skidding towards an area in which Flap knew there were parked aircraft full of aviation fuel, some urgent action was required. Flap's trained flying reflexes deftly used the rudder and a burst on the throttle of one engine alone to point his aircraft away from the parked aircraft. For a moment or two, Flap's Hampden was then skidding sideways, but still on a line of travel towards the parked aircraft. Flap therefore had to immediately give a burst on the throttles of both engines, to forcibly pull the Hampden onto a different line of travel, away from those petrol laden parked aircraft. However, having avoided that collision, it soon became obvious that the collision of the Hampden with something else less volatile was still going to be inevitable. The Hampden was by then fast approaching the airfield boundary that remained hidden in the rain and murk, and with the brakes remaining ineffective Flap shouted the order "brace for collision", as the aircraft ran on to collide with the airfield boundary wall. The subsequent collision with the wall ripped off the Hampden's undercarriage, but allowed the fuselage and the main bulk of the aeroplane to scrape over the top of the wall. There, the Hamden dropped onto its belly, before it finally skidded to a halt amongst the scattered ruins of the boundary wall and the scrubby surrounds of the airfield. Flap's Hampden was badly damaged, but the nearby parked aircraft and Flap's crew had all escaped unscathed!

Later that same day, 16 July, Hitler issued his orders to commence preparations for the invasion of Great Britain.

During the remainder of July, Flap and his crew set out on four more missions over Germany. Only two of those missions were successful, on 27 and 31 July, respectively.

Other missions on 17 and 24 July were abandoned due to engine problems on one count, and failure to even find the target due to a foul weather haze in the target area on the other.

In the meantime, on 29 July, and as the direct result of Hitler's order for his forces to prepare for the invasion of Britain, George and five other aircraft from 144 Squadron, in company with aircraft from 61 Squadron, were tasked with attacking the Dortmund-Emms canal in North West Germany. The mission was to drop special "vegetables" (mines) onto a specific part of the canal system, where it was hoped that two aqueducts could be smashed to render the canal unusable at those points. The attack was intended to prevent Germany from sending loads of equipment, motorised barges and small craft down the canal system from Germany, through Holland, Belgium and onward to the Channel ports, where fleets of barges and equipment were expected to be built up towards the invasion of Britain across the narrows of the English Channel. The vegetables were successfully planted without loss of aircraft. Later reconnaissance showed that one of the two aqueducts was severely damaged where mines had been detonated by passing barges, thus making that section of the canal unusable.

By mid-August, the Germans had made urgent repairs to the Dortmund-Emms canal. It therefore fell to other squadrons of Hampdens to immediately revisit the canal when, at great cost to themselves, they managed to smash up the German repairs that had been made. This caused further inconvenience to Germany by closing the canal down for another critical ten days.

July gave way to August, and from 12 August the aerial Battle of Britain got under way as intensive German air attacks started to fall on Britain's airfields in a determined German campaign to destroy the Royal Air Force on the ground.

Throughout August 1940, 144 Squadron had joined other squadrons of Bomber Command in nightly raids on targets in Germany. Those raids were directed specifically at North Western German industrial targets, oil refineries, canals and anything that might be useful to assist the German forces with their build-up of resources towards the threatened invasion. Canals and waterways always received special attention. Flap flew several sorties over Germany to bomb munitions factories at Essen, Dusseldorf Oil Refinery, canals and waterways at Magdeburg, Leipzig rail hub and station, Mannheim, and the canals and waterways that connected those centres to the Channel Ports, via Holland and Belgium.

By way of sudden change, on 23 August 1940, both Flap and George were detailed with four other aircraft for a night-time sortie to the captured French port of Brest. Some aircraft had been detailed to create a disturbance by dropping bombs on the port installations, whilst other aircraft, taking advantage of the distraction, and hopefully unnoticed, sowed vegetables (mines) in the harbour approaches, all with the intention of causing later damage and unexpected disruption to German shipping movements. Several aircraft suffered damage from enemy ground fire, and although none were lost, one damaged Hampden had to divert on return to Boscombe Down airfield where, although it was written off after a crash landing, the crew were all unharmed.

By 25 August 1940, the first bombs had fallen on London. Already overstretched Bomber Command was immediately ordered to retaliate with bombing attacks on Berlin, just to remind the German population that they were not going to be immune from attack.

On 3 September 1940, Flap received the good news that his temporary rank of Flight Lieutenant had been made permanent.

On the night of 5/6 September, during the nineteenth sortie of his tour of duty, George and his crew were detailed to bomb a target in Stettin. Neither George nor any member of his crew had ever heard of Stettin at that time, and it took a minute or two to establish that Stettin was near the very northern end of the German/Polish border. This meant that George had to fly his crew right across northern Germany, and back. This was the furthest distance that the fuel aboard a Hampden would permit, and not at all an ideal trip for the usual cramped conditions aboard. Anyway, George and his crew made it to Stettin, where they successfully bombed their target. However, the crew had heard and felt their aircraft being shot up over the target.

George's return trip seemed to take forever, but landfall was finally made over Norfolk after the long and exhausting flight. Sensing the fragile state of his aircraft and its dwindling fuel supply, George decided to divert to the nearest airfield to his landfall. This was quickly established to be the base at RAF West Raynham, Norfolk. A direct approach was therefore made to this airfield. However, due to damage inflicted on the aeroplane's control surfaces by enemy action, and the consequent need to keep his flying speed higher than normal during the approach to the unfamiliar airfield, George overshot his touch down point. Intending to abort the landing and circle the airfield once more, George opened his aircraft's throttles wide and retracted the wheels. He managed to get the Hampden to climb and regain some height. However, height had been gained at the expense of speed and exacerbated by the sluggish reaction of the damaged controls, the aircraft consequently stalled at the top of its climb. As the aircraft fell back out of control towards the ground, George managed to escape by parachute. However, his three crew were all killed in the crash and a very fierce fire that followed.

George was thoroughly shocked by the crash, and remorseful over the loss of his crew. However, he made himself get up in the air again by flying local trips on 10 and 12 September, before he was then rested from flying duties for a fortnight.

In the meantime, and since the fall of France, the Germans had been actively commandeering motorised barges, small craft and ships from all over Germany and the occupied territories and moving them gradually through the canal systems towards the Channel ports, ready to be prepared to act as armed transports for the invasion of Great Britain. As August had given way to September, high flying RAF reconnaissance aircraft had spotted a dramatic increase in the number of invasion barges sheltering in the Channel ports. Also, German warships were noted to be sheltering in the French Atlantic-facing ports of Brittany, from where they were an obvious threat to the lifeline of supplies being shipped to Britain from the USA, Canada, and the Commonwealth.

Accordingly, Bomber Command's attention was urgently redirected: on the one hand towards destruction of the invasion barges and small ships of all sorts then gathered in vulnerable masses within the Continental Channel ports, from which the invasion would surely come; and, on the other hand towards as much destruction and delay as could be caused to the larger warships in the more distant ports of Brittany.

The plan was for RAF Bomber Command's medium and heavy bomber force to give urgent priority to causing maximum damage to German invasion craft and military equipment in the captured French Channel ports by night, whilst the squadrons possessing the faster Bristol Blenheim light bombers, flying under cover of fighter escorts, were ordered to maintain daytime pressure on the Channel ports, thus continuously disrupting the Germans' invasion preparations by day and by night.

The heavy bomber crews were pleased to be allocated the new targets as it made their trips of shorter duration than having to fly to North West Germany. Also, when sowing mines and bombing by night, the reflective sheen from the harbour waters made it easier to identify the designated targets by silhouetting the various basins and landmark features of the harbours, the location of the targets having been previously identified from the well memorised daytime reconnaissance photographs taken by high-speed high flying aircraft earlier on the same day. The reflective nature of the waters also assisted the crews to avoid bombing the nearby port towns, where of course the citizens of our defeated French allies were still trying to live their lives as normally as possible, in spite of the occasional chaos that prevailed all around them.

Further reconnaissance photos, habitually taken the day following a raid, also enabled the crews to have the satisfaction of seeing the damage they had managed to cause.

During late August and on into September, Flap flew several successful bombing and incendiary raids against the barge fleet accumulations in the Channel ports of Ostend, Boulogne, Le Havre and Calais respectively, followed by mine planting raids against the Brittany ports of Bordeaux and St. Nazaire. Flap's crew enjoyed the raids against the barges, for the gunners could add their flying lumps of lead to the explosive bombing action, hopefully causing additional damage by firing their guns at the rows of motorised barges that were clearly contrasted against the reflective sheen of the still harbour waters.

During the mid-September climax of the Battle of Britain, as RAF Fighter Command was clearing the skies of the south-east, all available bomber aircraft from across the commands of the Royal Air Force were pressed into joining one massive all-out round-the-clock assault on the assembled German barge fleet in the Channel ports. Bomber Command had mustered all available aircraft, including the remains of the ill-fated Fairey Battles that had survived from France, and then the bombers of Coastal Command had joined in the fray as well. By the end of September, the combined Commands of the RAF had smashed up enough barges and shot down enough planes to convince Hitler that he would not be able to achieve sufficient supremacy in the sky as to enable him to invade Great Britain for the foreseeable future.

The official end to the Battle of Britain was declared on 31 October 1940.

The Battle of Britain, as it had raged to a crescendo, encompassed a much wider effort and sacrifice than that generally acknowledged or remembered today. No one would dispute that it was indeed "The Few" of RAF Fighter Command that shot the German Air Force out of the skies as the Germans had attempted to destroy RAF Fighter Command and demoralise the British city populations with its bombs. However, it must also be acknowledged that it was the men of RAF Bomber Command and RAF Coastal Command who, together, had set the French channel ports alight and smashed up a large chunk of the invasion fleet. All at some considerable cost to themselves when measured in lives lost.

The Battle of Britain Memorial at Westminster Abbey does therefore record the names of the aircrew across all three of the Commands of the Royal Air Force who lost their lives during this Greater Battle of Britain. The Memorial records the number of the lives lost as 537 Fighter Command, 718 Bomber Command and 230 Coastal Command – some 1,485 souls lost in total.

Flap was content to have survived to see the defeat of the German invasion threat at this point in time and, excluding minor shrapnel damage, without any apparent major damage by enemy action to the various Hampden aircraft that he had flown, and further, without injury to any of the crew members who had accompanied him.

As the threat of invasion had receded, 144 Squadron's efforts were directed back towards causing damage to the German war industry, general transport, communications, and shipping. Targets were varied between bombing and mining against German shipping in and around the occupied French ports, the bombing and mining of German ports in the Baltic, and the bombing of industrial and communication targets into Germany, as far as Berlin.

The success of Flap's early November 1940 raids into German territory were thwarted by continual poor visibility, and the severe icing of windscreen and flying surfaces, causing abandonment of three missions.

In the middle of all the chaotic activity, and following a trip to Hamburg on 17 November, Flap must have had some accumulated leave due to him, for on 18 November 1940 his engagement to Bernice Gain was announced, presumably with a gathering at the Gain family home in Sonning.

Back on station by 16 December, Flap and his crew, together with other squadron aircraft, were sent out on a mission to the historic town of Mannheim, Germany. Aircraft from other squadrons were also allocated to this raid, bringing the total of aircraft involved on the raid to a count of 134, all told. The action against this historical German town was ordered as tit for tat for unnecessary German damage recently done to British historical sites.

On 20 December, Flap and his crew were allocated to an operation directed against Berlin, with a midnight departure.

Flap's entry for that raid in the Squadron's Operational Record Book read as follows:

"**Hampden P2080** – Airborne from base at 00.29hrs. Set course for the German coast at 00.35hrs, weather excellent. Good pinpoint position on English coast and also on German coast. Positioned German coast at 3.26hrs. S/C (set course) Berlin at 03.30hrs. Snow over the whole track, weather very good for map-reading. Position Berlin at 05.00hrs. Bombed target at 05.05hrs. S/C for German cost at 05.41hrs. On the way back we shot up some trains, one railway siding, and an aerodrome. Positioned German coast at 6.16hrs. Landed 08.35hrs."

Following the customary crew debriefing session with the squadron adjutant, Flap found himself approached by several of the squadron's pilots who were curious to know about the sudden burst of activity on the part of his normally bored and inactive gunners who, like most Hampden gunners on night flights, rarely saw anything to shoot at, apart from occasional vain attempts to shoot-out active searchlights in and around target areas.

"Well," said Flap, "the weather on our return route had produced a brilliantly clear night, with snow on the ground. Visibility at ground level was so enhanced by the snow that, on spotting an active railway yard, I decided to drop the Hampden down low enough to give my gunners the Christmas present of being active directly against a visible enemy target for a change. The gunners were able to shoot up the railway sidings and two nearby goods trains, before we then came across a mobile goods train travelling in the same direction as ourselves. I then discovered that by dropping the Hampden's speed down to just short of its very low stalling speed of approximately 75 knots, I was able to slowly fly the length of that moving train, whilst the gunners whooped with delight as they shot it up! In fact, the gunners enjoyed themselves so much that they persuaded me to circle round behind the train and perform a second overhead pass for them to take advantage of.

"Then remaining low for another few miles, my gunners were unexpectedly able to shoot up an enemy aerodrome as we passed by. For a change, my gunners had some small reward for sitting in the very cold narrow confines of a Hampden for some eight and a half hours in the air. The only crew complaint came from my bomb aimer, who was moaning that he would have preferred to have had a couple of spare bombs handy to drop on to a target that they could actually clearly see for a change."

After a couple of days off for Christmas, Flap and the same crew were in the air again from 1.00am on 28 December, bound for Bordeaux. By way of contrast with their last pre-Christmas trip, on the outward journey the crew did not see the ground once and, after they arrived over the target area by dead reckoning, they found the target totally obscured by cloud. Abandoning the designated target, Flap found the docks at St. Nazaire through a gap in the clouds. The bomb load was promptly dropped there, rather than carrying the bombs home to base. Then, as Flap turned the aircraft for home, there was a loud clatter against the fuselage of the Hampden, but with no other apparent effect. However, on approaching home base after eight hours of flying, no radio contact could be made with base, and on landing it was discovered that enemy anti-aircraft fire had damaged the aircraft's heater air intake as well as knocking out the radio.

Flap's last operational mission with 144 Squadron was flown to Brest on the night of 4 January 1941, to bomb the German cruisers that were known to be sheltering in the port. The weather was foul, with poor visibility during the trip. However, navigation by direct reckoning brought Flap and his crew directly in over anti-aircraft fire, which they correctly assumed was over Brest. A quick circuit of the area gave enough glimpses through the clouds of the already familiar dock layout and nearby river, as to enable a bombing run to be made over the dock area where the ships were last seen to be located. However, the poor weather made it impossible to see the result of the bombs dropped, and Flap asked his navigator to set a course for home.

On arrival over the English coast, the crew discovered that it had snowed heavily. The reflective property of the fresh snow was enhancing the features of the landscape, which made it an enjoyable change to navigate over England by map-reading, all the way back to their Lincolnshire base. That operation completed Flap's designated first tour of thirty successful operational missions and entitled him to an immediate fourteen-day leave.

Before commencing his period of leave, Flap was notified of his next posting, that was to be to non-operational duties with 207 Squadron of No.5 Group, Bomber Command, at Waddington. Effective from 20 January 1941, that posting came with the challenge of having to familiarise himself with one of the three marks of a brand-new generation of more powerful heavy bombers that were then being hurriedly introduced into service with Bomber Command. In that respect, and once sufficiently familiar with handling the new aircraft, it was intended that Flap, as part of a small team, would then be transferred on to form a brand-new squadron to operate the relevant new bomber. There, Flap would be required to instruct other incoming pilots on handling the new craft.

Flap was soon relishing the challenge of getting his hands on something that had been specifically designed for a powerful ability to carry a large bomb load that, in the form of the all new Avro Manchester bomber, was designed to carry two and a half times the bomb load of a Hampden. However, Flap was not then aware of the magnitude of the most frustrating challenges that were to soon follow for him and all of the unfortunate crews that would eventually be allocated to fly the Avro Manchesters.

Chapter 8

Meeting the Manchesters

During 1936, the Air Ministry had challenged aircraft manufacturers to produce their design submissions for the production of powerful new heavy bombers, specifically capable of carrying much larger bomb loads, at greater speeds and over greater distances than previously possible.

Coincidentally, since 1935, and at the same time that the Air Ministry requirements were published, Rolls-Royce had been requested to design and build a powerful new aero engine, specifically to power the larger bomber aircraft that the Air Ministry then desired. However, it transpired that Rolls-Royce were maybe not very keen on developing totally new engines from a standing start, and much preferred to continuously and gradually improve the capabilities of their already successfully working engine designs. Therefore, it would appear that Rolls-Royce's solution to seeking the greater power required from a large new engine, was to amalgamate two of their smaller and already successful Peregrine V12 cylinder block engine arrangements into one large and potentially very powerful X24 cylinder block arrangement. The new engine layout was to be achieved by designing a method of joining two V12 cylinder blocks together, back-to-back, with the two conjoined cylinder blocks then sharing a single common crankshaft and crank case between them. The resultant huge engine design was promptly named the Vulture, possibly for the obvious reason that it would be quite the largest engine that Rolls-Royce had ever to that date had to name after a suitable flying bird. The new engine was confidently expected to produce at least double the power of one single V12 engine.

Meantime, the aircraft building industry's responses to the Air Ministry's invitation to submit designs to the preset specifications for the new bombers themselves eventually produced acceptable designs for three different bomber aircraft, with all three designs then being authorised to go forward towards manufacture:

1. **The Stirling**, from Short Brothers, designed as a four-engine heavy bomber, to be fitted with four Bristol Hercules fourteen-cylinder radial engines. This was the earliest of the three new aircraft to be completed, and was first delivered into RAF hands from May 1940.
2. **The Halifax**, from Handley Page, initially designed as a twin engine bomber to accept two of the aforementioned proposed new Rolls-Royce Vulture engines. However, during 1938 there were early doubts concerning the slow development of the huge Vulture engines, following early pre-production problems with that engine occurring at Rolls-Royce. It appeared that the Air Ministry, not prepared to let the Rolls-Royce problems delay the production of too many bombers, therefore ordered Handley Page to redesign their Halifax wings to accept installation of four of the smaller but already proven Rolls-Royce Merlin engines instead of the two larger Vultures previously proposed. The smaller engines were similar to those single engines successfully fitted to the Spitfire and Hurricane fighters. The first Halifax was duly delivered during November 1940 as a promising four engine bomber, fitted with four Merlin engines.
3. **The Avro Manchester**, from A.V. Roe, was also designed from the outset as a twin engine bomber to accept two of the newly developing Rolls-Royce Vulture engines. However, when Avro began experiencing development difficulties with the designs of both the Manchester airframe and its huge Vulture engines, their request to also allow them to redesign their Manchester's wings, and to accept four Merlin engines, was declined by the Air Ministry.

The Manchester/Vulture designs incorporated many interesting innovative features and gizmos, and it was assumed that the whole project was just proving to be rather slow to evolve. It could therefore be surmised that the Air Ministry possibly wanted to preserve the Manchesters as an ongoing development project, in the hope of eventually achieving a truly remarkable end result when the development difficulties of engines and airframes were finally overcome.

The first Manchesters were therefore delivered in the form of twin engine bombers as planned, during November 1940, straight into the hands of 207 Squadron of No.5 Group, Bomber Command, the very squadron that Flap was destined to join in the following January.

No. 207 Squadron, previously disbanded, had been specially re-formed within No.5 Group of Bomber Command at RAF Waddington, for the express purpose of being the first squadron to receive the new Manchesters for familiarisation and assessment, before then introducing the aircraft to personnel from other squadrons of No.5 Group. The introductory process was to be achieved by 207 Squadron, whilst also preparing to put the Manchesters into operational use on their own behalf.

The intention was that the Manchesters, with their expected capabilities of being able to carry approximately four times the bomb load of a Hampden, over a similar distance and speed as a Hampden, would gradually replace No.5 Group's Handley Page Hampdens to form a far more potent No.5 Group bomber force as the new aircraft entered into service.

The new Stirling and Halifax bombers were similarly deployed to other Bomber Command Groups and their squadrons.

Meanwhile, and well before the end of his rest period, Flap had heard disturbing rumours on the No.5 Group grapevine concerning the earliest Manchester aircraft that had already been delivered to 207 Squadron at RAF Waddington. Those rumours indicated that Avro and Rolls-Royce had been encouraged to push ahead too fast with the new technological innovations involved in the Manchester project! Consequently, the new Manchesters were being plagued with problems. The Manchester airframes and their Vulture engines were continually displaying a range of dangerously irritating faults, including the serious lack of power from the huge Vulture engines.

The facts of the matter later revealed that 207 Squadron, having only received delivery of the very first two of the new Avro Manchesters, on 6 November and 10 November 1940 respectively, had, by 12 November 1940, needed to summon the attendance of Rolls-Royce engineers to Waddington to try and sort out engine cooling faults, sudden hydraulic failures, poor engine performance and multitudinous other faults. Those faults were causing major problems on the Manchesters, such that they were preventing the squadron from safely carrying out the demanded schedule of flying trials on the new aircraft.

It was rumoured that, when Avro had earlier sought Air Ministry approval to redesign the Manchester's wings to accept four Rolls-Royce Merlin engines instead of the two Vultures, in the same manner that

Handley Page had already altered the Halifax design, Avro had been refused because the Air Ministry were wary of creating any more demand for Merlin engines in case Rolls-Royce would not have been able to produce the required total number of those engines fast enough. In short, it was better to keep the successful Halifax production line working flat out to ensure that, together with the Short Stirling production, at least two out of the three bomber manufacturers would then be producing much needed bombers. However, if only Avro had requested the change to Merlin engines before Handley Page, then preferences may well have turned out the other way around, in favour of Avro.

As it turned out, the year of 1940 ended with eleven Manchester aircraft at Waddington. However, due to the continuous plethora of aircraft faults, only a pathetic total of seventy-eight squadron flying hours had been achieved across those aircraft during the whole of the month of December 1940. Flap would soon discover for himself that the Manchesters had been delivered in the form of underdeveloped delinquents, complete with attendant multiple behavioural problems.

On 20 January 1941, Flap duly arrived on 207 Squadron at Waddington, at the same time as the arrival of several other first tour experienced and mostly decorated pilots, who had already successfully completed one tour of bombing operations. Flap and his associates needed to familiarise themselves with the Manchesters, by gaining sufficient flying experience on the new aircraft as to enable them to then instruct other incoming pilots on the operation of those unfamiliar Manchesters, thus creating further captain pilots to form new crews and squadrons towards the desired rapid expansion of the overall Bomber Command force.

To assist 207 Squadron's organisation, two separate flights were to be created. A Flight, designated to continue as a training flight for 207 Squadron's own future active operations, whilst continuing with their endeavours to iron out the Manchester's problems; whilst B Flight would also be a training flight, but providing familiarity training for those pilots who would go on to form another squadron and train more pilots on the routines of the Manchesters.

On 25 January 1941, a semi-permanent Avro engineering working party was established at Waddington, with the intention of facilitating the extensive list of modifications required on all the Manchesters so far received from Avro.

Over a short period of time, it had become apparent that the Manchester's engines were underpowered for the size of the aircraft and its load expectancy. The Vulture engines were also prone to dramatic mechanical failures, then leaving the aircraft trying to maintain height on the less than adequate power of one engine. Engine fires and hydraulic failures were also commonplace.

By 30 January 1941, there were fourteen Manchester aircraft and six full Manchester crews at Waddington.

In spite of the problems being experienced with the Manchesters, on the night of 24/25 February 1941, A Flight of 207 Squadron took the new Manchester bombers on their first raid, to Brest harbour. Six aircraft were detailed to attack the German cruisers sheltering there, and all reached the target area successfully and bombed. The bomber crews had all expected their aircraft to reveal typical Manchester faults during this operation, but surprisingly, and other than the task of having to work hard to gain height with their full bomb loads on board, only a couple of faults revealed themselves.

After dropping its bombs, one Manchester's bomb doors flatly refused to close due to a hydraulic leak. This aircraft was flown back to base with the bomb doors wide open. The added drag of the open doors slowed the speed of this craft considerably, for a while causing some concern that there might not be sufficient fuel aboard to carry the aircraft home. However, home base was reached, but all was not well! One leg of the undercarriage then refused to lower, possibly due to the same hydraulic leak that had prevented the bomb doors from closing in the first place. The manually operated emergency system would not lower the reluctant undercarriage leg either, with the result that a half wheels up landing had to be made. This was therefore the first Manchester to be recorded as damaged whilst on operational flying duties.

A second aircraft developed a serious leak that sprayed hydraulic fluid all over the windscreen. As a precaution, an early landing was made at an away airfield, without further damage.

On 25 February 1941, B Flight of 207 Squadron at Waddington was formally transferred out on paper to form a basic nucleus for the reformation of a previously defunct 97 Squadron. The administrative paper transfer comprised eight Manchester aircraft, complete with ground crews and flight crews, including Flap within a party of twelve officers.

The total available squadron assets at that time were barely sufficient to form a single flight for the new 97 Squadron.

By 27 February, the transfer of the assets of B Flight 207 Squadron to 97 Squadron was administratively complete, with the date of 10 March 1941 set for the physical move of the new 97 Squadron and its assets to its newly allocated base at RAF Coningsby. That move would be welcomed by all concerned, as it was expected to relieve what had slowly become an overcrowded situation at 207 Squadron's Waddington base.

However, come the dawning of 10 March 1941, only 97 Squadron's manpower and administration offices were able to move out of Waddington to the squadron's new base at Coningsby. The extremely wet, soggy, and fragile condition of the ground at Coningsby's grass-only airfield on that date prevented any guarantee of safe landing for the squadron's small allocation of rather heavy Manchester aircraft. The squadron's aircraft were therefore left in the care of 207 Squadron at Waddington, pending an improvement of ground conditions at Coningsby.

In the meantime, Flap had received notification that during February, he had been awarded the Distinguished Flying Cross (DFC) on account of his satisfactorily completed tour of active duty with 144 Squadron. He barely had time to add the relevant DFC medal ribbon to his uniform and acquaint himself with the new facilities at Coningsby before he went on a leave that had been long pre-arranged to enable him to fulfil a very important prior commitment.

On 14 March 1941, the day before his birthday, Flap married my mother, then Miss Bernice Gain, at the Parish Church, Sonning, being the village in which the Gain family home was situated. Due to the dire state of rationing and the war effort at that time, together with its effect of scattering families afar, there was a very limited guest attendance at the wedding, and the whole performance was carried off on a very tight budget. Even the confetti had to be home-made from chunks of second-hand gift wrap.

According to the photos in Flap's album, Flap managed to muster the greater wedding team, consisting of his mother, brother, an uncle and two aunts. His father was away as usual, on duty as Captain of a cable laying ship in faraway places. Bernice's team was only able to muster her brother and sister; her mother being away with her father, who was on Royal

Navy Volunteer Reserve Officer duties in Belfast, Northern Ireland, at that time.

It should be noted here that the members of neither family would ever refer to Bernice's new husband as Flap. He would always be John or Johnnie to them all, and it would seem to have been previously agreed that the nickname of Flap was to be reserved for use in a professional capacity only.

Flap's photo album does not reveal any clue as to where the bride and groom may have spent their honeymoon, but I think that the familiar Gain family home at Sonning, with the church and the Thames nearby, would have suited them fine as a honeymoon base!

During the early part of Flap's period of matrimonial leave, from 15 to 18 March, the ground at Coningsby dried out sufficiently enough to allow 97 Squadron's Manchester aircraft to be flown into their new base.

Chapter 9

Manchesters Go to War

Flap returned from his matrimonial leave on 4 April 1941 and, having been granted permission to be billeted off base in company with his new wife, he and Simba the dog moved off base into the care of a local family at nearby Egerton House, Iddesleigh Road, Woodhall Spa, to be joined by Bernice.

By then, 97 Squadron's base at Coningsby was much better established, and four of the squadron's Manchester aircraft had been declared fit and available for operational service.

In early March 1941, Winston Churchill had issued a directive to concentrate all available Naval and Air Force effort towards destruction of the German U-boats, capital ships, and long-range aircraft that were continually harassing the Atlantic sea convoys that Britain was depending on for the country's imported supplies of food and war materials. It was therefore no surprise that 97 Squadron were immediately assigned to provide their four serviceable Manchesters for the squadron's debut raid, destined to fall on Kiel dockyards in Northern Germany.

8 April 1941 – The previous night, a force of 229 mixed types of RAF Bomber Command aircraft, the greatest number of aircraft that had to that date been sent against a single target, had already given Kiel docks a good pounding. Considerable damage had then been done to German Naval accommodation and the U-boat production yards.

Now, on the night of 8 April, a further attack on Kiel by a force of 160 assorted RAF bomber aircraft was scheduled. Flap and his crew were allocated to fly Manchester L7291, to be joined on the raid by the three other available Manchesters from 97 Squadron and another eight Manchesters from 207 Squadron, together with aircraft numbers being made up to 160 by a mixed force of available aircraft drawn from across all Groups of Bomber Command.

Each aircraft flew to the target area independently of the others and, on approaching Kiel, Flap's crew could see fires already burning from 60 miles away; those fires resulting from the attention that Kiel had already received from the aircraft that had bombed ahead of them. The glare from searchlights made it difficult to find the precise targets, and Flap's attack was further hampered by being made through a very heavy concentration of anti-aircraft fire. The bombs were finally dropped without being able to see the final results because of the glare from searchlights and the glow from the multitude of fires already burning on the ground below.

However, the efforts of the combined bomber force and its crews did ensure another successful raid. Later intelligence reports indicated that this second attack on Kiel had fallen more on the town than on the dock areas. Buildings damaged included banks, an engineering college and the gasworks. Utilities were cut off and the water supply failed; 125 people were killed and approximately 300 injured, whilst 8,000-odd civilian workers were bombed out with many deciding to leave the city.

In April 1941, the effect of those two consecutive night raids on Kiel were regarded as possibly the most successful raids of the war to that date.

Of the cost of the raid to Bomber Command, four aircraft were lost, including one Manchester from 207 Squadron whose crew were captured by the Germans to survive as prisoners of war. A further nine already damaged aircraft were further damaged when crash landing in England.

Of Flap's Manchester, at some point the wireless became unserviceable, and on return to base the bombing gear was also found to be unserviceable, all damage probably being due to anti-aircraft fire whilst over the target area.

10/11 April 1941 – For 97 Squadron's second operation, five Manchester aircraft were dispatched to Brest, targeted directly at the German Navy's cruisers *Scharnhorst* and *Gneisenau* sheltering in that port. Flap and his crew were assigned a different aircraft, L7294, for this raid. All aircraft reached the target successfully, and although it was difficult to see the ships clearly, all aircraft bombed where the ships had last been shown on reconnaissance photographs.

The return trip to base was uneventful until, as Flap's Manchester approached the Coningsby flare path to land at 2am, it was fired on during a sudden eruption of cannon and tracer fire that passed to one side of the aircraft. Unbelievably, he had been attacked from behind by a German fighter aircraft! Fortunately, the German intruder's attack was well wide of its target, and Flap's intuitive evasive action was to yaw the aircraft sideways, away from the tracer fire. He then put the Manchester into a hard banking turn off the designated flight path and into the surrounding darkness, well away from the brightness of the flare path that had probably already assisted the German intruder by conveniently silhouetting the large Manchester target. Flap then opened the Manchester's throttles wide, retracted the undercarriage, raised the flaps, and climbed away from the Coningsby airfield.

Meantime, Coningsby's own defences added to the pyrotechnical display as they in turn fired at the escaping German aircraft which, it was later assumed, had flown off unscathed. Traffic Control diverted Flap to orbit a nearby radio beacon, well away from the home airfield, until it was judged safe to return and land.

The following day, Coningsby ground crews were able to pick up souvenirs, in the form of spent German machine gun and cannon shell cases, from around the airfield. There had been a lucky escape for Flap and his Manchester, as following the ground crew's inspection of Flap's aircraft, absolutely no damage was apparent. There was later some conjecture among the Coningsby aircrews as to whether the German aircraft might have shadowed Flap's Manchester all the way back from France, or whether the German had been deliberately hanging around the airfields of Lincolnshire, just waiting to pounce on the easy target of any slow-moving British aircraft conveniently silhouetted against the glare of an airfield flare path as it approached to land. Either way it was a close call!

On 13 April 1941, an order was received by all Manchester squadrons, again grounding their aircraft for engine modifications, and due to multiple failures of the main bearings revealed on the Vulture engines of several of the Manchesters.

Throughout the rest of April, 97 Squadron never had more than three Manchesters fit to fly at any one time; and then only for restricted local flying tests, gunnery practice and dual pilot tuition for the pilots that were still being newly introduced to the marvellous (sarcasm) Manchesters. Some crew members took advantage of the lull to take up their unused leave allocations, whilst others, for the want of something constructive to do, carried out occupational therapy in the form of gardening duties around the base.

As there were no squadron operations in hand during the period that the Manchesters' engines were being modified, on 29 April 1941 Flap was given the opportunity to attend an up-to-date BAT (Beam Approach Training) course at RAF Waddington. The Beam Approach was an audible landing aid that enabled the pilot of an incoming aircraft to find the end of a runway in little or no visibility. By flying along the merger line between two parallel radio signals, each transmitting a different intermittent signal beamed in line with the home base runway, the pilot of an aircraft, when correctly positioned mid-way between the two parallel signal beams, would then hear both intermittent signals together as one continuous sound.

Following Flap's return from the BAT course, the squadron's inability to get on with the war came to an end on 10 May when, after a strange start to the day following a rather random dropping of enemy bombs in the area of Coningsby, four Manchesters and their crews were scheduled for a raid on Berlin. Of the four aircraft that set out for Berlin, all were attacked by German fighters on route. One crew, after having numerous problems with their Manchester, bombed an alternative target before returning early. Two crews were wholly successful, returning later, whilst the fourth went missing.

Next morning, the Commanding Officer and his crew left base in company with another Manchester and crew to search for signs of the missing aircraft. The search was unsuccessful, but it later transpired the missing Manchester had crash landed into the sea, following a fire in a faulty engine. The crew had escaped into a dinghy, to be later picked up by Dutch fishermen before ending up as prisoners of war.

11/12 May 1941 – Flap's Manchester and two others were declared available for operations. However, one aircraft was unable to take off due to minor Manchester faults and problems. Therefore, only two 97 Squadron Manchesters were able to take off for a raid on Bremen Shipyards. Flap successfully bombed the Bremen Yards, but the other Manchester crew could not find the target due to low cloud. Both aircraft returned safely to base. Overnight, several sticks of enemy bombs and incendiaries were dropped in the immediate neighbourhood of the airfield. No real damage was done, and all the craters were promptly filled in by ground crew.

15/16 May 1941 – Flap, flying Manchester L7306, and three other 97 Squadron Manchesters were assigned for a raid on Berlin, in company with four Manchesters from 207 Squadron.

Of the four 97 Manchesters that had set out, one had to soon dump its bombs into the sea and turn back, due to severe loss of power on one engine. Then a second aircraft dumped its bombs and turned for home, after sending a radio message to indicate that one engine had failed whilst the second engine was running roughly. The pilot of the latter aircraft later issued an SOS message from somewhere near the Friesian Islands. This aircraft was not heard from again and was assumed to have been lost with all hands into the North Sea.

Of 207 Squadron's four Manchester crews allocated to the same raid that night, only one managed to bomb the Berlin target. Of the other three Manchesters, one made a very early return due to engine trouble, the second had to dump its bombs over Hanover and turn for home, following loss of engine performance and extra high fuel consumption, whilst the third had to bring its bomb load all the way home again for, having flown all the way to Berlin, it was then discovered that the bomb bay doors were securely jammed shut.

Therefore, only three Manchesters out of the total force of eight drawn from the two squadrons had actually managed to drop their bomb loads on or near the designated target.

Flap and his crew had managed to bomb the target area, but results could not be seen because of poor visibility. Then, on the return trip their Manchester ran into a severe thunderstorm, during which the entire crew of the aircraft suffered from the effects of St. Elmo's fire, as lightning danced on and around the most prominently exposed metal parts of their aircraft.

Apparently, thunderstorms create an electrically charged atmosphere, whereby there is an electrical charge difference in the air between the storm clouds and the ground. Those conditions then create an electrical pressure that changes the nature of atoms in the air, such that the air itself then becomes an extremely good conductor of electricity. In those circumstances, the phenomenon of St. Elmo's Fire is revealed when a dramatic difference in electrical charge between the air and another electrically charged object, such as a ship's mast or an aeroplane wing, reaches a critical point. The charged object in this case being the Manchester, the aircraft had suddenly discharged its electrical energy, and a dazzling bright blue light was emitted. The whole process lasted over several minutes, as the lightning danced around the most prominent parts of the aeroplane. The final flash of discharged electrical energy then temporarily blinded the whole crew who, whilst St. Elmo had been turning the outside of the Manchester blue, had in the meantime been turning the interior of the Manchester just as blue, with loud utterance of multiple swear words and various other assorted profanities.

The eyesight of the crew members that had been most affected by the brilliant light display gradually recovered over a period of several minutes. Hurried checks soon revealed that luckily no damage to the aircraft itself was immediately apparent, and Flap and his crew accordingly commenced the routine for a normal landing back at base. However, when attempting to contact base for landing instructions, it soon became apparent that the earlier fireworks display had rendered the aircraft's radio totally out of commission. Difficulties were eventually overcome to allow Flap to bring the Manchester down to a normal landing, and only then did he discover just how lucky he and his crew had really been. For after more than seven hours in the air and the prolonged confrontation with St. Elmo, it was revealed that there was basically only petrol vapour left in the Manchester's fuel tanks!

That Berlin raid was considered to be an absolute failure. The Manchester project as a whole was regretfully wasting the valuable time, and more especially the valuable lives of far too many well trained and experienced second operational tour crews. In seven months plus, since the Manchesters had first come into service, they had been beset by disaster after disaster; all mainly due to engine failures from multiple causes. Accordingly, on 17 May 1941 another "stop" order was issued, stating categorically that the Manchesters would not be used on operations again until the failures of the Manchesters' Vulture engines and their associated cooling and lubrication systems had been fully resolved.

The net result of the stop order was that there were no more Manchester operational flights for the remainder of May. The rest of that month, 97 Squadron's time was spent on cross-country flights for the purposes of maintaining crew training, whilst also carrying out altitude and load testing of the Manchesters following the various modifications being made by the Rolls-Royce engineers. During this period, and in spite of the continual modifications being made by Rolls-Royce across the squadrons that were cursed by having to fly the Manchesters, Vulture engine failures and engine fires continued to occur in abundance.

On 31 May 1941, 97 Squadron finally received an instruction from No.5 Group Bomber Command, stating that their Manchesters would be considered operationally fit from that same date. However, on the following two days, being the first and second of June respectively, two further serious Vulture engine failures occurred. Luckily, in both of these cases, when one engine had seized up and another engine had blown apart, the two aircraft were on the ground at the time of the respective events.

The foregoing 31 May order, intending to return the Manchesters to operations, was immediately cancelled. It would not be until 21 June that the Manchesters were finally able to return to operational service.

During this end of May period of squadron semi-inactivity, it was confirmed that Flap and his March bride Bernice were officially expectant parents.

21/22 June 1941 – Five 97 Squadron Manchesters, together with another thirteen Manchesters drawn from two other squadrons, were all declared fit to mount a raid against enemy shipping at Boulogne, France. The combined bomber force had not even cleared British soil before one of 207 Squadron's Manchesters, flown by a novice crew on their first operation, was tragically and mistakenly attacked by a British night fighter. The fatally damaged Manchester fell to the ground in Northants, and the entire novice crew perished as the bomb load exploded in a fierce fire.

Flap and his crew initially had some difficulty locating the target through the cloud and haze. However, the bombs were finally dropped on the target during two separate bombing runs, before the Manchester was set on a course for home.

Then, high drama for Flap and his crew on the return trip to base!

Having reached a position approximately fifty miles south of Coningsby base, Flap had gradually reduced his Manchester's flying height to approximately 4,000 feet, when the aircraft was fired on from beneath. An absolute hail of gun fire clattered and rattled through the aircraft in many places, whilst incendiary and tracer rounds added to the drama as they exploded in the darkness all around the aircraft.

Flap's immediate reaction was to yaw the Manchester off course to starboard, before then yawing back to port in order to spoil the aim of their potential adversary, whilst at the same time shouting the order to fire off a flare that would show the friendly forces pre-agreed identification colour code of the day. When fired, the correctly coloured flare had the desired effect, and the firing promptly ceased.

As the hail of fire had come from beneath the aircraft, and had immediately ceased on firing the flare, Flap and his crew suspected that one of the nearby ground-based anti-aircraft crews had made a bad mistake.

Amazingly, there were no injuries amongst Flap's crew, and for the ensuing few moments all aircraft systems still appeared to be functioning as normal. However, rather than risk remaining airborne any longer than absolutely necessary, Flap decided to skip the normal landing formalities and announced that he was making a beeline straight onto the runway flare path at home base. This turned out to have been the best decision, as unseen damage to the aircraft soon became apparent, as first one engine failed during the landing run, and then the second engine began to blow jets of steam from a severely damaged cooling system before also failing, just as the aircraft touched the ground.

Flap and his crew were very fortunate that they had been able to lower flaps, lower undercarriage, then land and apply brakes before both engines and the whole of the aircraft's hydraulic system failed completely. Then, immobile and stuck on the runway, they had to wait for a tractor to drag the Manchester away before any of the following aircraft could come in to land behind them.

An inspection the next day revealed more than three hundred holes in Flap's aircraft, and each of the crew members considered themselves most fortunate not to have been a casualty of gunfire; or worse still a spectacular crash.

It later transpired that Flap and his crew had not been attacked by friendly ground defences after all, but by an RAF Boulton Paul Defiant night fighter, or "Daffy" in Air Force slang, on patrol from its base at RAF Wittering. Unlike the single crewed Spitfire and Hurricane fighters, with forward firing guns that we are all familiar with from films and TV, the Daffy was a dual crewed fighter having a pilot with a separate rear facing turret gunner behind him, and no forward firing guns. This design was ideal as a night fighter, being able to stealthily rise up from below into an enemy bomber crew's blind spot, before firing into the aircraft's vulnerable underside. However, in this case Flap's crew thought it would have been better if the Defiant's crew had ensured that they were indeed firing at an enemy aircraft. The Manchesters after all, with their multiple failings, were of their own accord already proving to be a menace to themselves, without needing to be shot up by their own friendly forces.

It was unfortunate that the two-man crew of this particular Daffy had earlier been warned by their ground controller that there were in fact enemy aircraft about, that had already dropped bombs on seemingly random localities whilst attempting to hit the various bomber stations of Lincolnshire. Then, when the Daffy's crew spotted Flap's large, and possibly unfamiliar aircraft, they must have felt their adrenalin rise as they manoeuvred into an attacking position beneath it.

It later transpired that, before attacking, the Daffy crew had contacted their base to give their position, and to enquire if any friendly aircraft were then in their immediate vicinity. However, their control had advised the Daffy pilot that there were no friendly aircraft around, and an immediate attack was therefore pressed home.

Finally, in panic on seeing the colour of the day flare being fired, the Daffy crew again contacted their controller. This time the controller realised, from a more detailed description of Flap's aircraft, that it was indeed a friendly RAF Manchester.

The upshot of this event was that the Daffy crew were called before a Court Martial, and Flap and his crew were summoned to give evidence to the Court. However, all having given their account of the night's events before the Court, the Daffy crew escaped with a severe reprimand, and orders to urgently improve their aircraft recognition skills before taking to the air again. It was finally decided that the main fault for the unfortunate event with the Daffy lay with the sloppy ground controller, who gave out the erroneous information that led directly to the attack. That controller was subsequently dealt with through other channels, without being identified to either of the aircraft crews involved in the action.

So, of the total events that had occurred during the Boulogne raid of 21/22 June, the crews of the eighteen aircraft from the three squadrons that had been involved with this raid were furious. It was not as if they did not have enough problems already with their self-destructing Manchesters, without their own bloody air force shooting down two of their own number in one night.

On 30 June 1941, maybe by way of respite from the recent operational shambles, Flap, then promoted to acting Squadron Leader, and accompanied by Flight Lieutenant D.J. French of the same squadron, were both posted out on temporary detachment to RAF Swinderby. Here, 455 Squadron of the Royal Australian Air Force had recently arrived from Australia to be equipped with Handley Page Hampden aircraft. This Australian squadron had only been formed on 23 May 1941 in Australia, from pilots and crews from New Zealand and Canada, as well as Australia; all urgently trained to fly and crew under the Commonwealth Flying Training Scheme. Those crews then needed the immediate benefit of the experiences of Flap and French, both from their own active operations, and in particular Flap's time spent at 16 Operational Training Unit. The new squadron's crews needed to be familiarised with the Handley Page Hampdens, before later receiving their own squadron quota of Hampden aircraft.

For Flap, just over a week in the company of those mixed Commonwealth crews and their humour made for an enjoyable and pleasant distraction, well away from the Manchesters and their disastrous problems. The Commonwealth crews seemed to be full of enthusiasm for the job that they were soon to take on, and very keen to get going. During the week at Swinderby there was an amusing incident, when Flap was amazed to hear one of the Aussies complaining that he had been rudely awoken by a racket at some early hour; and all "well before bloody sparrow fart!"

"Where did you get that expression from?" demanded Flap.

"Common as Kangaroo do where I come from," replied the Aussie.

Following some further discussion, and the recollection that Australia was originally populated from Great Britain's unwanted convict exports, it was decided that the "sparrow fart" expression must have been exported to Australia by the Lincolnshire poachers that had been transported to Australia as punishment for their crimes.

In the meantime, back at 97 Squadron! On 1 July, another signal from HQ No.5 Group, Bomber Command, once again grounded all Manchester aircraft from operations, pending another enquiry into the continual malfunctions of the aircraft and their systems. Those malfunctions were then proving to be a bigger threat to the lives of the bomber crews than any of the enemy action being taken against them.

On 9 July 1941, Flap returned to 97 Squadron, with his rank maintained as Squadron Leader, to discover that the Manchester aircraft were still off operations. To maintain some operational effectiveness, many of 97 Squadron's crews had been flying Hampden aircraft borrowed from 106 Squadron, and this practice looked set to continue with twelve of the squadron's crew members detached to 106 Squadron for operations.

22/23 July 1941, Flap had been assigned to fly a Hampden for 106 Squadron, on a raid to Frankfurt in company with five other 106 Squadron Hampdens. The weather was so bad that only three out of the six aircraft managed to drop their bombs on a target. Due to worsening storms, Flap and crew made an early return after dropping their bombs on Bonn instead.

By the end of July, 97 Squadron had been split into two separate flights: "A" Flight, continuing to operate against the enemy in borrowed Hampdens, whilst "B" Flight were allocated any serviceable Manchesters, which at that time were all grounded.

By 2 August 1941, 97 Squadron had only five borrowed Hampdens available for operations. However, instructions received from No.5 Group, Bomber Command, authorised local flying of the Manchesters for operational training purposes only.

5/6 August 1941 – Flap and crew were allocated to fly Hampden AE300 to Karlsruche to attack the railway workshops there. However, this mission was abandoned due to a defective intercom, then followed by a distorted recall radio signal that caused some confusion as to whether the operation had been recalled to base or not.

7/8 August 1941 – Flap and crew flying in a borrowed Hampden set out in company with four other Hampden crews to attack the Krupps Steel Works at Essen. The raid was successful with several fires visible over the target on departure. One Hampden crew failed to return from the operation. On return to base, the Hampden crews learned that some of the Manchesters had been authorised for operations once again.

12/13 August 1941 – Flap and crew again flying in a borrowed Hampden against Magdeburg. One Hampden turned back after struggling to maintain operational height. Then, owing to bad weather and navigational errors, Flap could not find the target. An unknown aerodrome due south of the target was therefore bombed instead. Three of 97 Squadron's Manchesters, together with six from 207 Squadron, also operated on the same night against Berlin.

On 18 August 1941, in the midst of all the demoralising problems and disasters that the crews of the Manchester-equipped squadrons had experienced with their aircraft since November 1940, the Government sponsored Butt Report was then published. This report demonstrated that, in general terms and on the basis of photographic evidence produced during June and July 1940, only twenty-five to thirty per cent of bomber crews attacking German targets by night were managing to locate and bomb within five miles of their allocated targets.

The release of this report generated an immediate upsurge of anger, outrage and pure frustration from bomber crews generally, and from the Manchester crews and their ever-rising losses in particular. For if the thirty per cent success rate quoted in the Butt report was to be believed, then conversely these figures indicated that at least seventy per cent of the crews' bombing attacks were unsuccessful. The bombs from these unsuccessful missions were therefore falling harmlessly to the ground, whilst wasting valuable munitions and pointlessly generating ill affordable aircrew casualties and aircraft losses.

However, some good would eventually come out of the Butt Report for bomber crews in general. For it was an accepted fact that, in its splendid isolation of 1941, Britain had no other effective method of carrying the fight directly to the enemy, other than by bombing. It was therefore soon established that urgent governmental priority would be given towards the commitment of resources to build up the strength of Bomber Command, by investment into the development of superior aircraft and superior munitions, whilst also developing electronic navigation and bombing aids to more precisely guide those improved aircraft and munitions directly to their deserving targets.

2 September 1941 – As August gave way to September, newly manufactured Manchester aircraft were becoming available for delivery to 97 Squadron and others. It was decided that to accelerate crew expansion for the newly available aircraft, all second pilots would forthwith be trained as first pilots. Flap, together with Flight Lieutenant Price and Flying Officer H.S. Blakeman were then designated to remain on A Flight as dedicated Manchester flying crew trainers, whilst the whole of the remainder of A flight were transferred to B Flight, and B Flight was then placed under intensive ground training and operational training.

3 September – 29 September 1941 – Most of September was taken up with the testing of newly delivered Manchester aircraft and the training by both A and B flights of crews to man the new aircraft. Many of the new crews dreaded the reputation for unreliability that the Manchester had earned for itself, and such crews were pitied by the crews of much more reliable types of craft being flown by other squadrons. However, many crews did draw some comfort from the sheer size of the Manchester when compared with the smaller Hampdens that many had been flying previously. Flap, Price and Blakeman continued acting as full-time instructors throughout this period, and intermittently on through October and into the first week of November. Operational flying against the enemy did not involve them.

8 November 1941 – Dunkirk – Flap's first operational flight since mid-August. Flap and crew could not locate the docks due to the intense all-dazzling searchlight glare from below. Rather than bombing blind and risking the lives of the French civilians still trying to live their lives in the nearby town, they returned with their bomb load intact.

Trained crews were then given a break from operational flying because the squadron's Manchesters were once again banned from operations; this time due to hydraulic failures, and problems with their engine exhaust manifolds. Flap was thankful to temporarily return to his training and instructional duties until mid-December.

Chapter 10

Daylight Raid on German Cruisers

By the time the Manchesters of 97 Squadron were fit for operations once again, intelligence reports were being received suggesting that the German cruisers *Gneisenau*, *Scharnhorst* and *Prinz Eugen* were preparing to break out of the French port of Brest where they had been sheltering for some time. General concern was that the ships would disappear into the Atlantic to attack and destroy the allied shipping that was delivering the life-giving supplies of food, fuel and munitions being shipped across the Atlantic from the USA to the UK.

The trans-Atlantic shipping situation was now being described as desperate, with enough threat to our shipping from German U-boats without the additional presence of German surface raiders.

Japan had attacked Pearl Harbor on 7 December 1941, bringing the USA directly into the war, and on 11 December both Germany and Italy had also declared war on the USA. In this new situation, America, on which the UK was already heavily depending, was faced with the additional commitments of its own war effort against Japan. Continuing heavy shipping losses were therefore unsustainable, and an all-out effort to destroy the threat from the German cruisers was requested by the Americans.

Due to the lack of night-time bombing aids at this time, and the subsequent difficulty of finding targets in the dark anyway, continuous night-time raids on these ships by various squadrons of the RAF had been banging away over a long period of time without much decisive success. Most raids had only been sufficient to inflict a series of minor damage events on the ships, such damage not being sufficient to sink the ships or permanently prevent their departure, and only causing a succession of delays to departure through minor damages caused. Intelligence received reported that, much to the dismay of the French residents still trying to live out their lives normally, the town of Brest was gradually being wrecked by the bombs that had missed the ships and, apart from the minor damages caused to the ships, the only other real inconvenience to the Germans was that they were having to bus the ships' crews to out of town billets each night, as it was considered too dangerous to allow them to reside in town or onboard ship for fear of being killed by what appeared to be haphazard bombing.

Now, and in order to improve the accuracy of bombing and do some real damage, Bomber Command had been ordered to launch an all-out effort against these ships by daylight, and in clear weather when it should be possible to clearly see the targets. It was planned that the daylight bomber force would involve several different RAF Bomber Command squadrons, flying various available types of heavy bomber aircraft. The Manchesters' presence was requested on this particular operation because of its ability to carry a heavier bomb load than most other bomber types at that time, including two of the heaviest available armour piercing bombs, in an attempt to pierce through the thick armoured decks of the German ships.

When told of the planned daylight raid, the bomber crews' hearts sank as they recalled the disastrous daylight raids earlier in the war, when on one occasion a whole squadron of Hampden bombers had been destroyed on a single long-distance unescorted daylight raid into enemy territory. Since Bomber Command had suffered such losses, those long-distance unescorted daylight raids had been discontinued, and missions over Germany were only carried out under cover of darkness.

However, shallow penetration hit and run raids into nearby enemy occupied territory such as the French Channel coast were permitted in daylight. At this short range a nimble fighter escort could be provided to protect the slower bombers over enemy territory. Tried and tested short range raids had previously been tried out by using a mixed force of available bombers and fighter aircraft and termed "Circus Raids", the whole circus being designed to cause as much accurately targeted damage to German assets in France as possible.

However, in order for the fighter planes to successfully defend the bombers, it was necessary for the bombers to fly in a tightly disciplined formation, as opposed to night-time raids, when each aircraft was free to proceed to the target area separately and relied on the darkness to provide stealth. Daylight formation flying practice and daylight bombing practice was therefore commenced in earnest, and with immediate effect.

Determined plans for the Circus were urgently pushed ahead, together with prayers for a fine and clear weather window. The clear intention was to sink the *Gneisenau* and the *Scharnhorst*, with the use of nearly fifty bombers being drawn from no less than six different squadrons instructed to drop the most powerful of armour piercing bombs available at that time.

The raid was finally set for 18 December 1941, with up-to-date reconnaissance pictures of Brest harbour available, showing both the German ships *Scharnhorst* and *Gneisenau* present, plus the addition of the German ship *Prinz Eugen* in close proximity. A clear weather window was forecast for the whole of that day.

Come the day, the 97 Squadron formation was to consist of eleven Manchesters, including one spare, each carrying two 2000lb armour piercing bombs and two 500lb semi-armour piercing bombs. The Commanding Officer of 97 Squadron, Wing Commander Balsdon, whilst not really needing to, had chosen to join this operation as an observer in overall command. Leading the first flight, with borrowed aircraft and crew, he was flying as extra man in Manchester L7490 that was carrying the squadron marking OF-U. Flap, as second in command was flying Manchester L7492 OF-A and leading the second flight, with Flight Lieutenant Mackid in L7491 OF-C, leading the third flight.

The 97 Squadron Manchester aircraft took off in close succession from 9.30am, and in formation headed for a rendezvous with the formations of four-engine Sterling and four-engine Halifax bombers drawn from the other squadrons that were also designated to rendezvous over Lundy Island in the Bristol Channel, just north of Hartland, Devon. Soon after take-off, and as the ten Manchesters assigned to the raid had successfully joined the formations above Lundy, the spare aircraft returned to base. That early return was unfortunately a bit premature, as soon afterwards and whilst passing over Land's End, one of the force's Manchesters started to misbehave and developed faults that forced an early return. This reduced the Manchester force to nine aircraft only.

It had been pre-agreed that, as the Stirling and Halifax crews had previous experience of Circus raids, then they would lead the combined formations. The Stirlings therefore took the lead, followed by the seventeen Halifax, and then the remaining nine lumbering and unreliable Manchesters bringing up the rear.

The weather forecast had held good and produced a fine clear blue skied winter's morning, with stunning views. As the bomber formations passed over Land's End, the defensive escort of Spitfires and Hurricanes joined up to form a mini airborne armada. From their positions, towards the rear of the formation, the Manchester crews had magnificent panoramic views of the whole airborne ensemble. The mini armada made an impressive sight in the clear winter air. A sight not previously seen by many of the bomber crews, who had only ever flown under cover of darkness on night sorties.

As the armada drew nearer to Brest, the bulk of the Spitfires and Hurricanes accelerated ahead for a sweep of the Brest target area to tempt up the German fighter planes to scrap, and hopefully to use up the Germans' fuel and ammunition before the slow and vulnerable bomber force arrived on the scene.

As the leading Stirling bombers approached the target area, intense anti-aircraft fire opened up. The Germans also fired an obstructive smokescreen designed to drift over the harbour and disguise the whereabouts of the target ships. However, and probably to the intense annoyance of the Germans, the smokescreen appeared to be drifting away from the target area, rather than over it. Most of the bomber crews had in any case been to Brest so many times before, that even when flying by night they had become familiar with the layout of Brest harbour silhouetted against the sheen of the surrounding water. The recently taken reconnaissance photos confirmed exactly where the ships were then currently lying and, even if the smokescreen had been successful, it would only have needed glances of the harbour through any smoke to determine exactly where to bomb.

The Stirling and Halifax squadrons were the first to bomb. They held formation in a long staggered line as they ploughed through the intense trails of fire rising from the ground defences. They dropped their bomb loads and flew on through the gauntlet of wheeling fighters as the Spitfire and Hurricane fighter escort attempted to hold German fighter aircraft at bay. For the Manchester crews bringing up the rear, seeing the action in the bright sunlight presented a surreal scene not previously seen by them.

The Stirlings appeared to suffer the greatest punishment. Several appeared to be damaged, some badly, but it was not possible to tell if damage had arisen from ground fire, or the wheeling German fighter aircraft. The Halifax force appeared to fare better, and only one was seen to be in obvious distress.

Several fighter aircraft had appeared to be smoking from damage inflicted, and one was seen to fall into the sea. However, at a distance it was not possible to see if the individual fighter aircraft were British or German.

Then it was the turn of the Manchesters to bomb as they flew towards the target area in a long staggered line. Unfortunately, their arrival over the target coincided with the departure of most of the friendly RAF fighter force, that was by now running short of fuel and out of ammunition. The Manchesters were on their own! At the same time, the first German fighters that had earlier scrapped with the RAF fighter force had now had time to land, rearm and refuel, and were just then reaching the same height as the incoming Manchester force lumbering along at 15,000 feet.

An account of this raid in 97 Squadron's Operational Records shows that on arrival, the nine Manchesters flew straight into their bombing runs over the target area.

Flap and his crew in L7492 OF-A, leading the second flight of Manchesters, sustained several noisy strikes from anti-aircraft fire as they bombed, fortunately to no apparent effect. Then, whilst Flap's crew member Sergeant K. Williams was photographing the action below OF-A, their own bomb blasts were observed and photographed on the jetty right alongside the ships, with further blasts towards the end of the jetty.

Flight Lieutenant J.G. Mackid, leading the third flight of Manchesters, also pressed home a successful attack with visible blasts in the critical dock area on and around the ships.

The remaining seven aircraft also succeeded in dropping their bombs in the target area and several other on-target bomb bursts were observed.

However, no matter how successful the bombing runs of all nine of the aircraft had been, the raid was not without misfortune.

The lead Manchester of the 97 Squadron formation, L7490, with the Commanding Officer, Wing Commander Balsdon, as a guest aboard, had successfully dropped its bombs over the target area when there was a heavy burst of flak under the aircraft's tail unit. This burst caused heavy damage to the tail plane and rear gun turret. The rear gunner was severely wounded, and the aircraft then became difficult to fly as it turned onto a course for home base.

Manchester R5795, flown by Pilot Officer Stokes and his crew on their very first operation was damaged by flak on its approach, and consequently as it ran in to release its bombs it lost the power of one engine. As the aircraft, less bombs, then turned for home it fell behind the formation due to the loss of power from the failed engine. In this isolated position the Manchester then came under sustained attacks from German fighters that eventually set the aircraft alight amidships. The order to bail out was given, and four crew members were seen to leave the aircraft before it then crashed into the sea.

Manchester L7425 was flown by Flying Officer Rodley, who having successfully bombed, saw L5795 (Stokes) about to be attacked by the German fighter. However, Rodley was unable to warn Stokes of the fighter's presence, as his own radio had been knocked out by shrapnel from enemy fire.

Manchester L7460, flown by Flying Officer Blakeman managed to bomb the target before being hit by flak that holed the oil tanks. Lacking a supply of oil, the starboard engine then seized up. Unusually for a Manchester, Blakeman was able to continue flying the ailing plane on the one good engine as he turned onto a course for home.

Initially, it appeared that this daylight raid had cost 97 Squadron the total loss of one Manchester and its entire crew, one badly injured rear gunner, and considerable damage to a further two aircraft.

During the Manchesters' flight homeward, the observation of several four engine bombers struggling along at slow speed, and the sight of others that had ditched into the sea, indicated that the Stirling and Halifax squadrons might have taken even more heavy punishment from the German defences.

However, as the surviving eight Manchesters headed for home, further unfortunate events were about to unfold!

The Commanding Officer of 97 Squadron, Wing Commander D.F. Balsdon on aboard the lead Manchester L7490, had sensed problems with his aircraft following the anti-aircraft fire strike that had damaged the aircraft's tail unit. As the aircraft approached the home coast, he therefore decided to relinquish command of the squadron force to Flap, being the next most senior officer.

As the formation progressed, mist and fog began to appear. On making landfall, three damaged aircraft, including Blakeman still flying on one engine, were permitted to divert to the nearest convenient bases that were prepared to receive them.

The remainder of the Manchesters continued towards their Coningsby base where the wives of the bomber crews, including Mrs Balsdon the Commanding Officer's wife, had gathered to welcome their menfolk home for Christmas.

By late afternoon, just as dusk was falling, several aircraft had already landed safely at Coningsby, when the damaged Manchester L7490 carrying the Commanding Officer appeared on the circuit and made what at first appeared to be a normal landing approach. However, as the aircraft came in over the airfield boundary its path of travel was far too high to touch down in the right place on the runway. The pilot must have then decided to deliberately overfly the runway, with the intention of flying around the airfield perimeter a second time to attempt another landing approach, for the throttles of the Manchester were suddenly opened wide, and its engines roared! But, instead of accelerating away in level flight, the tail of the aircraft slowly fell downwards to position the Manchester nose up, diagonally to the ground. As the engines continued to roar under full throttle, the nose of the aircraft then began to rise steeply until the aircraft was momentarily stationary, vertically placed, nose up in the air and well above the airfield. It had stalled! As the aircraft dropped back towards the ground, it toppled over backwards into a nose down position, before crashing nose first, right into the centre of the airfield. On impact, the Manchester shattered apart and erupted into a vivid orange all-consuming fireball. The whole drama was played out right in front of the control tower staff; and worse still, right in front of the visiting wives of the crew members who had turned out to welcome the Manchesters home.

The following day, when the wreckage had cooled down, those paying their respects to the crashed crew members found it hard to accept that there was now absolutely no trace of the Commanding Officer of 97 Squadron and the seven other crew members that were aboard the crashed aircraft. The heavy metal parts of the aircraft had been driven deeply into the ground. All else, including their husbands and friends, was now an invisible part of the Manchester's finely powdered ashes. There were literally no mortal remains to search for.

It was assumed that the flak damage sustained to the tail plane of L7490 whilst over Brest must have damaged the control surfaces of the tail plane elevators badly enough to render them useless at the critical moment of landing, thus causing the total loss of control that inevitably led to the crash. If only the crew of this aircraft had earlier realised the true extent of the damage to their Manchester, they would then have been able to bail out of the aeroplane and take their chances with parachute drops to safety.

Of the damaged Manchester R5795, flown by Pilot Officer Stokes until crashing into the sea outside Brest, only three surviving members of the parachuting crew were eventually picked up from the sea by the Germans, some twenty miles out from Brest. The fourth crew member to bail out was never found and assumed drowned. The aircraft's captain, Pilot Officer Stokes, an Australian serving with the RAF, was assumed to have gone down with the aircraft and the other two crew members.

I don't think that Bernice, then my eight months plus heavily pregnant mother to be, can have been amongst the wives that had gathered at the airfield to watch the Manchesters come home. For if she had been there, then I reckon the shock of witnessing such a spectacular crash might well have meant that I was born in December 1941, instead of January 1942. She would in any case have been distressed to learn of the total loss of fifteen squadron members in the two lost aircraft, but not as distraught as those wives that had unfortunately witnessed the airfield crash first-hand.

Shocked by events himself, and then being the most senior 97 Squadron officer remaining, Flap found himself temporarily in command of the squadron. A new Commanding Officer (CO), Wing Commander J.H. Kynock was appointed the following day, pending his eventual arrival on station from 83 Squadron, Scampton. In the meantime, Flap, in his temporary position, prepared for the unenviable task of having to assist the new CO to write to the families of those fifteen 97 Squadron crewmen now missing or killed in action as a result of the Brest raid.

Of the thirty-five Stirling and Halifax bombers, flown by the other five squadrons that had bombed Brest ahead of the Manchesters, they had also suffered losses! Four of the Stirlings and one Halifax were downed. Some of those losses being the casualties that 97 Squadron had seen in the sea on their way home.

In the aftermath of the raid, and in spite of the photographic evidence of bomb blasts on the German ships and jetties at Brest, as taken by Flap's crew member and others, the 18 December bombing raid on these German ships was not acclaimed as being any more successful than previous raids. The damage to ships and jetties was described as superficial. Probably causing just enough damage to delay the intended departure of the German ships whilst damage repairs were carried out, but not damaging enough to sink or permanently prevent their eventual departure. Probability was, that the RAF's armour piercing bombs at that time were not heavy enough, or indeed powerful enough, to sink the German ships by piercing through the ships' thickly armoured decks before exploding; for that is what they needed to do. It was more likely that the bombs were bouncing off the thickly armoured surfaces of the German ships, even as they were exploding.

In spite of the foregoing, the determined leadership of Flap and Flight Lieutenant J.G. Mackid during their attacks on Brest harbour were recognised by a joint citation put forward for the award of the Distinguished Flying Cross (DFC) to both men; Flap's DFC to be in the form of a Bar to the DFC already earned on completion of his series of operations flown with 144 Squadron.

The new Commanding Officer of 97 Squadron, Wing Commander J.H. Kynoch arrived on Station from 23 December.

Flap's final duty as temporary commanding officer of the squadron was to sign a sheet in the Squadron's Operational Record Book, to certify that there had been no flying during the four days previous to 23 December, due to both the very poor weather conditions and the lack of serviceable Manchester aircraft.

The squadron sent a representative to the family funeral of the previous Commanding Officer, Wing Commander D.F. Balsdon, held at Portpatrick, Galloway, on Christmas eve.

Extraordinarily, some operational flying was scheduled for Christmas Day, but thankfully soon cancelled in favour of a training flight at the last moment.

Further intermittent formation and bombing training took place during the odd days running up to the turn of the year. However, unsuitable weather for operational flying ensured that squadron personnel were on station, or very nearby, to see in the New Year. All squadron aircrew carried the heartfelt mutual wish that the rumours they were hearing of the pending supply of better aircraft and improved munitions would materialise in the coming new year.

Chapter 11

New Year, New Babies, New Ideas

As the New Year of 1942 opened, it became common knowledge that 44 Squadron at Waddington had received the first production Avro Lancaster bomber to be issued to a squadron. It was also disclosed that, in order to preserve the secret of the Lancaster's existence for as long as possible, 44 Squadron had already trialled a Lancaster prototype under the name of Avro Manchester Mark 3 as early as the previous September. Further, rumours were now rife that 97 Squadron would be the next squadron to soon receive a brand-new production Lancaster.

The foregoing news meant that Flap, Bernice, and now the whole damned squadron were one way or another all in a highly expectant state; Bernice awaiting my appearance, and the squadron personnel awaiting the Lancaster's appearance. But as for poor old Flap, he was doubly expectant. He did not know if he was coming or going by mid-January! What a quandary? Which of the new babies would arrive first?

No. 97 Squadron records show that the painless delivery of the Lancaster beat my own delivery, by a mere two days, the Lancaster arriving very loudly at Coningsby airfield on the 14 January. Both squadron flight commanders, Flap and Squadron Leader J. Dugdale, were immediately given dual control tuition on handling the new Lancaster. Assembled spectators on the ground were suitably impressed with the smooth finish of the overall camouflage paint job, generally pleasing shape, and graceful appearance of the squadron's massive new baby that reputedly weighed in unloaded at 37,000lbs, or approximately sixteen and a half tons. Both squadron leaders were suitably ecstatic with their first experience of the power, stability, ease of control and overall performance of the new Lancaster. The Lancaster was joyfully eager to fly and, having become airborne, was most reluctant to come down again without having to be actively pushed down by the pilot. Even its exceptionally loud voice from its Rolls-Royce Merlin engines sounded right! Those attributes were the exact reverse of the sluggish Manchesters that had always been most reluctant to leave the ground and, once airborne, whilst often coughing and spluttering, then used the least excuse to head back to the ground again.

Following the Lancaster's arrival, most of the squadron's aircrew and ground crew spent the day as spectators of the most satisfying flying displays that they had ever observed. Then, during the evening of the 14 of January, there was much more celebration in the crowded officers' mess, as multiple toasts were proposed to the handsome new Lancaster.

Having to play second fiddle to an aeroplane, but not to be outdone by the foregoing events, my birth certificate shows that I turned up at my parents' newly rented family residence at Lingfield, Tor-o-Moor Road, Woodhall Spa, a couple of days after the Lancaster's appearance. On 16 January to be precise, and to a much smaller audience, and thankfully when all the other fuss had died down a little.

My arrival was much more painful, much less graceful, but a lot less noisy, and I weighed in at a mere seven pounds eight ounces only. Unfortunately, I needed immediate medical attention, having been born with a jaundiced condition that meant that my overall paint job was of totally the wrong colour with a lousy finish, being a wrinkly mess of jaundiced yellow. However, I probably received just as much welcoming attention as the newly delivered Lancaster, and I am sure that my arrival would have been used as an excuse for yet another booze up in the officers' mess, then being described as a head wetting ceremony. I am just thankful that Flap was sober when he registered my birth, for if he had been under the influence of alcohol, he might well have over enthusiastically named me Lancaster Sherwood.

Soon afterwards, and following the earlier announcement of the award of the Distinguished Flying Cross to Flap and Flight Lieutenant J.G. Mackid in respect of their actions over Brest on 18 December, a joint citation appeared in the *London Gazette* on 23 January, as follows:

> In December 1941, Squadron Leader Sherwood and Flight Lieutenant Mackid participated as leaders of formations of aircraft in a daylight attack on the battle cruisers *Gneisenau* and *Scharnhorst* at Brest. Extremely heavy and accurate anti-aircraft fire and opposition from enemy fighters was encountered, but although

Squadron Leader Sherwood's aircraft was hit several times by shell fire he skilfully kept his formation together and finally an accurate run was made over the target.

Flight Lieutenant Mackid admirably supported Squadron Leader Sherwood and pressed home a successful attack with great determination. Throughout the operation, which demanded a high degree of skill and courage, both these officers played a conspicuous part and contributed materially to the success obtained.

By the last day of January, and following further aircraft deliveries, 97 Squadron's total strength comprised of four Lancasters and four Manchesters. Operational flying of the Manchesters had by then been abandoned by the squadron in favour of intense crew training on the four Lancasters so far delivered.

However, a problem had arisen. In the sustained rain and snowfall of late January, the Lancasters proved to be far too heavy for the Coningsby all grass airfield. Their sheer weight, when loaded with crew and fuel, badly rutted the waterlogged all grass runways and taxiways. The airfield therefore had to be temporarily closed to traffic on 31 January.

On 17 February, with the aircraft score standing at eight Lancasters and one single Manchester remaining, the squadron were informed that they would soon be moving to Woodhall Spa, there to operate as a satellite of Coningsby. Woodhall Spa, being a recent purposely built all hard surface airfield, would then be capable of supporting the weight of the Lancasters in all weather conditions.

In the meantime, to the dismay of Flap and the squadron, they had learned that during the period 11/12 February, the German ships *Gneisenau* and *Scharnhorst*, the very ships that Flap had so recently been decorated for successfully attacking at Brest, had unbelievably achieved the unexpected by blatantly breaking out of Brest harbour in broad daylight, that being the most unlikely time of day that the ships would have been expected to breakout. The German ships had immediately rendezvoused with a German naval escort, and then successfully steamed off up the English Channel under an umbrella of German air cover, through the Straits of Dover, up the North Sea and away to the Fatherland. The whole operation was achieved without any effective opposition from a shamefully shambolic and tardy response from the Royal Air Force and the Royal Navy.

It was later reported that RAF Coastal Command, from St. Eval, in Cornwall, were supposed to have maintained a continuous airborne sentinel patrol over Brest harbour, in order to ensure an early warning of any attempted breakout by the German ships. However, the sole aircraft designated to patrol over Brest at the time of the breakout, had returned early to its St. Eval base with a fault, and without immediately being replaced by another aircraft. On hearing the news Winston Churchill was incandescent with rage. A later investigation blamed a totally shambolic lack of common communications compatibility between the various branches of the Royal Air Force and Royal Navy for the missed golden opportunity to destroy the *Gneisenau* and *Scharnhorst* once and for all.

By the end of February, 97 Squadron's Lancaster strength numbered twelve Lancasters, and the Manchesters had been totally banished. In the meantime, the squadron's ground crews and aircrews had moved into new living accommodation at nearby Tattershall Thorpe, and the Petwood Hotel at Woodhall Spa had been requisitioned as the officers' mess. On the map, Coningsby, Tattershall Thorpe and Woodhall Spa are all contained within a four mile square.

On 15 March it was Flap's twenty-fourth birthday. By then, there were sixteen Lancasters on the new base, but whilst crew conversion and general familiarisation training on the Lancasters continued apace, there was little time to celebrate personal birthdays.

Prior to 20 March, any thought of launching the Lancasters on a maiden operation had been abandoned due to the extreme weather conditions being experienced. However, on this date six Lancasters finally did take off on an operation to lay mines around the Friesian Islands. However, on the outward trip, and whilst still over home territory, the Lancaster piloted by Flying Officer Rodley lost both of its wingtips. Considering it unwise to fly on in a damaged aircraft, especially whilst carrying six huge sea mines and a full load of fuel, Rodley safely belly landed the Lancaster on the coastal sand flats near Boston. Whilst Rodley's crew were all unscathed, his Lancaster officially became the first one to be written off whilst engaged on operations.

Following on from the loss of wingtips from Rodley's Lancaster, some further Lancaster faults revealed themselves in connection with the landing gear. On two separate occasions, the lights that should have indicated that the respective landing gears had been safely lowered and locked into position failed to work. In the first instance, a quick radio discussion with flying control persuaded the crew that most probably the landing gear had lowered and locked, and it was therefore thought most likely that it was only the indicator lights themselves that were faulty. In this instance a safe landing was promptly made. However, when the same thing happened to the same crew again, only when flying in a different aircraft, they were in for a shock. Discussion again persuaded the crew that, as previously, it was probably the indicator lights that were the problem, not the landing gear itself. However, in that case, and just as the Lancaster landed, one side of its undercarriage completely collapsed. The crew escaped safely, but the Lancaster was burnt out in the ensuing fire.

There were also reports of various bits having fallen off a couple of Lancasters. In one case, one of the huge main wheels that were nearly as tall as a small man, just fell off. In a second incident, an even heavier item in the form of a whole Merlin engine just fell out of its wing mountings.

On 26 March, the few squadrons that had received Lancasters received an order grounding all of those Lancasters from operations until further notice, in order to rectify the faults revealed by the foregoing events. Those included skin wrinkling, the failure of the rivets attaching the Lancasters' wing-tips, the malfunction of the landing gear indication lights and a weakness in wheel and engine mountings.

During the period of this setback, the squadron's Commanding Officer, Wing Commander J.H. Kynoch, was posted away from the squadron, pending imminent arrival of Wing Commander John Collier DFC to take over command.

The grounding of the Lancasters caused an air of despondency to set in at Woodhall Spa and Coningsby, as the crews of both 97 and 44 Squadrons considered the possibility that the Lancasters may have inherited some of the unfortunate jinxes that had dogged the Manchesters for so long. However, and before the depression became too deep, the Lancasters were cleared for operational flying again from 8 April. Then, on 8, 10 and 11 of April some operational sorties were flown, but none involved Flap and his regular crew.

In the meantime, eight crews had been selected from each of the Lancaster squadrons for a special training programme, ostensibly to trial the Lancasters under various specific conditions. Flap, as second in command, was appointed to lead the 97 Squadron formation, and his instructions were to repeatedly engage the squadron's crews in daylight close formation flying at very low levels, whilst very low-level bombing skills were also to be honed to as near perfection as possible on the coastal bombing range at Wainfleet, just south of Skegness on the Lincolnshire coast.

During this intensive flying programme, and in spite of the recent faults revealed, Flap and his crews rapidly became convinced that the Lancasters were in actual fact going to be a great operational success. Although the Lancaster was a modified version of the disastrous Manchester, the radical improvements that had been made were exactly what were needed to transform the finished Lancaster aircraft into a roaring success. In order to make room to mount the Lancaster's four Rolls-Royce Merlin engines, as opposed to the Manchester's two clumsily ill-conceived Vulture engines, each wing of the new design had been necessarily lengthened by approximately six feet. This had added approximately twelve feet to the total wingspan and a beneficial additional square footage to the aerofoil flying surfaces of the Lancaster's wings. Consequently, the increased wing area had the fortuitous effect of considerably increasing the overall lift generated by the wings. Additionally, the flying crews considered that the four-engine layout would give them far greater security; for if they lost the use of an engine, for whatever reason, they would still have three-quarters of their engine power remaining, whereas previously on the twin engine Manchester, the loss of use of one engine, particularly when fully loaded, was quite often disastrous with sometimes less than half of the aircraft's normal power then remaining.

All things considered, the Lancaster felt right, sounded right, performed right and looked right. Whereas the old Manchesters were always reluctant to climb away from the ground to operational heights, the Lancasters were eager to just get going; up and away.

For the next few days, Flap and his eight 97 Squadron crews continued to hone their ever closer formation flying skills. Speculation gradually set in amongst the crews that, with all the activity centring on daylight close formation practice, they might well be in a process of being conditioned for some sort of special operation. Later, when 97's crews realised that 44 Squadron were also engaged upon the same flying disciplines with their Lancasters, they were absolutely sure that something was in the wind. Further speculation then followed as to the possible nature of any intended target.

On 14 April, this run of very specific training culminated in eight 97 Squadron Lancasters setting out on an extra-long distance low-level formation practice flight of an expected five-hour duration. The squadron formation consisted of two inverted vic's, or V's, of three aircraft each, flying one V behind the other. Flap, commanding the squadron formation, led the first V, flying in the point position, with Flight Lieutenant David Penman leading the second V in a similar position. Two spare aircraft tagged onto the rear of the formation, with Flying Officer Rod Rodley, who had previously lost the wingtips from a Lancaster, being the captain of one of them. The newly arrived incoming commanding officer, Wing Commander Collier, was keen to discover how well the Lancaster crews had progressed in their low altitude role, and therefore insisted on flying as a passenger in one of the aircraft for the duration of the exercise.

The 97 Squadron orders instructed them initially to rendezvous with the Lancasters from 44 Squadron over Grantham. However, the 44 Squadron aircraft failed to make the rendezvous for some technical reason, and 97 Squadron therefore pressed on alone. The designated route was then due south-west to Selsey Bill on the south coast, before returning north-east to Lincolnshire. Having returned to Lincolnshire, the heading was then north-west to Falkirk before then turning due north for a simulated low-level attack on Inverness. Finally, after turning over Inverness, the Lancasters were to fly south-east to drop practice bombs on the bombing range at Wainfleet, before returning direct to home base, after covering more than one thousand miles in total.

Unknown to the crews of the two Lancaster squadrons, the planners had already been at work to formulate the operation that they were at that stage unwittingly practising for.

To set the scenario, it was suffice to say that since long before the Japanese attack on Pearl Harbor had forced the United States of America into the war, the Americans had been extremely concerned at the magnitude of their shipping losses to German submarines whilst the American ships were trying to keep Great Britain supplied with war materials and food. Then, having been forced to declare war on Japan and Germany, the USA had as a consequence unfortunately opened the way for the German Navy and its U-boats to legitimately operate against allied shipping along the length of the USA's own eastern territorial waters. Long before the UK bound supply ships had even had a chance to set their course for England, they were being targeted by German submarines lying in wait in American home waters. Now, with Pacific as well as European theatres of war to contend with, the USA just could not afford the rapidly increasing shipping losses.

In short, the American president Franklin D. Roosevelt, had therefore appealed to Winston Churchill for British assistance in destroying, or at least seriously disrupting, the source of the German U-boat menace.

The difficulties of destroying U-boats at sea or trying to bomb them in their ports from high levels, whether by day or night, were well known. However, some careful thought at high levels had decided that, whilst the U-boats themselves might be an elusive and hard to destroy target, perhaps the component parts of the U-boats would be easier to destroy, especially if those parts could be reached long before they even became part of a U-boat. Accordingly, the think tank of British war planners had decided that if the supply of engines that powered the U-boats could be denied to the U-boat builders, then the supply of U-boats would be effectively strangled at source.

It was already common knowledge that the MAN Diesel engine works, situated in Augsburg, Bavaria, Southern Germany, were the main suppliers of diesel engines for the U-boats. That was it then! Decision made! Get the Royal Air Force to target the MAN Diesel engine works at Augsburg!

The target having been set, plans then had to be made to decide the method of attack. Accordingly, Bomber Command Operational Order No:143, and the Code Name "MARGIN", were allocated to the beginnings of such a plan.

A combination of intelligence reports and reconnaissance photos of Augsburg indicated the small size of the MAN Diesel engine assembly and machine sheds that needed to be destroyed. It was therefore immediately obvious that bombing from a high level in daylight or darkness would probably not even hit such a small target, never mind destroy anything important to the Germans.

It was therefore decided that the only way of being absolutely sure of destroying such a small target was to fly in extremely low, before then quite literally dumping the bombs very precisely, point blank, straight through the roof of each of the targeted buildings. Further, and to be so precise, the attack would have to be made in broad daylight!

After much careful consideration, it was decided that a successful surprise attack on Augsburg might well be possible. The precise situation of the MAN works in the middle of Augsburg was clearly marked by the presence of some high chimney stacks. Reconnaissance photos had also shown that there were some easy to follow natural geographical features that would allow a low-level attacking force to navigate visually almost right to the easily recognised factory gates, before revealing themselves only at the last moment, when already on their final bombing runs onto the target.

The main planning concern then centred on how to get the bombers safely down to Southern Germany to be able to carry out the attack in the first place. Daylight bombing operations with heavy bombers had already been abandoned because of the heavy bombers' vulnerability to attack by German fighter aircraft in daylight. However, brisk discussion with intelligence sources revealed the fact that, apart from the German homelands, the strongest, most experienced and efficient of Germany's air defences were concentrated in occupied French territory around the Pas de Calais and the eastern end of the English Channel, thus countering the threat of the main strength of our own air forces in the south-east of Britain. Conversely, the weakest and least experienced German air defences facing Britain were situated towards the more sparsely defended west of France.

It was therefore decided that, if the combined firepower of six tightly formatted low flying Lancasters could keep the least experienced German air defences at bay, then the daylight flying risks might well be acceptable.

The simplest western outline route to Augsburg was first set out as a simple line from Selsey Bill, straight across the Channel to a landfall on the Normandy Coast, just north-east of Caen. From there, then flying roughly south-east over France to outflank the best of the Luftwaffe's defences, and by-passing Paris, to reach the 48th Parallel, before then changing course to fly due east to eventually arrive just south of Augsburg in Southern Germany.

On 15 April, Flap and David Penman as the section leaders for 97 Squadron, and Squadron Leader Nettleton and Flight Lieutenant

Sandford as the section leaders for 44 Squadron, were summoned to Bomber Command HQ, High Wycombe, for a top secret briefing. Once there, they were informed of the nature of what initially appeared to them, and others, to be the suicidal nature of the joint Operation "MARGIN" mission that they and their crews were being asked to undertake in the near future.

On leaving HQ Flap and David Penman were ordered not to disclose any details of the planned raid to anyone else. In the meantime, they had plenty to think and talk about on the way back to Woodhall Spa.

On 16 April, the 97 Squadron's Lancaster crews were told that the attack for which they had been training would be launched in the afternoon of the next day, following a briefing on the operational plan. No further details were given and, to preserve secrecy, the eight crews were ordered to be confined to base overnight, with all outside contact denied and any consumption of alcohol banned.

During the morning of Friday, 17 April, the eight scheduled crews tested the engines and systems of their aircraft, and any necessary fine adjustments were immediately made by the closely attentive ground crews. Four 1000lb bombs were hoisted into the bomb bays of each aircraft, each with an eleven second delay fuse, to allow each section of the low flying aircraft to get clear before they were damaged by the explosion of their own bombs. A full load of fuel was also pumped into each of the Lancasters' huge tanks.

A mid-morning briefing was then convened, with the purpose of briefing the fully assembled crews with the finalised details of the mission, including details of the target, final route, and method of approach and attack.

On entering the briefing room, the wall map of Europe had been left with its cover on to conceal the details thereon from any unauthorised prying eyes. As the CO, Wing Commander Collier entered the room, and bearing in mind that the crews themselves had not previously been given any details of the route or eventual target, the cover was dropped from the wall map. Audible gasps were immediately heard as the route of the mission indicated by a coloured tape became apparent. There was nervous laughter from those crew members who, from the nature of their daylight formation flying practice, then realised the enormity of the mission that they were being ordered to undertake if they were required to fly the distance indicated on the wall map in broad daylight, especially if unescorted across occupied France, a chunk of Germany, and all the way to Bavaria!

Addressing the meeting, the CO commenced by exhibiting fine photographic details of the MAN factory target, whilst all emphasis was given to the utter importance of destroying the diesel engine assembly sheds situated at the factory. Finally, details of the bombers carefully planned outflanking route were disclosed to the assembled company.

Departure of 97 Squadron was planned for 3.00pm, to then rendezvous with 44 Squadron over Selsey Bill and head south of south-east from the Sussex coast to Dives sur Mer, Normandy, on the opposite French coast, flying absolutely as low as possible over the sea to avoid any radar detection by the enemy.

To reduce the chance of enemy fighter aircraft interference with the Lancaster force over the French coast, it was scheduled that the Royal Air Force would draw the Luftwaffe's fighter force into action elsewhere, by using formations of Boston light bombers under protection of an umbrella of Spitfire fighters to launch hit and run raids well away from the Lancasters' route into France, all distractions being timed to commence just before the Lancasters were due to pass over the coast.

Once over the French coast at Dives sur Mer, Cote Fleurie, on the Baie de Seine, the Lancasters' course was carefully laid to avoid known German airfields, by continuing south into France for a short distance before swinging diagonally south-east across the countryside of France, flying at a height of under 500ft to Sens, just south-east of Paris; then swinging east of south-east to a point just north of Lake Constance above the German/Swiss border. From Lake Constance, the course setting to be east of north-east to carry the formations to the easily recognisable Lake Ammer See, whilst hoping that any German detection of the bomber force on that direction of travel would give the impression that Munich was to be the eventual target. However, from Lake Ammer See, and following the feint towards Munich, the course was set to take the force on a very hard turn to port (left), to fly back on itself in a north-westerly direction to soon meet the river Lech, before then turning to starboard (right) and, flying absolutely as low as possible, to follow the course of the river Lech north to its intersection with a canal on the force's port (left) side. Turning to follow that canal, whilst remaining at extreme low-level, would enable the force to burst right into the centre of Augsburg as they rose up from the canal to position themselves to attack the target that would then be revealed right ahead of them.

The operation was deliberately timed to end as dusk was falling. The crews were briefed that, following the attack, they should then climb away from the target to gain height into the darkness and find their own individual routes back to home base, flying at high altitude on a north-westerly heading directly to Lincolnshire. However, should darkness be slow to fall, the order was then to retrace the outward route in a westerly direction until darkness did fall, and only then to turn to a more direct heading for Lincolnshire.

Photos and sketches of the target were shown, with particular attention being given to recognition of the most important parts of the target, most specifically the diesel engine assembly sheds. The crews were advised to expect only light defences over Augsburg and told that if they flew low enough over the target area, then it was unlikely that the German anti-aircraft defences would be able to depress their guns low enough to train them onto the attacking Lancasters.

Flap and David Penman, having already attended HQ, had then of course heard the operational briefing for the second time. The more they heard about what they were led to believe was the laying of such carefully detailed plans, the more they were inclined to believe that the raid could actually be a resounding success.

With take-off scheduled for 3.00pm, there was time for the crews to eat some lunch, whilst also grabbing flasks of coffee and packs of sandwiches to sustain them during the coming trip. Afterwards, there was a scramble to don the customary flying gear before the crew buses pulled up to take them out to their waiting Lancasters.

A few evenings previously, as Flap had fiddled around with his paperwork and logbooks, he had hesitated over the realisation that the impending trip to Augsburg would be the thirteenth trip of his second tour of active operations. However, not being particularly superstitious, and remembering that he had already successfully completed the thirteenth operational trip of his first tour of operations without serious event, he had dismissed any further thoughts of the matter.

Chapter 12

The Most Daring Raid So Far

By 2.00pm on Friday, 17 April 1942, at Woodhall Spa, the hard standings around eight stationary Lancasters of 97 Squadron had become the centre of much fevered activity. The crews of the Woodhall Spa aircraft were already aboard their aircraft and commencing their pre-flight checks, preparing for that day's planned trip deep into Germany.

A similar scene was also taking place at Waddington, as the Lancasters of 44 Squadron were brought to readiness.

All too soon at Woodhall Spa, a green Very light signal indicated it was time to start up the thirty-two mighty Merlin engines, four on each of the eight Lancasters, all needing to be warmed up to full roaring flight readiness. One by one the thirty-two engines were started, amid the attendant stink of exhaust smoke and the din that those actions always generated.

Aboard Lancaster numbered L7573, carrying the squadron ID prefix letters "OF" suffixed by the individual aircraft ID letter "-K", for King, Flap and his co-pilot, Pilot Officer Webb, were satisfied with their engine start up. However, on looking around his charges Flap noticed that the second aircraft in his section, piloted by Warrant Officer Harrison, had one very smoky engine that was running very erratically. On a hand signal from the ground crew Harrison's four engines were immediately cut. It appeared that Harrison would be at home for tea that night. The first reserve aircraft, piloted by Rod Rodley, he who had previously experienced the loss of a Lancaster's wing tips, would now have to take Harrison's place.

By the time Flap and P/O Webb had completed the standard series of pre-flight checks, ending with a check and tightening of their own personal seat belts and harnesses, it was time to taxi all the aircraft out to their take-off positions to await the green light for take-off.

The Most Daring Raid So Far   89

No. 97 Squadron's operational records for 17 April 1942 show Flap and his crew in L7573 OF-K (King) to have become airborne at 2.55pm.

Flap was then followed at one minute intervals by his wing men Flight Lieutenant Hallows and Pilot Officer Rodley, flying OF-B and OF-F respectively; all ahead of the second section led by Flight Lieutenant Penman and his wing men Flying Officer Deverill and Warrant Officer Mycock, flying OF-U, OF-Y, and OF-P respectively. All the Woodhall Spa Lancasters were airborne by 3.00pm precisely. The leading 97 Squadron aircraft held their speed down as they climbed away, deliberately allowing the later aircraft some time to catch up before forming up into two defensive vic's of three, as on the practice flights previously. A spare Lancaster piloted by Warrant Officer Rowlands then tucked into the open end of the rear vic'.

During the cross-country flight to Selsey Bill there was turbulent air that rocked the Lancasters about. It was a relief to pass over Selsey Bill, and drop down very low over the calm sea, as instructed, to avoid the possibility of showing up on the enemy's radar screens.

As no other problems had arisen with any of the aircraft, Warrant Officer Rowlands throttled the engines of the spare Lancaster aircraft back slightly, and then turned for home. Rowland and his crew would also be home for tea!

In the meantime, there had been absolutely no sign of the expected rendezvous with the six Lancasters from 44 Squadron. At one stage, Flap thought that he might have glimpsed them in the far distance, way off to port (left), but could not be absolutely sure. To keep the records straight, Flap asked his chosen navigator, Flying Officer Donald Hepburn, who had specifically been chosen by Flap for his already well proven navigational competency, to double check their own position. Hepburn replied that the 97 Squadron formation was exactly where it was meant to be. If the aircraft seen in the distance were indeed those of 44 Squadron, then it was definitely 44 Squadron that were well off their designated track.

At the pre-flight briefing, the crews had been told that it would not matter if the two squadrons did make their own independent ways to the target. Flap therefore gave the matter no further thought and concentrated on the task of leading his small Woodhall Spa force safely to Augsburg. Although the pre-set route to Augsburg had been carefully chosen to avoid all known German airfields, the pilots had all been briefed to fly over the open French countryside as low as possible to reduce the chance of visual or radar detection by enemy forces. As the 97 Squadron Lancasters thundered along over the French landscape, sometimes as low as fifty feet, they rose and fell with the contours of the different terrains encountered, often leaving the foliage of the countryside waving wildly in their wake as they passed. As they rushed onward, hypnotised by their sheer speed of 200 mph plus, and the close proximity of the ground rushing by beneath their aircraft, the 97 Squadron crews were totally oblivious to a terrible drama that was unfolding to the east of them.

The very event that the supposedly precise planning of the operation was designed to prevent was about to unfold. The Lancasters of 44 Squadron were flying at low-level, as ordered in the operational plan, but for some reason flying well off to the east of the operation's designated track. As they were passing an unnoticed German airfield, they were spotted by a flight of Luftwaffe Messerschmitt 109 fighter aircraft preparing to land at their base after their skirmishes with the very Bostons and Spitfires of the RAF's diversionary force that had been sent out to deliberately draw those same German fighters well away from the correctly designated track of the passing Lancaster force.

The German fighters immediately aborted their landings, snapped up their wheels and climbed to gain height. A running skirmish then developed as the Messerschmitts repeatedly ran in to attack the 44 Squadron Lancasters. The Messerschmitts caused absolute carnage, with their superior firepower that included cannons. The Messerschmitts' cannons were of a far larger calibre than the Lancasters' multiple .303 machine-gun arrays, and capable of firing impact exploding shells over a far longer effective range than the Lancasters' machine guns were able fire back with their simple inert lumps of lead; those in the form of non-explosive bullets that lacked any considerable punch, having lost effective momentum after travelling only two hundred yards or so.

Consequently, one by one the 44 Squadron Lancasters started to be hacked down, until there were only two out of the original six remaining in the air. The two remaining Lancasters, those of the leader, Squadron Leader Nettleton, and Flying Officer Garwell respectively, were only saved from a similar fate to the other four aircraft because the German fighters soon broke off the engagement to return to their base, having by then probably run short of fuel and ammunition.

Barely two and a quarter hours into the combined operation, two thirds of the original 44 Squadron strength, including two thirds of the twenty-four bombs that they were hoping to deliver to Augsburg, had been lost. That equated to a loss of one third of the combined force of the two squadrons that were heading for Augsburg. However, the two surviving Lancasters of 44 Squadron flew on, stubbornly maintaining their course towards Augsburg.

Meanwhile, Flap, leading the 97 Squadron Lancasters, had powered on unmolested. On the route over France, only slight deviations had been made to avoid built up areas, and navigator Hepburn had no difficulty in finding the next turning point south-east of Paris, over Sens. A fresh course was then set for Friedrichshafen, situated just above the Swiss/German border on the northern shores of Lake Constance. At Lake Constance the visibility was good, and the course was again reset, this time for Lake Ammer See. As Lake Ammer See came into view, Flap's still intact formation opened out slightly to make ready for a tight turn to port (left) that would then lead them on to the course of the river Lech, where they were to then to turn to starboard (right) in order to follow the river due north to its intersection with a canal on the port (left) side. Turning to port to follow the canal north-west, would then lead the formation right into Augsburg and directly onto the MAN factory.

Unknown to Flap and the crews of 97 Squadron as they turned onto the course of the river Lech, the remaining Lancasters of 44 Squadron, of which they could not be sure of having had any sight of since leaving base, had already passed through ahead of them.

In Augsburg that evening the light was still bright, and there were crowds of people thronging the streets whilst enjoying the traditional annual spring festival. As the two remaining Lancasters of 44 Squadron rose up from the canal and over the wooded margins of Augsburg to view the target, many amongst the Augsburg crowds waved to them. The crowd had not heard the German air raid sirens wailing above the sound of the festival's brass bands. However, when the sound of eight Rolls-Royce Merlin engines reverberated low overhead and combined with the racket of the German anti-aircraft defences as they started to fire, then the crowds soon realised that there was a big problem!

Nettleton, and his wing man Garwell, were both able to instantly recognise the target, the images of which were still fresh in their minds from the models they had seen at their recent operational briefing. The Lancasters' bomb doors were then opened. Over the internal intercom system, the respective bomb aimers called out their minor course adjustments to their pilots, to ensure that the bombs fell right onto the target. The three gunners aboard each of the two aircraft contributed to the general din above Augsburg by firing at the various rooftop anti-aircraft gun emplacements. Satisfyingly for them, those gun positions turned out to be much more susceptible to lumps of flying lead than the Luftwaffe fighter planes had been during their earlier engagement with the enemy's fighters over France.

Then, the two Lancasters bucked and rose slightly as they were relieved of their bomb loads.

In his head Nettleton counted down the seconds of the pre-programmed eleven second delay bomb fuses, to the occurrence of the multiple explosions that soon followed, and as he turned his aircraft away he surveyed the satisfying, but very expensive, result of 44 Squadron's hard day's work. However, when he looked around for his wing man, Garwell's aircraft was not there anymore.

Garwell's aircraft had been hit by anti-aircraft fire early on during the bombing run, and a fierce fire was already burning in the aircraft as his bombs were dropped. Rather than turn away earlier, Garwell had made the conscious decision that, having come all this way and seen his comrades pay such a dear price over France, he would carry on irrespective of the onboard fire to ensure that he dropped his bomb load on the target.

As Garwell turned away, he did not have any time to watch for explosions on the target beneath. He was now desperately looking for some open ground on which to put his burning and difficult to control aircraft down. Spotting some open ground, Garwell landed his Lancaster on its belly and it started to break up. As the front end of the aircraft separated from the rear and slithered to a halt, Garwell and three other crew members were able to scramble out on to the grass.

It was not yet as dark as the operational plans had assumed that it should have been, as Nettleton, now flying the one and only surviving Lancaster of 44 Squadron's initial force of six aircraft, headed west to retrace the route by which he had arrived at Augsburg, whilst awaiting nightfall before he could gain height and fly a more direct route home under cover of the promised darkness.

The Most Daring Raid So Far 93

Some few minutes later, as Flap led the Lancasters of 97 Squadron low along the river Lech, there was no way of knowing whether the planned element of surprise had already been lost by an earlier arrival of 44 Squadron over Augsburg, or not. As the first section of 97 Squadron roared along over the waters of the river Lech, the crews wondered whether they might still possibly be holding an element of surprise, or whether the German anti-aircraft gun crews had been fully alerted and were just waiting for them to appear.

As the Lancasters of 97 Squadron rose up from the river Lech over the outskirts of Augsburg, only then did they know by the sight of the smoking target and the instantaneous arrival of German anti-aircraft fire, that Augsburg had already been stirred up by the arrival of an unknown number of 44 Squadron Lancasters before them.

As Flap was leading his section of three 97 Squadron Lancasters to close in on their target, his wing men, Flight Lieutenant Hallows and Flying Officer Rodley, had both dropped their respective aircraft back from their leader in order to space themselves out from each other. As well as gaining fore and aft space, that manoeuvre then enabled them to move their Lancasters slightly inwards to narrow the width of their overall formation, thus ensuring as far as possible that all three of their section's aircraft would be able to pass comfortably right over the narrow target that they were rapidly approaching. As the section of three huge aircraft rose up over the tall chimneys of Augsburg and dropped down to attack, Hallows and Rodley could hear and feel multiple strikes on their aircraft from the fierce enemy anti-aircraft fire. At the same time, they both witnessed strikes on Flap's aircraft, OF-K, ahead of them. Those strikes had immediately produced a stream of white vapour that was trailing behind the aircraft. Then, just as Flap's bomb aimer had released his bombs, right on the target, it became obvious to the following onlookers that there was a fire building on board their leader's aircraft.

As soon as Flap's bombs had fallen away, the onlookers observed Flap's apparent reaction to the fire as he immediately dropped his Lancaster right down to rooftop level. His probable intention being to avoid any further hits on his aircraft as he turned away from Augsburg towards the outskirts of town; probably in the hope of finding a clear space where he might be able to pancake his Lancaster onto the ground. However, as Lancaster OF-K levelled out at minimal height away out over the outskirts of Augsburg, the senses of Flap and his crew would then have been totally overwhelmed by a most tremendous roar. For the half load of aviation spirit then remaining in the Lancaster's fuel tanks, the very fuel that should have released its energy gradually to power the aircraft home to Lincolnshire, had instead been triggered by the heat of the fire to release the entirety of the latent energy stored within it to fuel the creation of one enormous cataclysmic orange fireball, as Lancaster OF-K flew straight into the ground and exploded. For Flap and his crew, the last thing that their senses would have known would have been a roar of such crescendo that it could not possibly have got any louder, whilst at the same time being accompanied by an impossibly brilliant white light before, for them, it was total oblivion…

As Flight Lieutenant Hallows had followed in to bomb immediately behind Flap, he had also felt his aircraft take hits from the fierce barrage of gunfire then rising in defence of the MAN works. However, in his case there did not appear to be any immediately visible damage to his Lancaster, but the close proximity of the exploding shell had put his bomb aimer completely off his aim, just at the critical moment.

Flying Officer Rodley, bringing up the rear of the section, had just dropped his bombs on the target when he saw the smoke and petrol vapour trailing back from Flap's aircraft as it rapidly lost height. Then, as the smoke turned black and fierce flames appeared, it became obvious that a serious fire had quickly taken hold of the aircraft. Both Rodley and Hallows, together with their respective crews, would later relate how, before any of the section's delayed fuse bombs had even detonated, they had the horror of witnessing Flap's aircraft flying straight into the ground and exploding into an all-consuming orange fireball. So fierce was that fireball, that it re-brightened the fading evening light of what had been the day of the Augsburg spring festival celebrations; and then Lancaster OF-K had, quite simply, been King no more!

As Rodley and Hallows turned westward to fly away from the target, Flight Lieutenant Penman was leading the final section of three Lancasters along the river Lech towards Augsburg. Penman had held the section back over Lake Amer See to give the first section time to clear, whilst at the same time avoiding any chance of the second section being caught in the blasts of the first section's delayed fuse bombs as they detonated.

As the last three Lancasters were on their final run in to the target, the aircraft of both of Penman's wing men were hit by gunfire. On the left, a shell went right through the wing of Flying Officer Deverill's aircraft without at that time appearing to have caused any other damage. Almost simultaneously on the right, the aircraft of Warrant Officer Mycock received a hit that, judging by the colour of the billowing dark smoke being emitted, appeared to have set fire to the aircraft's oil supply. In spite of the damage sustained, all three of the Lancasters stayed stubbornly on course to drop their bombs on the target.

However, as Flight Lieutenant Penman closed his bomb doors and led the section away from the target, he had to watch with horror as Mycock's damaged and already fiercely burning aircraft, with its bomb doors still gaping wide open, veered out of the formation and flew straight into the ground to create yet another massive orange fireball over Augsburg.

The two surviving Lancasters of the last section then turned for home, with Flight Lieutenant Penman leading Deverill's damaged aircraft that, as a result of the earlier shell damage, was by then flying on only three engines with most of its defensive guns knocked out due to a loss of the hydraulic pressure needed to drive the gun turrets. Deverill managed to maintain protective contact with Penman, flying in formation at a wider distance than usual and, as darkness fell, being guided in that darkness by the exhaust glow from the Merlin engines of Penman's aircraft. That same darkness enabled the two aircraft to soon rise to a much higher and much safer cruising height on the most direct course for the long trip home to Woodhall Spa.

According to 97 Squadron's operational records, and in spite of flying home separately, 97 Squadron's four surviving Lancasters all joined the Woodhall Spa airfield circuit within half an hour of each other, and by 23.25hrs the survivors were all safely landed. As the crews were bussed in from the aircraft dispersal points, they realised that there were more people than usual gathered on the tarmac waiting to welcome them home.

After disembarking, and whilst their memories were still fresh from the action, the crews were immediately ushered away into a debriefing session; as if most of the day's horrific events would not have remained vividly burnt in their minds for weeks afterwards, or more probably for forever. To keep the crews alert as they answered questions on the day's events, copious amounts of coffee, tea, biscuits and cigarettes were handed out during the debriefing session, all whilst a traditional homecoming fried breakfast was being prepared in the Woodhall Spa messes.

Many in the assembled throng of well-wishers were shocked at the loss of two of the most popular 97 Squadron crews. Especially in the case of Flap, who of course had been a popular founding member of 97 Squadron since its reformation in February 1941, when the squadron was first set up to receive and operate the Lancasters' predecessors, the Avro Manchesters, from which the design for the more successful Lancasters had eventually evolved. Others in the throng were relieved that the squadron's casualties were not higher, as many had considered the whole trip to Augsburg to be a ridiculously suicidal mission from conception anyway.

When the Woodhall Spa debriefing team made early contact with the 44 Squadron debriefing team at Waddington, the news then received numbed everyone into far greater shock. For at half past midnight, not a single one of 44 Squadron's Lancasters had returned to their Waddington base. However, within another hour, at 01.30am, just as the Woodhall Spa crews were finishing their breakfasts and were about to head off for some rest, news came through that the sole surviving Lancaster of 44 Squadron, that of the leader, Squadron Leader Nettleton, had survived, whilst wandering off course to port (left), yet again! After becoming totally lost on the return trip, the crew had used SOS radio procedures to obtain a radio fix of their true position. That positional fix revealed that they were somehow well out over the Irish Sea. They had in all probability passed right over the west of England and Wales before, being unable to recognise any landmarks, they had grown concerned as to their true whereabouts. Then, having established their true position, a following radio message advised Nettleton's navigator to set a course for the nearest available diversionary airfield at Squire's Gate, near Blackpool, where the sole surviving Lancaster of 44 Squadron finally landed safely at approximately 01.00am, after being in the air for a total of ten hours solid.

Chapter 13

The Cost of the Daring

In Augsburg

On the evening of 17 April 1942, when the fires had died down or been extinguished, and it was realised that no more bombers were going to come, one citizen of Augsburg had decided that it was safe to take his dog for its usual walk. As he passed along a tree lined avenue on the outskirts of the town, near to where one of the burning bombers had crashed, he noticed a large object tangled up amongst some broken branches in the trees. As the walker moved closer, he could make out that it was some sort of seat, enclosing what looked to be the slumped body of a dead man. Rather than interfere with his find, the citizen hurried to find the nearest property with a telephone, where he roused the occupants and requested them to summon the relevant authorities, before returning to guard his find.

Not many minutes later, the local police and the German equivalent of the Home Guard were on the scene. On disentangling and retrieving the cumbersome seat, it was established that its occupant was wearing the battle dress uniform and insignia of an RAF pilot, who turned out to be unconscious rather than dead. With the realisation of the seat's connection with recent events, the military immediately took charge of the situation, making the decision to remove the seat from the scene complete with its comatose occupant in situ, simply to avoid the possibility of further aggravating any unknown injuries that might have already been sustained.

The following morning of 18 April 1942, some twelve hours after the last of the surviving RAF bombers had flown away, the citizens of Augsburg were still aghast at what had occurred the previous day, and big questions were being asked.

Had not Hitler and Goering promised that no enemy aircraft would ever penetrate so far into Germany as Bavaria?

How could the RAF, in broad daylight, have penetrated so deeply into Germany without, as far as they were concerned, any Luftwaffe opposition whatsoever?

As the RAF had approached from the south, might they indeed have flown in from Switzerland?

However, the majority of the population of Augsburg were relieved that the RAF appeared to have confined their activities to bombing the specific target of the MAN Diesel works only. The few deaths that had resulted were incidental to the attack on the actual works themselves. The RAF had not bombed any residential properties, nor fired their guns upon the citizens on the streets. In fact, the only real damage to their individual properties had been caused by their own German anti-aircraft gunners, who had managed to depress their guns so low that they were knocking great chunks out of the architectural features of the nearby historical buildings of their own very quaint historical town.

Some citizens even expressed a certain admiration for the way that the giant Lancaster bombers, previously unseen over Germany, had been impressively flown at such a low level. It had appeared to them that the huge bombers had materialised from nowhere to drop their bombs; before the surviving aircraft had then simply disappeared again.

The German Information Ministry described the raid as a pointless propaganda exercise, expected to cost the MAN factory only a few days of lost production. However, the real propaganda value might have been greater than German High Command had realised, for many citizens of Augsburg were immediately concerned that it did not look too good for their future if the RAF could drop by anytime they chose, unopposed, and in broad daylight. But of course, those citizens did not know what it had actually cost the RAF in lost men and machines to just "drop by" on that one day.

Of the damage done to the MAN works itself, out of the seventeen bombs later known to have reached Augsburg and landed on the factory, five disappointingly had failed to explode. Therefore, of the total of forty-eight bombs transported from Lincolnshire, only twelve (25%) were effective in causing some damage.

In Lincolnshire

At Woodhall Spa and Waddington, on the morning of Saturday, 18 April 1942, it became apparent that there would not be any more surprise returns from Augsburg. The stark truth had then registered that, out of the total force of twelve brand new Avro Lancasters, as collectively drawn from 44 and 97 Squadrons respectively for dispatch to Augsburg, only five had returned. A fifty-eight per cent loss rate that would remind the Air Ministry why they had previously abandoned unescorted daylight bombing raids into enemy territory.

That same morning, David Penman went to see Bernice, my mother, to offer his condolences for the loss of her husband Flap over Augsburg the previous night. He described to her what had been witnessed by the crews of the surviving Lancasters of 97 Squadron and stated that in his own mind he was quite sure that there would not have been any survivors from the catastrophic fireball crash of OF-K that had been witnessed. However, David Penman was totally taken aback by Bernice's reaction to the news that he gave her. For there were no tears, and no fuss! She simply stated that she knew Flap so well that she would have known immediately if he really had died. Therefore, as she had absolutely no such intuition, she was adamant that Flap was still alive.

On Station at both Waddington and Woodhall Spa, the respective squadron commanding officers and their adjutants (administrators) were busy at their desks. The up-to-date information on those crews that had not returned from Augsburg needed to be put forward to the Air Ministry, to enable the relevant notifications to be issued to the next of kin. Also, accurate debriefing information had to be collated, to enable the Air Ministry to issue an official communiqué on the same day to assist the Sunday press with their headlines for that weekend.

Both squadron commanding officers were also putting forward their recommendations for decorations on account of the outstanding valour and bravery shown during the previous day's operation. Both commanding officers recommended the immediate award of a Victoria Cross to each of the respective squadron leaders who had led the two squadrons' formations of Lancasters on the Augsburg operation: namely – Squadron Leader John Dering Nettleton of 44 Squadron, and Squadron Leader John Seymour Sherwood of 97 Squadron (Flap).

Of Flap, Wing Commander Collier, the Officer Commanding 97 Squadron, wrote:

> "Squadron Leader Sherwood, D.F.C. led his squadron on the daylight attack on the important Diesel Engine Factory at Augsburg, Southern Germany. With great skill and ability Squadron Leader Sherwood led the formation at very low level across 900 miles of enemy occupied territory – eventually leading all his aircraft directly on to the target. On the approach to the target itself, heavy and accurate anti-aircraft fire was experienced but, with extreme daring and cool-headedness he pressed home the attack with his Section. Scoring direct hits on the factory with his bombs from a very low level.
>
> "While bombing the target his aircraft was hit by anti-aircraft guns and caught fire.
>
> "Squadron Leader Sherwood continued to lead his section away from the target with one wing well alight and until such time as the aircraft became uncontrollable.
>
> "By extreme devotion to duty, Squadron Leader Sherwood ensured the success of the operation with which he was charged and continued his daring leadership until the end. His conspicuous bravery on this occasion crowned a long and distinguished career in the service of his country."

Having been signed by Wing Commander Collier, Flap's recommendation was forwarded to Group HQ, where it was signed and endorsed by Group Captain H.A. Haines as follows:

> "This gallant leadership deserves the highest recognition. His example will always be remembered in the Group and in the Royal Air Force."

On reaching HQ No.5 Group Bomber Command, the recommendation was both signed and endorsed in the handwriting of Air Marshall A.T. Harris as – *"Strongly recommended"*.

However, it would eventually be realised that on reaching the Air Ministry somebody had added the following unsigned pencilled condition to the recommendation of a Victoria Cross for Flap:

> *"To be rec'd (recommended) for DSO if later found to be alive."*

The commanding officers of the two squadrons also prepared a group citation, in support of the additional decorations that they were recommending for the heroic actions of other officers and ranks that took part in the operation. The 97 Squadron recommendations included a DSO for Flight Lieutenant David Penman, who led the second section of 97 Squadron and a DFC for Flight Lieutenant Hallows who took over command of the first section when Flap's aircraft was shot down. Strangely, there was no recommendation at all in respect of Warrant Officer Mycock and his crew who, in spite of their damaged aircraft being well alight, instead of jettisoning the bombs and seeking to force land their Lancaster in the open countryside, had stubbornly kept on course to place their bombs on the target before their aircraft had also plunged into the ground to create a second fireball.

The squadron citation was signed and dispatched on the following day, Sunday, 19 April.

Also, on Sunday, 19 April, and the days immediately following the raid, the newspapers rushed to get their Augsburg stories into print, all as based on the official Air Ministry communiqué issued early on 18 April. That communiqué had gone into greater detail than was usual, thus enabling the press to name many of the crew members who had taken part in the operation. Consequently, official pictures of a very serious looking Flap appeared in most of the papers under several different headlines, such as: "RAIDER HERO MISSING", "NO LIFE WAS LOST IN VAIN" or "WAR'S MOST DARING RAID." In most cases the reports were accompanied by the following quotation, as extracted from Prime Minister Churchill's message, as sent to the Commander-in-Chief of Bomber Command, immediately following the raid:

> "*We must plainly regard the attack of the Lancasters on the U-boat engine factory at Augsburg as an outstanding achievement of the R.A.F. Undeterred by heavy losses at the outset, the bombers pierced in broad daylight into the heart of Germany and struck a vital point with deadly precision.*
>
> "*Pray convey the thanks of his Majesty's Government to the officers and men who accomplished this memorable feat of arms in which no life was lost in vain.*"

Immediately following the raid, it was directed that the surviving crews from 44 and 97 Squadrons should for the time being be completely rested from operational flying duties, pending possible requirement for interviews by the press. There was in any case a shortage of serviceable aircraft, as in addition to those aircraft that were lost and needing to be replaced, the surviving Lancasters were all suffering from multiple damages, mainly caused by anti-aircraft fire over the target that had inflicted damage to airframes, hydraulic systems and engines. The gun turrets on several of the Lancasters had also seized up, or inexplicably ceased to work.

During the rest of April and on into May, interesting, and sometimes very interested, VIP visitors were received by the two squadrons. Early visitors included the Secretary of State for Air, soon followed in early May by the "Father of the Royal Air Force" himself, Viscount Hugh Trenchard, Marshal of the Royal Air Force and an ardent supporter of the obvious need for a determined strategic bombing campaign.

During their rest from operations, the 44 and 97 Squadron crews found plenty of time to occupy themselves by holding their own unofficial post-mortems to discuss what had caused such heavy losses to the 44 Squadron formation over France. Relatively early on in the war, the decision had already been made to avoid sending heavy bombers on unescorted daylight missions due to the ease with which they were outgunned by the greater effective range and firepower of the cannons fitted to the enemy's aircraft. At the briefings before the raid, it was solely the planners' explanation of their carefully laid plans, including precise timings, diversions, and outflanking routes, that had given the crews the real confidence to believe that they would be able to fly all the way to Augsburg in daylight without interception by the enemy. Indeed, Flap *had* led his 97 Squadron formation all the way to Augsburg unmolested!

It was therefore most unfortunate that a series of compounding errors had conspired to cause the destruction of two thirds of the 44 Squadron formation so soon after it had entered enemy occupied territory. The Operation Margin route over France had been precisely plotted to avoid flying over or near German airfields, yet the 44 Squadron formation had passed right along the boundary of an already stirred up and active German fighter base.

Inter squadron pub chat had soon revealed that whilst 97 Squadron's crews were correctly briefed to cross the French coast over the seaside town of Dives-sur-Mer, in accordance with the operational orders, the crews of 44 Squadron at Waddington were fairly sure that they had in fact been briefed to cross the French coast at the different seaside town of Villers-sur-Mer. Somewhere along the chain of command a misunderstanding had occurred that then placed 44 Squadron some six miles further towards the east of France than the track that they should have been on. Consequently, as they were following a straight course from Villers-sur-Mer to the next designated turning point at Sens, it automatically took 44 Squadron's formation right along the boundary of the already active German fighter base at Beaumont-le-Roger, near Evereux. Retrospectively, it is easy to see how such place name confusion could have occurred, as the coast of Normandy is thick with little seaside towns bearing the suffix "sur-mer" ("on-sea").

Also, retrospectively, there was a chance that the foregoing error might not have mattered at all if all else had gone to plan. However, the first error had been compounded by a further misunderstanding. In this instance there was some confusion over the timing of the diversionary raids that had been arranged to draw German fighter forces away to the east. Inexplicably, the diversionary raids were carried out much earlier than had been planned. All timings for the operation were based on the assumption of an addition or subtraction of a few minutes either side of a "zero hour", calculated from when the combined forces were expected to cross "the coast". However, there would seem to have been some confusion over which "coast" the plan was referring to; the coast of England, or the coast of France? Either way, the confusion meant that the German fighters had already been out to intercept the RAF's distractions to the east, and they were therefore arriving back to land earlier than predicted by the Augsburg raid's planners. Consequently, the German fighters then found themselves right on top of 44 Squadron's easily spotted formation of large Lancaster aircraft, passing right along the perimeter of their very own Luftwaffe base.

Apparently, if 44 Squadron had been correctly briefed to follow the same designated route as 97 Squadron, then the whole force of twelve aircraft and their full bomb loads could well have managed to sneak through to arrive unmolested over the Augsburg target.

A study of the designated route shown in Bomber Command Operation Order No. 143, in respect of Operation Margin to Augsburg, as held in the National Archives under the reference AIR16/757, reveals how, through the planners' poor attention to place name details, operational results could have possibly turned out to be even worse! The planned route listed on the Order shows that after Sens, the next designated turning point on the Augsburg bound bomber force's route was listed as Ludwigshafen, therein purporting to be on the shores of Lake Constance. There is indeed a town ending "...shafen" on the shores of Lake Constance, but that is Friedrichshafen, not Ludwigshafen. Ludwigshafen is approximately one hundred and twenty-five miles away, north by north-west from Friedrichshafen, near Mannheim. The fact that this error could have remained unnoticed on the operational order, before issue to the participating squadrons, might therefore lead one to suspect that other erroneous directional orders could well have been issued at the respective squadron briefings. Therefore, as the route to Augsburg had been most carefully planned to avoid alerting the Germans, any force setting a course that relied on erroneously briefed place names was quite likely to blunder into trouble, simply by flying over far more heavily defended German territory on the way to Augsburg than was intended.

Chapter 14

Into Enemy Hands

The almighty roaring noise had faded away, and the impossibly brilliant white light had dulled. As Flap stirred and stretched, he realised that he was in a comfortable bed and wondered if he might have been dreaming of recent events. However, before he had the chance to even try and open his eyes, he just knew that there were problems. He could feel the bandages on his head and face and, worst of all, the voices that he could hear were talking in German! He opened his eyes very slowly and discovered that he could see. Eye slots had been left in the bandages, and he looked gingerly around.

Flap's movements had been noticed, and a nurse came over to his bedside and spoke to him in rather curt but fairly good English. She explained that he was in a German military hospital having sustained a concussion and burns to his face when his aeroplane had crashed. She offered him a drink of water and told him that she would call the duty doctor to look him over now that he was awake.

The doctor soon came to check Flap over to ensure that he had recovered, or was likely to recover, the full use of all his faculties. Flap was immediately apprehensive to learn that he had been burnt, but soon relaxed following the advice that his burns were not too deep or serious, and that they would probably not scar him as his pilot's leather flying jacket, helmet, goggles, earphones and oxygen mask had between them given him some good protection from the heat of fire or explosion. As Flap had absolutely no recollection of the crash, the doctor suggested that a few more days of rest were required before he might be ready for discharge from hospital care. In the meantime, the doctor authorised that light meals should be taken.

Within the next few days a uniformed German official dropped by to inform Flap that he was officially a Prisoner of War (PoW) in the hands of the German Reich. He was also advised that an escort would soon be arranged to transport him to an interrogation centre, where the necessary forms would be completed to register his PoW status with the International Red Cross, before his onward transmission to a Prisoner of War camp run by the Luftwaffe (German Air Force).

However, before Flap's discharge from hospital could be arranged, his skin broke out in a vivid red rash that was accompanied by a very high fever and periods of delirium. The hospital immediately diagnosed the rash as scarlet fever, an infectious disease that had probably entered his system through burn damaged areas of skin.

In 1942, without the availability of today's refined antibiotics, scarlet fever was regarded as a far more serious debilitating infectious disease than today, capable of quickly causing widespread epidemics.

The last thing that the Germans needed would have been a scarlet fever epidemic running out of control amongst two thousand odd prisoners and personnel in the confined spaces of a PoW camp, and possibly beyond. The PoW camp would in any case have had only limited medical facilities of its own to hand. Consequently, the Germans immediately postponed any thought of transferring Flap to a PoW camp, and he was immediately placed into the hospital's isolation ward.

A total of just over six weeks therefore elapsed, after Flap was shot down, before he was eventually declared fit enough to be transported to a German interrogation centre near Frankfurt for processing. There, whilst the necessarily compliant Red Cross forms were duly completed, it was the real intention of the German interrogators to gather as much useful information as possible from the many captured Allied aircrew passing through their hands. To that end, skilful techniques were employed by the inquisitors to lull their aircrew victims into unwittingly divulging sensitive information that might be of benefit to the German Reich. Many captured aircrew were already deeply traumatised by their recent experiences of seeing fellow crew members killed and injured during the drama of being shot down and, in such circumstances, the Germans hoped to easily gain useful intelligence from this vulnerable and sometimes very pliable source of information.

As Flap's six week hospital stay had given him some time to recover from the initial trauma of his crash experience, he felt confident that his interrogators would not manage to trick him into discussion of any sensitive information during the interrogative process. However, in spite of knowing that he had dreamt all manner of absolute nonsense during his hospitalised periods of unconscious delirium, Flap could not have realised that he had also been muttering all sorts of incoherent nonsense during those same periods. It therefore took him totally by surprise when the interrogating German officer suddenly demanded to know, "Was ist sparrow fart?"

Trying not to look too surprised, or amused, Flap had started to reply with the intention of explaining that "sparrow fart" was simply an idiomatic slang expression used in the Lincolnshire and Yorkshire countryside of England. However, before he could offer his logical explanation of the derivation and literal meaning of the said expression, and before he could speak any further, his interrogator demanded to know why one would have to be "up before sparrow fart." At that point, it occurred to Flap that the Germans just might believe that, irrespective of the truly intended meaning of the words, "sparrow fart" might in fact be a coded name for some sort of significant process or operation, possibly involved with being "up", as "up" into the air and flying, rather than simply leaping out of bed!

Flap therefore decided that it was not his job to deter the Germans from any erroneous and potentially time-wasting beliefs. He therefore simply stated that he had absolutely no knowledge of any process or operation named "sparrow fart", in anticipation that his use of the words "process" and "operation" might just further encourage the Germans to think that there could indeed be some mysterious significance to the phrase.

Following completion of matters over several days at the interrogation centre, Flap was then transported with other aircrew PoWs to the purpose-built German Prisoner of War Camp designated as Stammlager Luft III (Main Camp For Aircrew), usually known as Stalag Luft III for short, at Sagan, Lower Silesia, Germany, situated one hundred miles southeast of Berlin. That PoW camp, then only recently opened for business from 21 March 1942, had been set up specifically to enable the German Air Force (Luftwaffe), rather than the German Army (Wehrmacht), to be responsible for the housing and care of captured allied aircrew as their own special responsibility, supposedly on the basis of ensuring that the sporting and chivalrous mutual respect that had arisen between the opposing fellow knights of the air during the First World War might still be permitted to continue during the Second World War.

When Flap arrived at Stalag Luft III, he discovered that the camp consisted of two separate compounds, known as East Compound and

Centre Compound respectively, together containing a PoW population of some 2,500 men that had been created by gathering all allied aircrew PoWs to one central place from the various PoW camps situated across Germany and occupied Poland. The East Compound housed British RAF and Fleet Air Arm officer aircrew, inclusive of Polish, Czech, French, Belgian, Dutch, and Norwegian aircrew who had previously escaped their occupied homelands, specifically to become British subjects, which had then enabled them to join the Royal Air Force. The Centre Compound housed NCOs only.

The whole camp had been constructed on a previously forested site that had been cleared of its pine trees and had been carefully chosen by the Germans for its natural escape deterrent features. The visible ground within the compound consisted of a dull dusty grey soil composed of rotted down pine needles, which in turn lay above a bright yellow sandy subsoil. The bright sand was therefore contrastingly obvious against the pale topsoil if either soil layer was disturbed by any attempt at tunnelling into it, whilst the friable nature of the sand itself left any tunnelling attempts hazardous under the threat of a sudden collapse of sand.

Both camp compounds were surrounded by ten-foot-high double fences, all topped with razor wire, beyond which the forest growth had been cleared back by a further thirty yards. The space between the double fences had been filled with coils of razor wire, and forty-foot-high guard towers which, as the PoWs usually referred to the Germans as "Goons", had consequently become known as Goon boxes. Those boxes had been placed around the compound perimeter at fifty-yard intervals. Ten yards inside the main fence, there was also a low tripwire that the prisoners were forbidden to cross, at the risk of being shot at from the goon boxes above.

In order to further reinforce the camp's natural escape deterrents, the huts within the compound had been deliberately built well away from the perimeter fence, specifically to extend the required distance of any prospective tunnelling project that might originate from those huts. Additionally, each of the compound huts had been built on top of a series of two-foot-high pillars, specifically designed to leave any under hut activity immediately visible to the patrolling guards. On top of all of the foregoing precautions, microphones had been secreted into the ground around the compound at periodic intervals to detect any underground vibrations that might be linked to tunnelling activity.

The reception process at Stalag Luft III involved the photographing, fingerprinting, identification, and numbering of each individual prisoner, for German camp records. Flap was allocated a Prisoner number (in German: *Gefangenennummer*) 385 which, when attached to his prison ID, entitled him to receive his personal issue of bedding, towel, cutlery, bowl and mug. To his disgust, he had become a *Kriegsgefangenen* (war prisoner), generally shortened by the prisoners to Kriegie during conversation. His photograph and his fingerprints had then been filed upon his *Personalkarte* (personal card), as held within the camp records.

With German formalities completed, Flap was then introduced to the population of the East compound of the camp. There, he soon discovered that there was to be a secondary reception process, conducted by the Kriegies themselves, for their own security and protection. The process had been set up following the early discovery of German efforts to obtain useful intelligence information from allied aircrew by introducing English speaking stool pigeons with false Kriegie ID into the prisoner population. The Kriegies own secondary process therefore quite simply involved the expectation that at least one existing Kriegie would, from a previous RAF association, usually be able to readily recognise and vouch for genuine incoming newly captured RAF personnel. Failing that, a series of difficult questions had been designed to weed out any prospective impostors. That combined process had the dual purpose of providing a good reference for recognised and approved Kriegie incomers when possible, as well as then providing a friendly face to show the new arrival around the camp and introduce him to the humdrum routine of a Kriegie's life. In Flap's case, the system worked out well, for he was instantly recognised by Flight Lieutenant John L. Nunn, from when they had served together flying the Manchesters of 97 Squadron, until John Nunn had been shot down.

John Nunn related to Flap how he had been captured by the Germans, when, on the night of 16/17 August 1941 over Belgium, and outward bound to bomb a target near Dusseldorf, his Manchester had been held in a cone of searchlights before being attacked by a German night fighter. He had already been struggling to gain height in a typically sluggish Manchester with a full bomb load aboard, when the unexpected fighter attack had set fire to one of the Manchester's engines, damaged the aircraft's hydraulics and undercarriage, and in doing so had destroyed all hope of Nunn keeping the aircraft aloft. On issue of Nunn's order to bail out of the doomed aircraft, five of his crew parachuted away. However, the front gunner had been so badly wounded by the fighter attack that he was unable to jump. John Nunn therefore decided that, rather than desert the front gunner to his fate, and as the aircraft was going down anyway, he would stay at the controls and attempt a controlled descent and forced landing that might then save both the front gunner and himself. Luckily, Belgium is low lying and fairly flat, for it was such a dark night that, unable to see the ground at all, Nunn had to rely solely on his altimeter to tell him when he was nearly at zero height.

As the reducing altimeter reading passed one hundred feet and approached a reading of fifty feet, Nunn gently pulled up the Manchester's nose to allow the tail end of the aircraft to meet the ground first, before then closing the throttles and allowing the front end of the aircraft to slump noisily to the ground. Luckily, the Manchester dropped into an extensive area of thick undergrowth and small trees, the springy resistance of which was sufficient to cushion the fall of the aircraft as it flopped down, as well as then bringing it to a gradual halt without too much destruction to itself. Fearing the possibility of fire and explosion from the large amount of fuel and munitions still remaining aboard the aircraft, Nunn somehow managed to get himself and his gunner out of, and away from, the aircraft before collapsing into a heap on the ground. John Nunn and his gunner were not located by the Germans until the following morning. Both were then hospitalised by the Germans, when it was discovered that in addition to his gunner's severe injuries, Nunn himself had breaks in both his arms and several lesser injuries. His gunner, Sergeant H. Currie, unfortunately soon died of the gunshot wounds to his chest that had been received in the fighter attack. John Nunn was subsequently awarded the Distinguished Flying Cross (DFC) for his selfless act of remaining with the crippled aircraft in the attempt to save the life of his helpless gunner.

Flap and John Nunn were genuinely pleased to see each other again, and both knew that they would have plenty to talk about, albeit that they were now both frustrated by the captive situation that they found themselves to be in. Nunn was particularly keen to hear details of how the dreaded twin engine Avro Manchesters, such as he himself was flying when shot down, had morphed into the very impressive sounding four engine Lancaster that had successfully transported Flap to Luft III. And of course, John Nunn was keen to hear such details of the Augsburg raid that Flap was able to remember, bearing in mind that there were some details that Flap would not have been aware of at that time.

Nunn gave Flap a tour of the East Compound before showing him where his allocated quarters were to be, in one of the fifteen single storey huts within the compound. Each of the twelve main bunkrooms within these huts was designed to sleep twelve men in double decked bunks, and the bunk rooms themselves were arranged around the separate day rooms, cooking facilities and central solid fuel stoves.

Nunn made Flap aware that there were inquisitive German administrative and security personnel continuously active in and around the prison compounds. In Stalag Luft III those security personnel were led by a German Sergeant Major in the form of one Hermann Glemnitz, nicknamed Dimwitz by the Kriegies. Glemnitz, who was himself an ex First World War Luftwaffe pilot, was assisted by four NCOs, and as well as responsibility for security, also kept records and administered the twice daily roll calls (Appells). Dimwitz had so far proved himself to be a man of good humour, who enjoyed a good joke, always apparently with a sporting sense of fair play. The Kriegies had already very early on decided that, whilst Dimwitz was obviously a German patriot, he was most definitely not a Nazi!

Together, Dimwitz and his security team had earned the Kriegie nickname of "ferrets" from their habit of ferreting in and around the Kriegies' huts, in the roof spaces and under the floors, whilst looking for signs of clandestine activity and forbidden items. Ferrets were usually easy to spot when out and about, dressed in their heavy blue overalls. However, the ferrets also had a happy knack of secreting themselves where they could invisibly eavesdrop on prisoner conversations for intelligence information, and/or observe what they might consider to be any form of suspicious activity. There were even camouflaged positions in the undergrowth outside the camp perimeter, from which the ferrets could secretly observe the Kriegies' outdoor compound activities.

Prompted by Nunn's description of the ferrets' inquisitive activities around the camp, Flap related how the German officer at the PoW reception centre had questioned him about the significance of the phrase "sparrow fart", that he himself must have apparently uttered in an unknown context whilst unconscious. Nunn found Flap's story amusing, and they agreed that it might be good sport to keep the phrase alive during occasional conversations held, especially if ferrets were known to be in their vicinity.

The brief of Dimwitz and his ferrets was to co-operate with the Kriegies as best they could, all in order to ensure Kriegie contentment whilst securing the smooth and peaceful running of the camp. To that end some of the security staff were very co-operative in obtaining materials required to keep the Kriegies well absorbed in their hobbies, sports and keep fit activities. Flap was surprised to discover that, for the duration of his stay, the Germans would actually pay him a small salary in cash that could, with prior approval, be officially used to arrange outside purchases of permitted goods via the compound administrators. Unofficially, Flap's fellow Kriegies soon advised him that his cash, when combined with the availability of a further currency in the form of Red Cross cigarettes and chocolate, could enable him to obtain just about anything that he might require from some of the German personnel, especially those who were already conditioned and known to be easily approachable in exchange for some small reward.

To counter the activities of the ferrets, the Kriegies were continuously developing their own counter security system. This consisted of at least one Kriegie, designated duty pilot of the day, always being on duty to keep a log of the movements of Dimwitz and his staff. By simply logging all German staff entering or leaving the compound, in and out, the Kriegies were then able to ensure that there were no unseen ferrets remaining in secreted positions around the compound.

The duty pilot was always supported by one or more duty stooges, who were briefed to keep ferrets away from any sensitive areas of the compound where illicit Kriegie activities might be taking place. Ferrets were easily distracted, usually by mock Kriegie fights and animated disputes, and for long enough to enable others to hide whatever forbidden items might have been open to imminent discovery.

Unfortunately, it was a ferret that, just before Flap's arrival in the compound, had caused the only existing contraband radio set in the East Compound to be confiscated. However, Nunn was able to inform Flap that confiscation of the radio had not occurred before the Kriegies had heard the BBC's morale boosting news announcement of the RAF's first one thousand bomber raid delivered to Cologne, Germany, on the night of 30/31 May 1942.

By the time of Flap's arrival in Luft III, captured aircrew from the Cologne raid were already beginning to arrive there. Over the following weeks Flap would hear details of that momentous raid from them and the clandestine BBC news bulletins.

The RAF's first one thousand bomber raid had been carried out on the industries of the German city of Cologne and, in addition to the damage caused to German industry, the raid was designed to be a successful psychological hammer blow against Germany as a whole, giving a hint of what might eventually be delivered to Germany on a regular basis. However, it soon became obvious that the planning for that raid had in fact entailed the absolute scraping of the RAF Bomber Command barrel to achieve the required number of aircraft that were made available. As it happened, a number actually exceeding the magic target of one thousand aircraft was eventually achieved for the raid, but to this end, even the operational training units of the RAF had been raided for their aircraft, together with some of their operationally inexperienced pilots and crews. Many crews that flew that night had not even completed their training, before eagerly jumping at the chance to take part in a small piece of history in the making.

Nunn was also able to update Flap on some 97 Squadron news. Most of which had occurred during Flap's period of hospitalisation and had also been most recently received from new intakes of RAF PoWs to Stalag Luft III. Among such news, Flap learned that Flight Lieutenant J.G. Mackid, with whom he had shared a citation for their respective awards of Distinguished Flying Crosses following their joint actions during the daylight raid on the German capital ships in Brest harbour on 18 December 1941, had been killed in action. Mackid had been lost during the 27 April 1942 raid on the German capital ship *Tirpitz*, that had been sheltering in the Norwegian Fiords, near Trondheim.

As Flap's first day of Stalag life drew to a close, it was agreed with Nunn that there would be plenty of time ahead for them to discuss their own individual falls from the sky. Nunn was also looking forward to hearing more about the morphing of the dreaded twin engine Manchester aircraft into the amazing Lancasters that Flap had spoken so enthusiastically about, and Flap was certain that they would soon be hearing a lot more news of the Lancasters anyway.

It was just bad luck for the 97 Squadron Kriegies to have been removed from the game, just as the Royal Air Force was on the verge of obtaining quantities of what was promising to be its strongest and most capable bomber, in the form of the superlative four engine Lancasters.

Finally, Flap now had time to reflect on whether mission number thirteen of his second tour of operations had been unlucky, or not! He was certainly unfortunate to have been shot down in the first place. However, good fortune had fought back, and he was very lucky to have then been thrown through the windscreen, away from his exploding Lancaster and the fierce petrol fire that followed. He was even luckier to have remained securely strapped into the protection of his armoured seat; and luckiest of all, to have then had his fall gradually broken by the branches of the trees that he had finally landed in, which more readily yielded to the combined weight of Flap and his seat than the solid ground would have done. Consequently, when those facts were debated with Flap's fellow Kriegies, the general consensus was that good luck had prevailed over bad for Flap, in a ratio of three to one! He was after all alive and kicking, and back amongst like-minded friends.

Chapter 15

Home Life Continues

On 4 June 1942, out of the blue, and nearly seven weeks after she had last seen Flap, Bernice received the following telegram from the Air Ministry, at the Woodhall Spa address where she had remained.

For the sake of clarity, the words of the scrawled and difficult to read Air Ministry telegram are repeated herewith, as follows:

"6.14am London Telex 54 (Postmarked Woodhall Spa, dated 4 JU 42 Linc's)

"Mrs JS. Sherwood Lingfield Tor-o-Moor Rd Woodhall Spa Linc's from Air Ministry Kingsway P6182 3/6 further information now received through the International Red Cross Committee states that your husband Squadron Leader John Seymour Sherwood DFC is a prisoner of war in German hands stop.

"Letter confirming this telegram follows.

"His mother is being informed. 1500"

On becoming the properly registered guest of the Germans at Stalag Luft III, Flap's presence in Germany, and his Prisoner of War (PoW) status, had automatically come to the notice of the International Red Cross. The Red Cross had then in turn notified the British Air Ministry of Flap's survival, together with a note of his Stalag Luft III address and PoW (Kriegie) number.

Bernice had been proved right all along of course!

But how had she known that Flap had survived?

With Flap stuck in Germany, Bernice and I, in company with Simba the dog, were left occupying a space at Woodhall Spa that would soon be required by an incoming replacement aircrew family. Therefore, Bernice and I, no longer having any direct connection with Woodhall Spa, and needing to conserve cash anyway, decided that it was time to move back to Bernice's family home at Sonning. However, the pre-war family house itself, Turpins at Sonning, had by then already been commandeered to house an American Forces Administrative Unit, but there did appear to be a vacancy in Lilac Cottage, situated in the same grounds as Turpins, into which familiar surroundings Bernice was happy to move, with me and Simba the dog.

On Tuesday, 30 June 1942, in accordance with the revelation of Flap's survival, and in acknowledgement of his successful leadership and actions over Augsburg on 17 April 1942, the *London Gazette* carried an announcement of his citation for the award of the Distinguished Service Order (DSO). The citation was worded in a similar style to that already revealed earlier, and a copy contained within a letter dated 7 July 1942 was forwarded to Bernice by the 97 Squadron Adjutant (Administrator) on behalf of the Commanding Officer of 97 Squadron. On 30 June and 1 July, the press used the DSO announcement as a good reason to fill up some more news space with a re-run of their Augsburg raid stories, some being accompanied by maps of Germany and speculation as to where exactly Flap's prison camp might be situated.

For Bernice, it was obviously settling to have knowledge of the fact that, whether imprisoned or not, she still had a live husband, and I still had father. Also, better the live man decorated with a Distinguished Service Order, rather than a dead man awarded a posthumous Victoria Cross!

Postal communications between Kriegies in German hands and their families and friends at home were both possible and permissible, via the International Red Cross. However, because the mail was necessarily sent by indirect routes in both directions, it could take as long as seven or eight weeks for items to reach their final destination. Consequently, following the telegraphed announcement of Flap's survival to my mother, initial communications by post were a bit slow to get going. It was therefore the end of June 1942 before lines of postal communication were established between Flap in Stalag Luft III and Bernice at home.

In the meantime, Bernice had been forced to give Simba the dog up for adoption. For following Flap's departure, Simba had seen fit to take over as the family pack leader but had then started becoming too possessive of my mother and me. This was alarmingly demonstrated on the night a policeman had knocked on the door of Lilac Cottage to advise Bernice of a fault with her blackout curtains that was causing light to be shown outside.

The policeman was calm and polite, but unfortunately had a rather deep growling voice. Simba cocked his ears and stood listening to the policeman growling at Bernice for a little while, before deciding that enough was enough. He had then decided to join the conversation with a bit of growling of his own, as he slowly advanced on the growling policeman with his teeth bared and ushered him out of the door backwards. The policeman immediately stopped growling, before fleeing the house unscathed. However, in an official police phone call to Bernice the following day, some helpful suggestions were made concerning Simba's threatening behaviour.

Generally, officer prisoners in Stalag Luft III were allowed to send three letters and four postcards per month. All such outgoing correspondence was checked by two censors. One censor was a fellow prisoner, appointed to ensure that no information of benefit to the enemy was inadvertently revealed to the Germans within homeward bound Kriegie correspondence. The second censor was a German *Postzensur*, acting to obliterate in black ink anything showing the prison camp, Germany, or the Germans in a negative light, whilst at the same time seeking out the slightest inadvertently revealed item of intelligence information that might be of value to themselves. Finally, all of the correspondence was then screened by German cipher experts, looking out for the possibility of coded messages or code words being hidden within the correspondence. Any suspected written passages were promptly blacked out. All incoming mail addressed to the Kriegies was treated to exactly the same censorial procedures by the Germans.

The earliest evidence of Kriegie correspondence from Flap that I have discovered is a copy of a German approved and supplied Kriegie postcard that was sent home to the 97 Squadron Adjutant, Flight Lieutenant Hind, on 26 June 1942, worded as follows:

"26/6/42"

"Dear Hind – Just a line to let you and the boys know that I am OK, but not a little "Browned Off". I got away with a burnt face followed by Scarlet Fever. I have no news of the rest of the crew & fear the worst. However, it is good to think that we had done our jobs well. I hear that we are all "Heroes" at home. Please congratulate the crews that made it! I think that Rodley and crew blew up in the air. Nunn sends regards, I told him you got his card. All the best to all Flap."

It is interesting to note that at the time of writing this card, Flap obviously believed that, of the two 97 Squadron aircraft shot down, it was the Lancaster of his wing man Flying Officer Edward Rodley, in addition to his own aircraft, that had also been shot down in flames over Augsburg. Whereas it was in fact the Lancaster of Warrant Officer Thomas Mycock DFC, the right-hand wing man of Flight Lieutenant David Penman who was leading the second section of the squadron's formation, that, having been set alight by anti-aircraft gunfire, was then flown on regardless of the raging fire on board, to place its bombs squarely on the target. The Lancaster then veered away and exploded on the ground. Mysteriously, and in spite of the gallantry of Mycock's most persistent attack, no citation was ever put forward to acknowledge the gallantry of Tommy Mycock, or his crew.

I do not know when Bernice might have received her first prisoner communication from Flap, because I would imagine that their personal letters were probably destroyed years ago. Consequently, the earliest dated items sent home from Stalag Luft III that I have discovered addressed to Bernice, are photographs simply dated October 1942. The photo shows Flap on the right of a group outside his accommodation hut within the East Compound of Stalag Luft III. He is still wearing the same clothes that he was wearing under his flying suit when he flew out to Germany; namely RAF battledress over a white polo-necked pullover.

This photo had probably only survived for so long because it was in the back of an old photograph frame and masked by more recent pictures when I discovered it. The reverse of the photo carries the German censors "GEPRUFT 46" ("INSPECTED 46") stamp, together with Bernice's address at Lilac Cottage, Sonning on Thames, and a note of the sender as:

"S/L J.S. SHERWOOD, GEFANGENENNUMMER 385, STAMMLAGER LUFT 3".

The Germans only allowed photos that showed the camp and its inmates in the most pleasant and well cared for of camp surroundings to be enclosed within outgoing Kriegie mail. Consequently, and in an endeavour to retain control of all Kriegie photography within the camp, prisoner ownership of cameras was officially prohibited. Any unapproved enclosures within Kriegies' letters were intercepted and rejected by the postal censors immediately.

1936 Newly commissioned Pilot Officer J.S. Sherwood. (*Author's collection*)

1942 Press release picture following capture in Germany. (*Author's collection*)

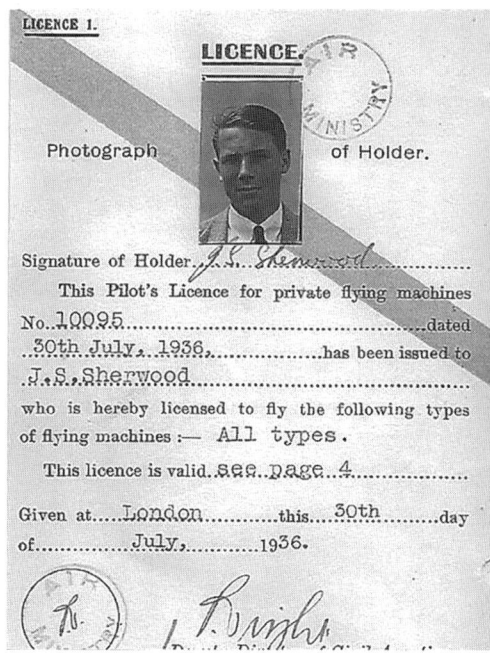

New personal pilot's licence. (*Author's collection*)

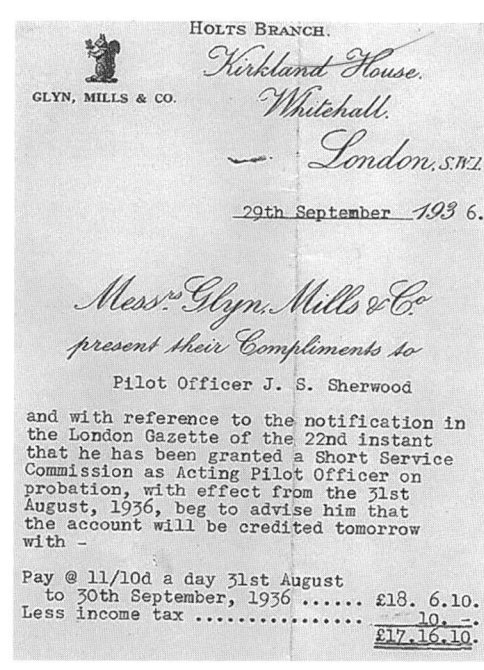

First month's pay letter. (*Author's collection*)

A Hawker Fury. (*Author's collection*)

A broken undercarriage trailing before … (*Author's collection*)

… tripping over that broken undercarriage. (*Author's collection*)

Air Service Training Ltd, Ansty – June 1936 pupil intake. Flap in back row 3rd from left. (*Author's collection*)

Less fortunate. No survivors! (*Author's collection*)

A very happy Acting Pilot Officer J.S. Sherwood by his plane. (*Author's collection*)

The Standard Nine Avon coupé motor car. (*Author's collection*)

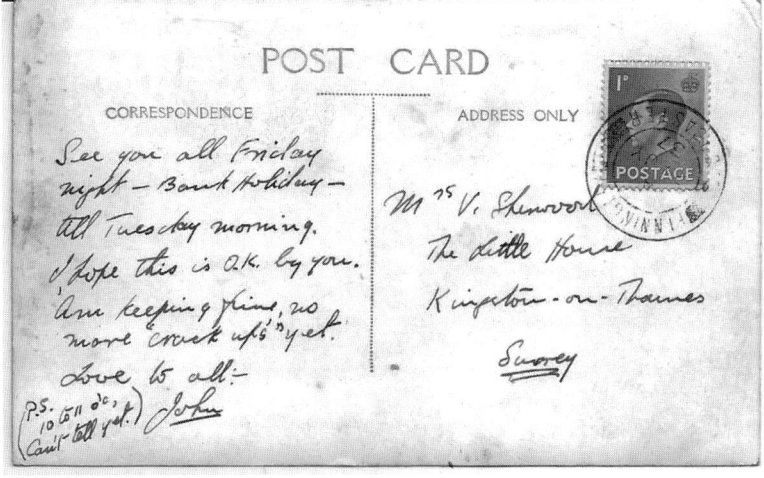

Flap's Bank holiday postcard home. (*Author's collection*)

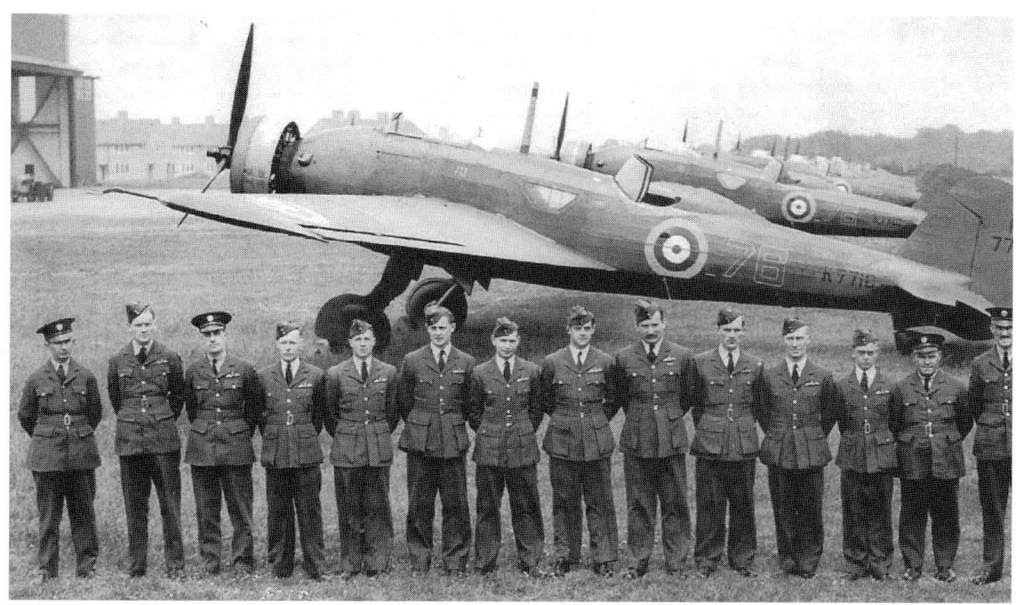

An official picture of 76 Squadron Wellesleys and crews 1938. Flap 5th from left. (*Author's collection*)

Handley Page Heyford – a Behemoth of an aeroplane that unbelievably remained in service until the 1939 outbreak of war. (*Author's collection*)

de Havilland Dragon Rapide – Flying Classroom. (*Author's collection*)

Simba and Roger (the dogs). (*Author's collection*)

The Gain family table at Middlesex Yacht Club's Annual Dinner Dance, December 1938 – Flap and Bernice left, nearest to the camera. (*Author's collection*)

The first Handley Page Hampden to arrive at Finningley. (*Author's collection*)

Fairey Battle light bomber. (*Author's collection*)

Avro Anson – Navigational trainer. Note rooftop observational astrodome. (*Author's collection*)

MY *Matoya* (2nd from left) and sisters on Thames moorings, at Middlesex Yacht Club 1939. (*Author's collection*)

Mid-1940, 144 Squadron crews with a Handley Page Hampden. Flap seated two places left of Simba the dog, who had taken centre stage as the self-appointed squadron mascot. (*Author's collection*)

Flap and Bernice leaving Sonning Church amidst large chunks of coarse home-made utility confetti. (*Author's collection*)

Group of 97 Squadron officers, during an MP visit on 21 September 1941. Flap seated, second from right, flanked by the C.O. Wing Commander D.F. Balsdon and Squadron Adjutant Flight Lieutenant Hind. (*Author's collection*)

The 97 Squadron Avro Manchester "OF-A" flown by Flap. (*Digital composition photo created and donated by A.C. Sherwood*)

18 December 1941 – Bomb bursts on and around the *Gneisenau* and *Scharnhorst* in Brest harbour. (Photo taken from Flap's Manchester L7492 OF-A at 15,000ft, by crewman Sgt. K. Williams.) (*Author's collection*)

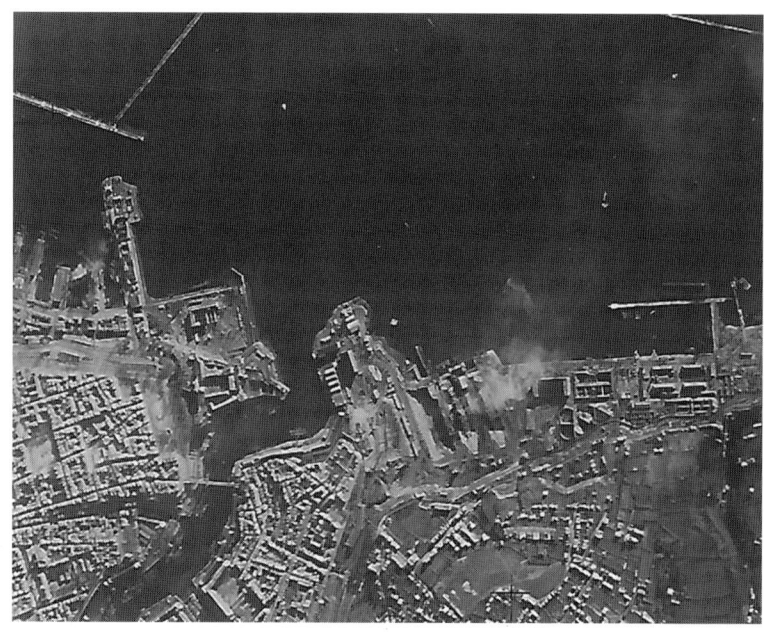

Avro Lancaster showing Flap's "OF-K" markings. (*Digital composition photo created and donated by A.C. Sherwood*)

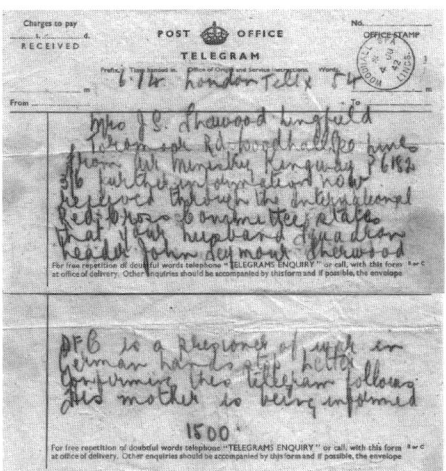

A photo of the original 4 June 1942 Air Ministry telegram. (*Author's collection*)

97 Squadron Commanding Officer's letter to Bernice; issued soon after revelation that Flap was alive in enemy hands. (*Author's collection*)

Outside their Luft III Kriegie hut (Flap on right of group). (*Author's collection*)

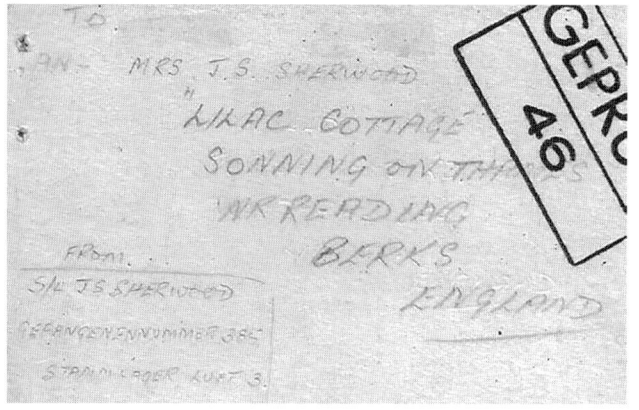

Rear of Luft III photo showing censor's stamp etc. (*Author's collection*)

Henri Picard's caricature of Flap dated 16-1-43. (*Author's collection*)

Some of the Kriegie physical training fanatics. Flap on extreme left. (*Author's collection*)

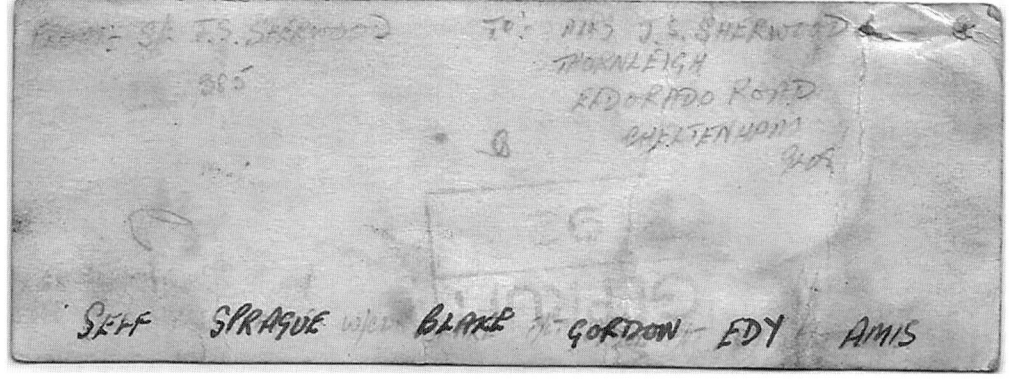

The rear of the physical training group photograph, listing names of the participants. Several of whom were Royal Canadian Air Force officers (RCAF). (*Author's collection*)

Front and back of Kriegie postcard. (*Author's collection*)

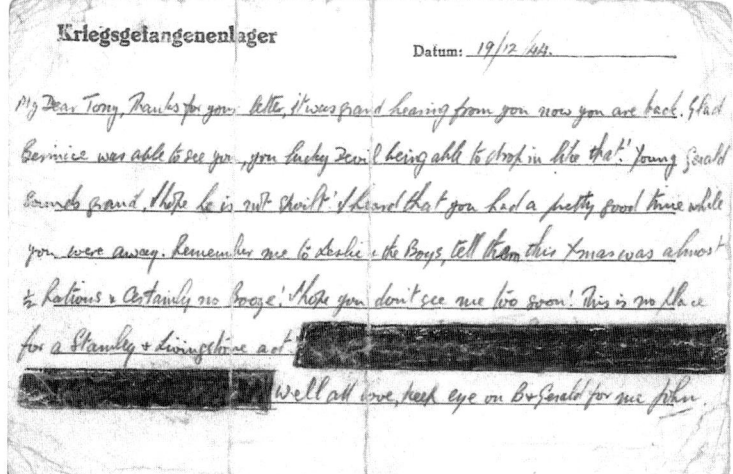

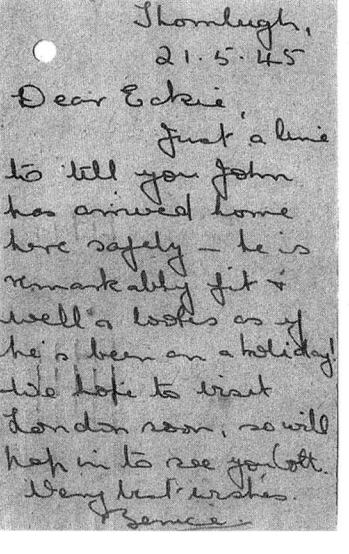

Bernice's postcard to a family friend (her father's business manager) re' Flap, who, after all he had been through, was looking as though he had just been away on holiday. Note the Victory Bells postmark. (*Author's collection*)

Triple gabled Turpins Cottage, Sonning, 1940s. (*Author's collection*)

The deserted Middlesex Yacht Club – previously home of M.Y. *Matoya* and her Dunkirk sisters. (*Author's collection*)

An immediate post European war letter to Bernice's father, Lt. Commander Kenneth. E. Gain RN, who was still on station in Colombo, Ceylon, pending the end of Japanese hostilities. The letter warning of the depleted state of the Gain family's business affairs. (*Author's collection*)

> 35 Mexfield Road
> East Putney. S.W. 15.
>
> May 16th. 1945
>
> Dear Mr. Kenneth,
>
> I have not heard from you since Mr. Forbes came home, with the good news that you are now a Commander in charge of a cruiser. No doubt like me you have been fully occupied.
>
> Well the war in Europe, as you know, is over and the flying bombs have stopped -- which is saying something; we never knew when one of the shops would go west, or whether we ourselves would go west for that matter. As it is most of the shops are damaged.
>
> The ration is still 1/2d, enough to keep us going, but there is still a possibility that it is going to be cut shortly, which won't be too good for the old Firm. We have insufficient staff still and no one gets more than a few days holidays -- I think we are all feeling the strain.
>
> Eric is still allocator for Paddington. Rationing seems certain to go on for a couple of years yet. Poor old Goad has passed away after an operation in St. Mary's hospital
>
> I wonder how long the Japanese war will last. Don't know whether it will be over very quickly or last quite a long time. What do you think. Surely after being away for such a long time you should be able to get demobbed, but whether there is anything to come back to is another matter. I see in your letter you talk about "turning over to Royal Navy" ?
>
> I know you had a letter from Mr. Lewis. Just what it all means I don't quite know. Just what the shareholders are going to do or what they can do, I don't know.
>
> I have seen Mrs. Kenneth once or twice and had some news of you; also that on the whole you have been keeping in good health, that is apart from prickly heat. I have not seen Peter since he left the Navy.
>
> Well I have nothing more to say just know. We are waiting to see what is going to happen, just as we have been during the past four years.
>
> All the best wishes,
>
> Eckie

> AIR MINISTRY,
> WHITEHALL GARDENS,
> LONDON, S.W.1
>
> 28th January, 1958.
>
> Dear Wing Commander
>
> I have it in command from The Queen to convey to you, on leaving the Active List of the Royal Air Force, the thanks of Her Majesty for your long and valuable services.
>
> Yours Sincerely,
> George Ward
>
> Wing Commander J.S. Sherwood, D.S.O., D.F.C.

Her Majesty the Queen's letter of thanks for Flap's long and valuable service. (*Author's collection*)

The Rock of Gibraltar with an Avro Lancaster in the foreground, and Vickers Wellingtons beyond. All aircraft showing the "FGG" & "FGE" markings of RAF Central Navigation & Control School. Circa 1950. (*Author's collection*)

Catamaran "Cat-a Bat" hitched to the VW Beetle. (*Author's collection*)

The last known picture of Flap and Bernice together, with a friend between them. Mevagissey Harbour, Cornwall. Circa 1972. (*Author's collection*)

Chapter 16

Settling in to Kriegie Life

It did not take Flap long in his new surroundings to decide that the Stalag food left a lot to be desired. The staple foods issued by the Germans consisted of rather dubious potatoes and a very rough and heavy black bread that took a lot of getting used to. Fresh vegetables were in very short supply, and then only akin to root vegetables of a poor quality and type that might usually be fed to a farmer's livestock at home. An intermittent supply of poor quality meat, usually containing fifty per cent bone and sometimes of rather dubious origin, was available. Sometimes the meat ration was replaced by an issue of a poor quality blood and gristle sausage. Theoretically, the Kriegies were supposed to receive the same rations as German enlisted troops. If that was true, it probably meant that, with the addition of regular deliveries of PoW food parcels from the International Red Cross, the Kriegies' diet might well have been superior to that of their German guards.

The East Compound of Stalag III had been opened long enough for the earliest prisoner arrivals to have created the beginnings of small vegetable gardens outside some of the accommodation huts. Subsequent bartering of Red Cross goodies with German Guards had then managed to secure a small supply of seeds to enable some salad crops and a few small vegetables to be produced over the summer months, those being used to perk up the flavour of the Kriegies' rations. Flap felt he needed to tell Bernice that he was missing her good old English grub, but thought it pointless to mention it in any correspondence, as the *Postzensur* would surely have blacked that comment out immediately.

Flap soon settled into the humdrum routine of the East compound of Stalag Luft III. At least the company was composed of many like-minded souls, and a new compound radio must have been obtained, as regular news bulletins were being circulated around the Kriegies' huts again. To protect the radio and its whereabouts, only one person was designated to listen silently to the BBC news on headphones, whilst memorising the news content. The news was then relayed orally by that listener to several other persons, before each of these then became runners responsible for further oral deliveries of the news bulletins to other groups of Kriegies; preferably in the open air, and well away from the possibility of being overheard by the skulking ferrets. By using this system, the radio set and its listener were well protected, and its actual location was known to very few people.

By September of 1942, the German Command and general administration of Stalag Luft III was gradually being overrun with problems. Firstly, the East compound of Luft III was becoming very overcrowded due to the ever-increasing number of prisoners arriving at the camp from the downed Allied aircrew then falling into German hands. Secondly, during the summer of 1942, there had been multiple escape attempts from the East Compound, as co-ordinated and approved by a Kriegie escape committee headed by Lieutenant Commander James Buckley of the Fleet Air Arm, who was assisted by Squadron Leader Roger Bushell, RAF, acting as his administrator. The escape attempts had been carried out by means of tunnelling and some cleverly staged walkouts from the camp sporting various disguises. In spite of the fact that all of the escapees, including those from only one successful tunnel, were soon rounded up and returned to the camp, it was obvious that the German ferrets were struggling to keep track of what was happening in such crowded conditions.

The Germans soon announced that, to relieve the overcrowding in the long term, an additional new compound would be constructed. The new compound, because of its proposed position would be known as the North Compound, and was expected to be ready for occupation from the spring of 1943.

In the meantime, and to immediately reduce overcrowding in the East compound, the Germans had decided to transfer roughly two hundred of the East Compound Kriegies to a newly opened Kriegie camp designated Oflag XX1B, situated at Schubin, in the north of Poland. The Germans took advantage of this transfer to include the many Kriegie troublemakers already known to them from recent escape attempts. The troublemakers took the form of escapees, tunnel diggers, general troublemakers, and the overall escape organiser himself, Lieutenant Commander James Buckley. For the Germans had deliberately selected the site of this Oflag for its very remote, desolate and inhospitable location, which they hoped would act as a big deterrent to any further escape attempts by the selected troublemakers.

At this point in time, the Germans did not seem to recognise the involvement of Roger Bushell in the administration of escape activities. Due to a previous scrape with the German Gestapo following an earlier escape from a camp in Lubeck, when the Gestapo had promised Bushell that if he ever came to their attention again he would be shot, Bushell had taken great care to maintain a very low profile at Luft III. However, he soon realised that the Kriegies now expected him to take over as the natural successor to James Buckley but for the time being he insisted that his low profile should be maintained during the winter months, pending the promised springtime move to the new North Compound, when ready.

To maintain some sort of physical fitness, it was customary for the Kriegies to take brisk walks around the perimeter of the camp compound. There, if walking with company, there were no ferrets in earshot to overhear the subject of any discussions. However, Flap, having been on rugby and gymnastic teams during his school days and early RAF training days, preferred to keep active by joining in with the various groups of Kriegies who engaged in ball games, jogging, gymnastics, and general physical training exercises around the compound.

As the autumnal daylight hours began to grow shorter, the Kriegies had to create their own forms of indoor occupational therapy to keep themselves busy during the long dark winter evenings. Red Cross parcels and crates were rich sources of wood, plywood, paper, cardboard, string, and tin, that the Kriegies relied upon to produce the materials useful for various handicrafts and model making skills, as well as the manufacture of some illicit items. As a scratch modelling fan already, Flap was immediately in his element and taking notice of the skilful and ambitious projects that some of the Kriegies already had in hand. However, the Kriegies as a whole had not at that time fully realised or organised the potential power of their collective knowledge of do-it-yourself skills, or the problems that those skills would later cause for their Germans captors.

Over a period of several days during December 1942, the RAF sergeants that had been held captive in the Centre compound of Stalag Luft III were moved out to a different camp, and in their place United States aircrew began to arrive into the Centre Compound of Luft III.

Also during December, the second radio was somehow "ferreted out" and consequently confiscated. There was immediately a determined resolution amongst the Kriegies that any replacement radio would have to be much better secreted. In the meantime, the East Compound was deprived of the benefit of the BBC news once again.

As 1942 drew towards its close, it became apparent to Flap that an already cold winter was going to get even colder in Sagan, Lower Silesia. The small iron stoves situated in the East compound's huts struggled to produce enough warmth to maintain a reasonable temperature in the prisoners' quarters. As the weather grew colder, there was often an overnight build-up of frozen condensation on the inside of the walls and windows of their huts, mostly arising from the moisture content of the Kriegies' own exhaled breath during the night.

A kind of Kriegie Christmas came and went amid sad thoughts of those at home. All being well disguised by as much self-enforced joviality and enthusiasm as it was possible to muster in the circumstances. There was a heavy reliance on the contents of stockpiled Red Cross parcels to enable something approaching a festive meal to be prepared. Father Christmas did not show up, but small token gifts were exchanged between mates. The gifts were mostly handmade craft items, such as wooden sliding lid anti-crush cigarette boxes made from recycled scrap wood, and able to comfortably hold a packet of ten or twenty Red Cross cigarettes. Additionally, assorted Christmas decorations were crafted from whatever was readily obtainable from around the compound from the wrapping and packaging contained in Red Cross parcels.

As the new year of 1943 opened, the weather immediately became even colder, but at the same time the days were almost imperceptibly beginning to grow longer again. Whilst out on a brisk midday perimeter walk, Flap found himself in conversation with an interesting young Belgian pilot named Henri Picard; Gefangenennummer: 685. Henri turned out to be an accomplished caricature artist and, on learning that the first anniversary of my 16 January 1942 birth was fast approaching, he offered to sketch a caricature of Kriegie Flap to commemorate the occasion. Flap took Henri up on his kind offer.

The original picture is drawn in pastille colour, upon what I suspect is slightly yellowed Red Cross supplied paper. It is clearly signed "Henri Picard", dated "16 January 1943", still uncreased, and still in remarkably good condition today. There is a photo of the Henri Picard caricature in the plate section of this book.

Whilst chatting to Henri Picard, Flap would have discovered Henri's own interesting short history, as follows:

At the age of twenty Henri Picard had joined the Belgian Royal Military School, but for some reason soon found himself more interested in flying. He therefore sought a transfer to the Belgian Military Air Service, joining Aviation School in late 1938. Soon deciding that he definitely wanted to be a pilot, he managed to secure a place at a Belgian Flying School, before graduating on to the Advanced Flying School at Goetsenhoven, Belgium, where he was situated when the Germans commenced their invasion of Belgium. Ahead of the German advance, the Advanced Flying School was immediately moved to France, before soon having to be further moved on to French Morocco, as it became obvious that France was on the verge of capitulation to the Germans. Henri was then one of a large group of like-minded men who decided that they wished to carry on the fight against Germany from Great Britain. Henri arrived in England in mid-July 1940 to apply for British citizenship, and by mid-August he had already been accepted for the Royal Air Force Volunteer Reserve. It then took nearly a whole year to pass along the RAF's military flying training programme and operational training schemes before he was finally posted out to fly with 131 Squadron. A further posting took him to fly with his compatriots at 350 (Belgian) Squadron RAF, where he saw action flying Spitfire fighters. On 29 June 1942, he destroyed two German Focke Wulf 190 fighters, and subsequently, on 21 July 1942, he was awarded the Belgian Croix de Guerre for his actions. He then went on to share credit with another pilot for the destruction of a further FW190 on 19 August 1942. However, a week later his luck ran out when he was injured as he was shot down over the English Channel. Able to successfully bail out of his aircraft, he had then struggled to get into his dinghy because of leg injuries. Then, having spent nearly a week at sea, that included riding out two storms, he was finally washed up on a French beach. By the time he was discovered by the Germans, he was dehydrated, hungry, and barely conscious. However, in a similar fashion to Flap's experience of falling into captivity, the Germans treated him well by immediately carting him off for urgent treatment at hospital, where he remained until he was fit to be forwarded along the German administrative route to Stalag Luft III.

Some time during February a new radio receiver began to operate in the Kriegies' hands. It had been decided that the radio needed to be much better secreted than the previous set, as that appeared to have been much too easily "ferreted" out. Accordingly, various Kriegie skills were utilised to build the radio receiver itself invisibly into the structure of a rustic home-made wooden table. There, totally hidden within the woodwork of the table, any electrical contact with the radio for battery, aerial, earphones etc, could only be made via various strategic nail and screw heads situated around that table. Each exposed nail or screw head had in turn been invisibly wired back to the radio within the framework of the table. It therefore left only the smaller items associated with the radio to be suitably secreted elsewhere around the compound huts.

During February, it became obvious that the promised superior new North Compound was progressing rapidly towards completion. The new compound was some half a mile from the East compound and separated from the East Compound by the Centre Compound and an area which housed the overall camp administrative HQ and German living quarters. As the three compounds and HQ area were all contained within one overall fenced, gated, and guarded area, voluntary Kriegie work parties were already permitted to visit the new North Compound area for the purpose of clearing the open ground between the new buildings of tree stumps and other obstacles, before then levelling out in order to make room for unobstructed recreational areas and gardens. The new compound was going to be much larger than the East Compound, with a projected boundary circumference of about a mile in its own right.

Labouring on the Kriegie working parties, in addition to their own regular gymnastic and physical training exercises, helped to maintain the fitness of Flap and his fellow Kriegie fitness fanatics. Work continued in earnest around the new North Compound throughout March and, by 27 March 1943, the Germans had declared the new compound ready for occupation.

Chapter 17

To The North Compound

The move of the East Compound Kriegies and their official belongings into the new North Compound of Stalag Luft III took place over a period of several days following 27 March 1943. Of course, the presence of Kriegie working parties in the new compound over the preceding weeks had already given the Kriegies the opportunity to secrete any unofficial contraband belongings in and around the new compound and its buildings. Consequently, nothing of real contraband value was lost during the move. The only real Kriegie disappointment was having to leave behind the results of previous multiple do it yourself projects such as various fixed built-in furnishings and improvements that had been created in the East Compound over the previous twelve months or so.

However, to offset any disappointments resulting from the move, the Kriegie inmates soon realised that they were going to be more than compensated for their losses by the improved facilities offered by the new North Compound. There, the kitchens, washrooms and lavatories were all integral within the living quarters; whereas previously the Kriegies had been forced to cross extensive outdoor areas in all weathers to use such facilities. Earlier Kriegie involvement on the site had ensured that the sports field was nearly complete, and the Germans had even granted permission for a theatre to be soon built within the new compound.

Furthermore, as all of the individual Luft III compounds were contained within the one overall guarded perimeter, the Germans were content to allow the Kriegies to have some inter compound contact and interaction in respect of various sporting, cultural and educational activities, all in an endeavour to ensure that the new facilities would give the Kriegies maximum satisfaction and contentment, and thereby act as a distraction from any escape activities.

The ability to maintain contact with the East Compound was very welcome, as a small nucleus of existing Kriegies had been left behind in the old East Compound, ready to assist the settling in and integration of the next Luft III intakes of RAF Kriegies that were then expected to be moved in from various other camps in due course. When the new intakes did arrive, they included several of the Kriegies that had previously been sent to Schubin but did not include any of the previously blacklisted troublemakers.

On the opening of the North Compound, it was said that the German Camp Commandant genuinely believed that he had created a Luxury Luft resort, offering such amazing recreational facilities and superior accommodation that his Kriegie guests would be so contently distracted as to then wish to comfortably sit out the rest of the war, with absolutely no further wish to attempt any premature departures.

However, contrary to the Commandant's beliefs, and whilst there was absolutely no doubt that for the time being the Kriegies were very pleased with the overall improvements to their surroundings and living conditions, there was never going to be any change in the Kriegies' overall desire to inconvenience the Germans by escaping. Mainly in the hope of a home run to then fight again another day; or, at the very least to waste valuable German time and resources on grand games of hide and seek around the German countryside.

Indeed, in their determination to maintain an escape programme, and during the time that the East Compound Kriegies had been allowed to work prematurely on the new North Compound site, the Kriegies had taken the opportunity to hoard all manner of goods stolen from that site. The stolen goods included tools, building materials, clothing, and German documents in preparation for their escape programme, all having been taken from under the noses of the German civilian workers and guards employed on the new site. Nothing was sacred if left unattended, for very early on it had been realised that the German civilian workers were reluctant to report such losses to their employers, for the fear of their own carelessness being blamed for such losses, and the punishment that might then follow. The Germans were therefore oblivious to the vast amount of material and equipment that had gradually fallen under Kriegie control.

At the beginning of April 1943, it was ironic that the Camp Commandant was still congratulating himself on his achievements when, long before they had even been moved out of the East Compound, the Kriegies whilst awaiting the move into the North Compound had already held a series of meetings with the specific purpose of setting up an escape committee ready to operate within the new compound.

In that respect, before the move from the East Compound had taken place, the Kriegies had already agreed that the East and North Compounds would in future act independently of each other in respect of escape planning and execution, although some co-operation and sharing of tools and materials over both compounds would continue wherever possible. Squadron Leader Roger Bushell, having been listed as included in the move from the East Compound, was immediately elected to be the Head of the new North Compound's Escape Committee. It was then requested, as a precaution against anti-eavesdropping ferrets, that Bushell should thereafter be known only by the code name of "Big X" in respect of any conversations concerning escape matters. The East Compound were then left to select their own new Escape Committee and Head thereof when, as expected, the East Compound became re-populated with intakes of new Kriegies.

Having been elected to lead the North Compound's Escape Committee, Squadron Leader Bushell then appointed his choice of suitable Escape Committee members on merit, giving preference to those Kriegies already known to have the knowledge and skills that would be of immediate benefit to any escape effort. An agreement was also reached, whereby individual freelance escape projects were banned unless sanctioned by the Escape Committee, thus avoiding any conflict of interest with the main agenda and ensuring that the maximum effort was concentrated unhindered through the Escape Committee. There also followed a clandestine process that encouraged approximately two thirds of the prospective North Compound Kriegies to immediately register themselves with the Escape Committee as interested in taking some part in escape activities, together with a note being made of the useful skill or specialist knowledge that each individual possessed.

Roger Bushell proposed that, rather than planning a multitude of small escapes, it would be to the Kriegies' benefit to place all their energy towards one sudden and unexpected mass escape via multiple tunnels, although this would not in the meantime preclude consideration of any other viable suggestions, as long as they were controlled directly by the appointed Escape Committee. However, the main thrust of escape effort was always to remain with the intention of a mass escape via tunnels, with all such tunnels being so designed as to aid the rapid exit from the compound that would be required to saturate the Germans' local resources with an absolute tidal wave of Kriegie fugitives.

It was finally agreed that the overall main escape plan would involve three simultaneous tunnels that were to be named as Tom, Dick and Harry respectively; each tunnel to start from a different place in that sector of the North Compound that was furthest away from the German barracks. And further, to avoid taking the unnecessary risks and pressures of building tunnels to a deadline, there would be no set time limit to build the tunnels. Additionally, at the least hint that the Germans might have become suspicious, then work was to immediately cease until such time as any German interest had receded again.

From that moment on it became of paramount importance that the three tunnels were only to be referred to by their respective names and, as an anti-ferret eavesdropping precaution, the word "tunnel" itself was therefore banned from use during any Kriegie conversations.

In the meantime, the process of settling into and bedding down the new compound was still generating much German activity around the North Compound. There was plenty of coming and going of German civilian contractors, as the finishing touches were made, and whilst surplus materials and rubbish were cleared away. This fevered activity gave more opportunity for the Kriegies to pinch tools and materials, together with any workmen's passes and travel documents that could be copied and forged for the use of future escapees. Also, the Kriegies were able to carry out a clandestine survey of the whole of the North Compound under the pretext of planning their own compound improvements in the form of provision of vegetable and flower beds, and the possible installation of a mini golf course or putting green.

Following the move in, progress on the Kriegies' North Compound Escape Committee decision to build three tunnels was such that, by 11 April 1943, three sites had been selected for the entrances to the respective tunnels from within the compound's huts. Further, the required trap door entrances and their frames were already under construction. The mainly wooden floors of the camp's huts were all elevated above the ground, to allow the German ferrets to periodically check for signs of any excavations beneath. Therefore, to achieve invisibility, the tunnel traps could only be situated where some small areas of concrete hut flooring were necessarily supported directly on to the ground. Those situations were limited to the plinths and slabs beneath barrack room stoves, washrooms and drainage installations, through which each of the tunnel shafts would have to be driven before reaching the sandy ground beneath, thus enabling the Kriegie tunnelling to commence. The slow task of starting the tunnel shafts by painstakingly chipping away at the concrete by hand was then put in motion. The sounds of stolen hand tools chipping away at concrete were muffled on site as far as possible, whilst the playing of rowdy ball games generated lots of alternative noise outside the huts in order to overwhelm any of the noise that might escape from the works within.

On implementation of the overall scheme, Flap had immediately volunteered to involve himself among the teams of Kriegies who were already engaged on the bespoke manufacture of tools and equipment that would be required to successfully work the tunnels. There, Flap's already proven improvisation skills, of making use of what he could scavenge from around him to utilise for the scratch modelling world, was simply scaled up to be of beneficial use to the overall escape plan.

A case in point were the air pumps that would be required to pump fresh air to those that would eventually be working within the long tunnels. Those pumps had been designed to take the form of cylindrical hand operated concertina bellows, all to be manufactured from standard issue kitbags with simple in and out flap valves at either end, designed to alternately suck fresh air in at one end of the cylinder, before then blowing it out of the other end on the return stroke. In addition to the kitbags, other parts for the pumps, and the mounting frames to hold them, were being built from stolen wood, various scrap materials and Red Cross KLIM dried milk tins. If simply viewed as outsized models, the pumping equipment was subject to the same manufacturing principles, but without being so fiddly to handle.

Work on the promised compound theatre was already well in hand, and at this stage of its construction was of immense benefit to the tunnelling preparations. There were so many tools and materials lying around the theatre site that there was very little chance of the ferrets noticing the diversion of certain items to the Kriegies' alternative underground projects.

In order to carry the pumped fresh air along to the working face of each tunnel, further teams were manufacturing ducting from the Red Cross branded "KLIM" dried milk tins. Those same milk tins were also being used to manufacture various implements for digging, excavating, and generally moving the large quantities of sand that were expected to be generated by the tunnelling. There again, Flap was able to demonstrate his ability, by obtaining lead and solder from the joints of the dried milk tins, and then reapplying it as a liquid solder to the joints of the remodelled tin cans to turn them it into any form of useful implement required. Reclaimed solder was also valued for use in the casting of forged badges and uniform buttons that were required for fitting onto various imitation German uniforms that some of the potential escapees were planning to wear whenever they might finally be lucky enough to escape Stalag Luft III.

However, on 17 April 1943, Flap had good reason to stand aside from the foregoing Kriegie activities for the day. For 17 April 1943 was the first anniversary of his lucky escape from Lancaster OF-K (King) when, following the bombing of the MAN factory at Augsburg, the remainder of his entire crew had perished during the ensuing explosive crash that completely destroyed the aircraft. Apart from reflecting on feelings of guilt over his sole survival, Flap had recently received an inquiry from the family of one of his lost crew. For on that same day in 1943, Flap wrote a German-supplied Kriegie postcard in reply to that inquiry, and addressed it to the mother of Sergeant Arthur Cox, one of his own Lancaster crew members that had been killed during the Augsburg raid on 17 April 1942.

On that April evening in 1942, Arthur, for a short while, had been the very busy front gunner on Flap's Lancaster OF-K (King). In that unenviable crew position he was very exposed to the enemy, being perched way out front of the aircraft in a clear Perspex turret, right on the very nose of Flap's leading aircraft; situated forward of Flap's feet that were at the Lancaster's rudder controls, on the flight deck above and behind Arthur. As the Lancaster ran in to the attack, at roof skimming minimal height, Arthur was trying to suppress the German opposition by furiously firing his twin .303mm machine guns at the opposing German light anti-aircraft gunners that were situated on various rooftops and towers surrounding the MAN diesel engine factory. The German gunners on the towers would have been plainly visible to Arthur, as they would have been almost on the same level as him and the low flying Lancaster, and those German gunners were in turn hosing back their return tracer fire from multiple machine guns and light cannons. In his very exposed position, Arthur Cox must have felt that the incoming fire was being very personally directed right at him. However, at the same time, the bomb aimer in his position directly beneath Arthur, lying face down flat on his stomach with his face pressed against his bomb sight, would probably have felt the most vulnerable of all the crew.

On the very limited space available on the Kriegie postcard, Flap had written as follows:

"17/4/43"

"Dear Mrs Cox – There is little I can tell you of the actual flight to Augsburg owing to my present position. Your son was killed when we crashed and is buried near Augsburg in Bavaria, which is very beautiful country in Southern Germany. I do not remember much about the crash myself but the rest of my crew must have been killed instantly –
Yours sincerely, J.S. Sherwood, S/L"

In January 1943, Arthur Cox's mother and father had already been advised that, on order of the King, their son was to be Mentioned in Dispatches for his outstanding gallantry on the day of the Augsburg raid.

On that first anniversary of the Augsburg raid, Flap also reflected on how, in the meantime, he had since learned so much about the overall results of that raid. Most of the information having been gathered through conversations with the almost continuous incoming stream of newly shot down Kriegies arriving at Luft III. Flap had already learned that the loss of his Lancaster OF-K (King), and one other, were the only two losses from his 97 Squadron formation, with the other four of his charges having survived the trip. He was therefore truly shocked to learn that 44 Squadron's foray to Augsburg had resulted in only the single Lancaster and crew of 44 Squadron's formation leader, Squadron Leader John Nettleton, the appointed leader of the whole operation, surviving the raid. Retrospectively, Flap had therefore been very pleased with his choice of Flying Officer D. Hepburn as his navigator for the Augsburg trip, and even more pleased that he had chosen to follow Hepburn's positive assertion that 97 Squadron's Lancasters were bang on the designated track over France on their outward trip to Augsburg, thus avoiding the German fighters from Evereux that so decimated 44 Squadron's Lancasters.

In the meantime, at Luft III, work on the three tunnels was progressing apace. The well disguised trap doors had been manufactured and were already in place. The next stage, of sinking the initial shafts to the required depth of twenty-five to thirty feet for each tunnel had then commenced. The extreme shaft depth had been agreed in the expectation that the German listening devices situated around the compound would then be unable to detect the vibrations of the digging at such great depths. As the shafts were driven down, their walls had to be shored up by building squared wooden box sections in situ. The shoring consisted of wood that was purloined from the bed frames, bed boards and floorboards of various huts around the compound.

By 31 May 1943, the shafts for all three tunnels had been completed. Each of the tunnels themselves had then been excavated to the length required to install and line three chambers off to the side of each tunnel; those chambers were required to accommodate an air pump and its operator, an on-site workshop, and a waste sand storage facility respectively, all within each tunnel.

A leisurely paced digging campaign then commenced into the summer months of 1943. To assist the disposal of the large quantities of sand that were going to be removed, railways comprising of flat wooden trucks carrying sand boxes, and running with wooden wheels on wooden rails, had been designed to carry the sand from the tunnelling faces to the foot of each shaft. The prefabricated component parts of the railways had already been manufactured by the Kriegies before being secreted around the compound, and those were then installed into the respective tunnels as each tunnel reached a sufficient length to be able to benefit from the operation of its own railway.

The outside disposal of so much sand from the working of three tunnels at once was always going to be a problem. Extreme care was needed because of the way that the bright orange colour of the freshly tunnelled sand contrasted so sharply with the compound's visibly greyish topsoil. Immediately following removal from the tunnel, the sand was placed into an assortment of small bags at the shaft head. Those sandbags were then collected by an intermittent stream of passing Kriegies who, after secreting the bags by various methods within their clothing, then covertly transported the sand to the various favoured disposal sites dotted around the compound.

For quick disposal, some of the sand was placed into the roof spaces of the compound's huts. However, the bulk of the waste sand had to be disguised by being buried under, or blended into, the compound's own topsoil. The mixing method was most simply applied by trickling sand down in the midst of pre-arranged sporting groups as they played around the compound. The players then used their feet to shuffle the fresh sand about until it blended with the topsoil. However, burying the sand under cover of any horticultural process provided a much faster bulk disposal. Accordingly, burial pits were dug out in the various flower and vegetable beds situated around the compound. Tunnelled sand was then placed into each pit, before re-covering with topsoil and finally replanting the sites.

As the North Compound excavations progressed, other Kriegie teams were manufacturing and storing the quantities of various items of equipment that would eventually be required by the potentially large number of escapees. Travel documents, maps, compasses, clothing and disguises were the usual requirements.

With some amazing skill, outfits of civilian clothing were created from items of the Kriegies' own uniforms, blankets, and bed sheets; not forgetting abundant clothing and materials previously stolen from German civilian workers, during the construction of the North Compound.

In order to produce forged travel documents and passes, the Kriegies had already accumulated a stock of originals, mostly stolen from the German civilian workers. Various grades of card and paper were saved from the packing within Red Cross parcels and crates; whilst inks and dyes were manufactured from various food stuffs, minerals and medicines. Anything not readily available from improvisation, including up to date versions of the various documents required for copying, were obtained or borrowed from some of the guards and ferrets, that from previous careful conditioning, or even blackmail, were already known to be susceptible to accepting bribes in the form of Red Cross cigarettes and chocolate.

So, over the summer of 1943, the clandestine industries of Luft III became an absolute hive of humming human activity.

Chapter 18

Over the Wooden Horse

Following their move from the East Compound, the North Compound Kriegies had been able to maintain close contact with the Kriegies of the East Compound, whose inmate numbers had in the meantime been restored by further intakes of new Kriegies. The North Compound Escape Committee members were therefore aware that the East Compound Kriegies were also planning a tunnelled escape of their own.

However, the East Compound Kriegies had decided upon a different approach for their tunnelling scheme. As their compound huts were set so far back from the perimeter wire, they had decided that instead of intense tunnelling, either deeply or over long distances, they could more quickly dig a shorter and shallower tunnel starting from a position much nearer to their compound's perimeter wire than their Kriegie huts were situated.

The plans for East Compound's tunnelling operation had been thought up by Flight Lieutenant Eric Williams who, as a German speaker and intending to escape himself, had appointed two other German speaking officers to escape with him. His audacious plans were so designed as to commence tunnelling into the open ground of the compound from as near to the perimeter wires as possible. To disguise this tunnelling operation Eric Williams had designed a gymnastic vaulting horse that, when built, would be carried out to the same place in the compound every day. In situ, the horse would be used for physical training exercises. However, whilst Kriegies were to vault over the horse, two men secreted within the horse were to carry out the actual tunnelling operation itself, with reliance on the noise generated by the vaulters' feet pounding on the ground to confuse the operators of the German ground listening devices. The Germans had previously installed such devices around the compound, but those would easily be persuaded that all the noise was generated by the vaulters alone.

With the use of plywood and timber obtained from the crates that had contained deliveries of Red Cross parcels, together with other softer finishing materials and packing scavenged from bedding around their compound, the East Compound Kriegies had already built the "Wooden Horse". The Horse's sturdy construction on a rigid timber inside frame, when combined with two long removable carrying poles, ensured that it was strong enough to safely carry two men together with their digging equipment to and fro around the compound, even with a full load of dugout sand also aboard.

Initially, and to acclimatise the Germans to the horse and its pre-designated position in the compound, it was carried out for use daily over a week or so, with no attempt being made to dig. During that period, the horse underwent various inspections by the ferrets and various German officials. Then finally, on 8 July 1943, tunnelling from under the horse commenced when the tunnel shaft trap door was set into its frame at a depth of some two feet below the surface of the ground, and at a distance of some fifteen to twenty feet in from the perimeter warning wire. The trapdoor was then buried again, under a pre-mixed soil that was matched to that of the compound's surface. Before removing the horse, the carrying crew had to carefully note various co-ordinates in relation to the trapdoor's position in order to make certain that they would be able to blindly re-relocate the horse in its correct position, exactly above the hidden trap, for all future sessions.

In the following days, as more and more East Compound Kriegies took an interest in the horse as a new method of exercising, excavations from under the horse commenced in earnest. Metal bowls were used to dig out sand and form an initial shaft below the previously installed trapdoor, down to a total depth of six or seven feet only. A narrow tunnel of barely two foot square dimensions was then started in the direction of the perimeter fences. It was obviously going to take some time for the tunnel to reach the required length, mainly because the speed of operation was governed by the small amount of sand that could be removed and safely carried away after each day of tunnelling.

The wooden horse tunnel did not have the benefit of a railway and, as the sand was dug out, it had to be placed into a wash basin that could be pulled back and forth along the tunnel by long ropes attached either side of it. At the foot of the shaft, the sand was then transferred into old socks and small purpose made bags that, when full of sand, were hung on hooks within the horse to be carried away with the operators at the end of each session.

After each tunnelling session, the horse was returned to its home in the compound's canteen building, where firstly two dirty diggers had to be removed for a shower and a change of clothes. The horse's remaining contents, in the form of several bags of sand, then had to be removed and placed into the hands of the sand disposal teams, who used similar methods as the North Compound to dispose of what was obviously expected to be a far smaller total volume of sand from their short and narrow tunnel.

In the meantime, appreciative interest in the horse continued to grow amongst both the German staff and the inmates of the Luft III compounds alike. Various duty ferrets on occasion added to a very noisy and enthusiastic audience, actively applauding some of the energetic, skilful and entertaining exercises performed over the horse, whilst all the time failing to guess what further energetic Kriegie activity was taking place right under their very noses, beneath the horse.

An early interest in the horse also came from the Kriegies of the North Compound, as just for the hell of it, Flap and his fellow followers of physical exercise regimes threw down the challenge of a vaulting competition against the East Compound, on condition that the North Compound competitors would be granted some practice sessions before the day of the competition. So intense was the continuous distraction caused, as the training and competitive activities over and around the horse became the centre of activity, that tunnelling from beneath the wooden horse of the East Compound was able to continue at a pace nearly every day throughout the summer of 1943.

Chapter 19

Kriegie Life Continues

During the summer of 1943, the hidden Kriegie radios kept the residents of Luft III well informed of the progress of Allied land forces against the underside of the Axis powers of Germany and Italy, in the form of a succession of seaborne landings on Sicily, and then the toe of Italy and Salerno.

News of any positive Allied progress was always an encouragement to the Kriegies, and by mid-August of 1943 the Kriegies of the North Compound estimated that, with their supreme efforts and efficient tunnelling systems they had excavated a total of just over one hundred and sixty tons of sand from their three tunnels; and all had been safely carried away and disposed of by more than two hundred appointed sand carriers that had so far managed to work unnoticed by the ferrets.

For a while longer digging and disposal continued uninterrupted, until such time that rumours fed back from friendly German personnel indicating that a decision had been made to add yet another compound to Luft III. Problematically, the vacant site chosen for the new compound was exactly where the Escape Committee had determined that the tunnels of Tom and Dick should surface. Rumours of the development were soon confirmed as fact when German workers started to clear the trees away from the proposed new site.

Roger Bushell hurriedly convened an Escape Committee emergency meeting to discuss the new situation. The outcome of that meeting was a decision to immediately switch all efforts towards the swift completion of threatened tunnel Tom, which at that time was the most advanced of the three tunnels then in progress, and therefore able to give some hope of completion before construction of the new compound was commenced. To hasten the work on Tom, it was decided to increase the number of work hours by introducing relays of shift workers, and further, as the entrances to Tom and Dick were situated in two huts in close proximity to one another, it was decided to abandon any further tunnelling in Dick and use it as a very handy sand dump to speed up the rate of sand disposal from Tom.

Unfortunately, further setbacks then occurred. Firstly, the few Americans that were billeted amongst the Kriegies of the North Compound, who had greatly contributed to the overall escape effort, were moved out to join their countrymen in their own American compound; thus depriving them of ever benefiting from all the effort that they had put into the North Compound's escape plans.

Then secondly, and much worse, the new fast track system of working on tunnel Tom soon backfired. The concentrated activity generated by both tunnelling and sand disposal in and around one small area of the compound had caught the attention of the ferrets. The ferrets were immediately convinced that something was going on that they ought to know about. However, after several days of persistent searching and ferreting around, they still had not located the entrance shaft to either Dick or Tom. It was eventually by pure chance that a crack in the passage floor of one of the huts gave the game away to the ferrets, and Tom's entrance trap was discovered.

Having discovered the extent of Tom, the Germans seemed undecided as to what to do about such extensive underground workings. They finally decided that they would simply blow the whole tunnel up, to ensure that it was then rendered completely useless. There then followed an act of such extreme demolition, that it turned the Kriegies' disappointment at losing their tunnel into a spectacle of some considerable entertainment. Probably due to some miscalculation over the amount of explosive required to do the job in a confined space, the Germans caused an enormous explosion that did considerable damage to various structures around the compound. Then to the delighted cheers of the watching Kriegie audience, the stilted supports of one of the perimeter Goon Boxes slowly sank into the ground, leaving the tower leaning over at a drunken angle as the ground subsided beneath it.

Immediately following the destruction of Tom, the Escape Committee were convinced that the Germans thought that they had destroyed the North Compound Kriegies tunnelling dream in its entirety. The Germans, whilst condescendingly busy congratulating themselves on the destruction of Tom, seemed to be oblivious to the existence of either Dick, that was then being used as a sand storage tunnel, or Harry that was the one surviving tunnel that still held some potential promise of being driven through to completion.

The Escape Committee's immediate reaction was to therefore push on with all haste in tunnel Harry while the Germans' guard was down. Accordingly, the hut that contained Harry's entrance shaft became very busy as the tunnelling operation became live again. Harry's entrance shaft was well hidden beneath the plinth that supported the hut's wood burning stove. To enable access to Harry, a flue extension had been manufactured to enable the stove to be moved into another position away from the tunnel trap, even whilst remaining alight. In the event of any danger, Harry's shaft was easily and swiftly re-covered by the plinth, with an added deterrent to any interference being afforded by the hot burning stove replaced above it.

However, after only a few days of working on Harry, the Kriegie compound duty stooges reported a noticeable increase in ferreting around in the compound. With no wish to lose Harry, and with concern that any further delays would reduce the chance of finalising any escape before the coldest part of the approaching winter set in anyway, the Escape Committee decided to put the whole North Compound tunnelling project on hold until the following spring.

The stove and plinth over Harry's trap were therefore resealed for the winter, whilst those who had hoped to escape resigned themselves to facing another freezing winter in the draughty huts of Luft III.

However, as October 1943 came to an end, three Kriegies in the East Compound had already decided that they would definitely not be staying for the cold Sagan winter. The Wooden Horse escape project had come to fruition after one hundred and fourteen days of undiscovered, slow, steady tunnelling for just over one hundred feet. At midday on 29 October, Michael Codner was carried out in the horse with a spare man who sealed him into the tunnel, before the spare man then returned within the horse to its canteen base. Then later, at five o'clock in the evening of the same day, Oliver Philpot and Lieutenant Eric Williams were carried out in the horse with another spare man who finally sealed them all into the tunnel for the last time, before the horse returned once more to the canteen.

As darkness fell Codner, Philpot and Williams broke out of the tunnel outside the compound, in fully prepared civilian disguises, and carrying their light luggage headed for Sagan railway station to catch their respective evening trains. All three of the escapees spoke fluent German, and expected no difficulty buying tickets, catching trains and negotiating travellers' checks en route to their favoured Baltic port destinations, from where they had all planned to stow away on departing Danish or Swedish ships.

Only then was the 1943 tunnelling season truly over in the various compounds of Stalag Luft III.

All three of the Wooden Horse escapers managed to successfully acquire individual passages on ships. When their chosen ships reached their respective home ports, all three of those escapers successfully applied for repatriation to England.

The fully detailed story of their escape is told in books entitled "The Wooden Horse" *by Williams, and* "Stolen Journey" *by Philpot. A film entitled* "The Wooden Horse" *was also made.*

Chapter 20

Kriegie Winter of 1943/44

As October of 1943 turned into November, and although further direct work on tunnel Harry had been postponed, the North Compound continued to be a productive hive of escape activity. For whilst Harry was dormant, with its entrance trap now guarded by the permanently lit wood burning stove on the plinth above its entrance trap and shaft, it was only the actual act of tunnelling that had stopped. There was still the opportunity to press on with activities associated with the manufacture of a whole range of escape equipment, all of which needed to be ready for use by whatever date that Harry might eventually be completed and ready for use.

Therefore, immediate advantage was taken of the intense activity surrounding completion of the compound theatre and its preparation for a programme of Christmas entertainment. Such intense theatrical activity and its attendant distractions gave the Kriegies a welcome cover to continue manufacturing the various illicit items that would eventually be required for their planned escape. Clothing for various disguises was easily worked on, being naturally well camouflaged amongst the array of legitimate theatrical costumes already being prepared. Also, the artistic uses of paints, dyes and inks by the theatrical scenery and backcloth artists were easily diverted to alter the colour of any cloth or paper that might be required by the tailors and forgers, as they worked on their respective escape projects.

Recalling the chill of the previous winter at Luft III, the North Compound Kriegies had obtained, from some of the American Kriegies, details of a simple recipe and process that enabled them to manufacture a form of moonshine alcohol. This was made out of Red Cross tinned fruit, combined with discarded vegetable matter that was easily collected from the compound kitchens. There was therefore some immediate hope of generating more warmth and cheer than was apparent over the previous Christmas.

Christmas of 1943 came and went, amid some enforced joviality and the usual exchanges of some small, handcrafted novelty gifts. Hand forged lucky charms, made from the lead and solder salvaged from Red Cross Klim tins, seemed to be the favoured gift that Christmas, especially for those Kriegies hoping to soon take a one-way trip through tunnel Harry.

Immediately after Christmas, there occurred a distraction from the humdrum of the winter routine. A burst pipe in the wall of one of the washrooms in the North compound's huts had somehow overnight sprayed water onto a level part of the compound, before then freezing to produce a large sheet of firm ice. On seeing the ice, and for the sheer novelty of something different to do, a small party of Kriegies were taking it in turns to run at the instant ice rink and slide swiftly across the ice. Dimwitz then happened to pass by and, seeing the joviality surrounding the mini-ice rink, he ordered a hosepipe to be brought out into the compound. Additional water was then sprayed onto the ground to enlarge the makeshift ice rink over a greater area as the water froze. Unbelievably, Dimwitz soon reappeared with a box of ice skates that he had managed to conjure up from somewhere. Then Dimwitz and his ferrets stayed to watch the ice show, whilst smugly congratulating themselves for ensuring that the Kriegies were well occupied in the harmless pursuit of winter fun. The ice rink soon became a well-used novelty that held the Kriegies' attention over several days, and sporadically on into the new year when the right conditions prevailed.

It later transpired that some Kriegies who had made exaggerated mention of the ice rink in their letters home, in addition to having already previously mentioned the existence of the camp theatre, the football pitch, and the golf course, must have given the wrong impression to some of their family members. For several Kriegies received very sarcastic letters in return, suggesting that those Kriegies might indeed have been "living the bloody high life", whilst those at home were alone in suffering the effects of rationing and general wartime deprivation.

In the meantime, a meeting of the Escape Committee had decided that several weeks of work would probably be needed to drive tunnel Harry to completion. It was therefore agreed to open and inspect the tunnel to ensure that it had survived the worst of the winter. Accordingly, on 10 January 1944, Harry's hatch was opened up for an inspection that revealed an immediate need to replace some of the shoring that had slipped out of place due to a movement of sand.

The necessary maintenance work was immediately to put in hand to restore the incomplete Harry to good order, whilst the fortunate discovery of an unattended spool of electrical cable also enabled electric lighting to be added at suitable locations within the tunnel.

From 15 January, tunnelling recommenced in earnest. However, as the compound still remained frozen, thus preventing the disposal of excavated sand by shuffling it into the compound's surface, it was decided to store sand in the cavity beneath the theatre's tiered seating for later disposal if necessary. The decision to dump sand in the theatre also avoided any increased activity in that area of the compound that contained the entrance shaft of demolished Tom and the previous sand dumping ground in the shaft and tunnel of the abandoned but still undiscovered Dick.

The tunnelling in Harry continued apace into February, and the tunnel's length reached two hundred feet by the end of that month. Then quite out of the blue, on 1 March, and without any explanation, the Germans pulled twenty Kriegies out of the morning parade and sent them immediately to a new compound some three miles away from Luft III. Unfortunately, amongst the twenty banished Kriegies were a number of key escape plan personnel, which caused the Escape Committee some concern that the Germans might somehow know more about their escape plans than they were letting on.

However, it soon came to light that Dimwitz, the senior ferret that had habitually been most successful in the escape busting stakes and tunnel discovery, was due to depart on fourteen days of leave. From past experience, it had become apparent that, in the absence of the senior ferret, the rest of the ferret team were quite content to take things easy. Most of the lesser ferrets were happy to be distracted by profitable fraternisation with the Kriegies, whilst themselves being unwittingly interrogated for any useful information as they gorged themselves on Red Cross chocolate and chain-smoked Red Cross cigarettes. An urgently called meeting of the Escape Committee therefore decided to take advantage of the senior ferret's absence, by calling for an all-out Kriegie effort to complete Harry and all excavating activity related thereto before the senior ferret's return to camp.

Over the following days, a supreme effort by all involved with the Harry project ensured that the tunnel was driven through to the required pre-calculated length of three hundred and sixty feet. The wooden railway, now in the form of two separate lengths, in total reached all the way to the rising shaft at the end of the tunnel, which in turn had been capped at a mere foot below the surface of the ground outside the compound. Also, all traces of sand had been cleared from the hut containing the entrance trap.

By 14 March 1944, Harry was complete, and the wood burning stove was permanently back on its plinth, standing guard over Harry until the tunnel was required for the final act of escape!

Coincidentally, the very next day, 15 March 1944, was Flap's twenty-sixth birthday. When he awoke on that morning, he found that his only birthday present was to be a lazy day off from any escape activity. Indeed, there appeared to be a lazy and overbearingly still atmosphere of anti-climax around the whole compound after the pressures of so much intense clandestine work over the preceding days. Over six hundred persons had been directly or indirectly involved in some way with the overall tunnelling enterprise, and then suddenly all that activity had stopped. It was so quiet around the compound that some on the Escape Committee feared that the Germans might detect that something was afoot. Therefore, some visible compound activities had to be hastily arranged to ensure that an air of apparent normality prevailed around the compound.

As well as the tunnel being completed, most of the escape equipment, in the form of clothing, disguises, forged documentation, maps and compasses had been completed during the tunnelling lull of the winter months. All that remained therefore was to issue specially prepared travelling food rations and the individually forged travel permits. However, as the travel permits could only be used on the one date shown thereon, they could not be date stamped until the very last hours before departure, when there had to be absolute certainty that the escape was going to go ahead on that particular date.

In the meantime, not everyone had taken the day off. The Escape Committee held a conference that included all their technical advisers and specialists in an endeavour to agree the date for the mass escape of Kriegies. In that respect, there were many things to consider, each of which needed to be at or around its optimum condition at the appointed time. For a start, it was agreed most suitable if the big escape could coincide with the night duty watch of a lazy, chain smoking, chocolate munching, lesser ferret, rather than a senior man; and further that the weather should ideally be dark, moonless, noisy and dry; and be on a day that avoided any need to travel on Sundays, when very few trains ran.

Whilst realising that not all of their requirements could possibly be met on any one night, the Escape Committee's meeting decided that the most important requirement was for absolute darkness. The Committee therefore provisionally fixed "Escape" day for the forecasted moonless night of Friday, 24 March 1944, with an attendant proviso to postpone all activity if the weather should otherwise prove hopelessly unsuitable on that night.

Then, after some reference to the hours of available darkness expected on the night of 24 March, some simple calculations indicated that up to two hundred and twenty escapees would be able to pass through the tunnel in close succession before dawn. Therefore, out of the six hundred odd listed Kriegies that had been involved directly or indirectly in the overall project, decisions had to be made as to how to decide who should be allowed to escape, and in what order of priority. Out of the six hundred, and for reasons of their own, approximately one hundred decided against taking part in the escape anyway. Thereafter all those of the small number with a fluent command of the German language were automatically prioritised as having the best chance of overall escape success. That total was then boosted to one hundred by a lucky draw of names from amongst the listed key workers of the overall escape scheme. There was then a final draw against the remaining listed names to boost the total to the two hundred and twenty maximum required.

Only then were those who knew that they had been selected to escape able to set about making their final preparations. Individual disguises, clothing, maps, compasses, and food rations, all had to be prepared and readied for use. The last items to be distributed would be the travel permits and an issue of German currency drawn from funds built up by trading Red Cross chocolate and cigarettes with certain of the compound's guards.

Chapter 21

The Great Escape

Long before the allotted day, the Kriegies that had been selected to escape were thoroughly briefed on how to use the tunnel to the greatest advantage. The briefing included specific and careful instructions regarding the permissible size of luggage, backpacks and bedrolls that it was possible to take through the tunnel, and many pieces of luggage were immediately checked to ensure compliance. Also, as many escapers would not have previously had the opportunity to venture into the tunnel, great emphasis was placed on promptly obeying any instructions given to them by the various experienced key workers that would be stationed along the escape route out of Luft III. That escape route included the marshalling area within the barracks hut that contained the entrance to Harry, and then on down the tunnel shaft, through the actual tunnel, and up to the exit; along which the least delay caused by any argument or thoughtless action would waste valuable time that might cost others their chance to escape.

Come the morning of 24 March 1944, the weather was unsettled enough to be causing some wind noise which, if maintained, would combine with the expected moonless night to produce the ideal dark and noisy conditions for escape. The final decision to mount the escape was soon announced, and the forgery department immediately geared itself up to date stamp two hundred and twenty sets of pre-prepared travel permits.

An eerie atmosphere then descended upon the North Compound, as those scheduled to escape became engrossed in finalising their preparations, ably aided and abetted by those that were not going. Fearing that the Germans might notice the sudden change of atmosphere, the Escape Committee once again had to request the non-escapers to generate some racket and create an air of normal activity around the compound.

Immediately after evening roll call, the tunnel was staffed and checked by the key workers who had been allocated to crew the escape complex in the various roles that would assist the escapers through the tunnel. However, there was immediately some delay, when those appointed to break out of the tunnel's rising end shaft discovered that the exit hole was not in the expected pre-planned position that would have enabled the exit to be obscured from view by the woodland scrub surrounding the compound. However, a hurried consultation with the tunnel managers quickly set up a watch station and signalling system that would enable each escaper to know when it was clear to exit the tunnel.

As a consequence of the delay, it was past ten p.m. before the first escapee actually entered the tunnel and moved forward. It soon became apparent that, in spite of the recent careful briefing, many escapees had not followed instructions regarding the size of their luggage. Hold up after unnecessary hold up was caused by the jamming up of outsized cases and bundles in the narrow tunnel confines. The net result of the combined delays so reduced the rate of departure that, by the time it was necessary to close down the operation because the sky was beginning to lighten, only eighty-seven men had passed through the Luft III barracks departure point.

It was then that a single shot rang out!

The tunnel exit had been discovered!

A lone sentry patrolling outside the compound wire had by chance veered away from his usual path and almost walked into the recently opened exit shaft of the tunnel, before nearly falling over some prone human forms that were lying on the ground nearby. Luckily, the single rifle shot then fired by the astounded sentry was a warning shot that did no damage. Rather than being fired at the escapers, the shot had been indiscriminately fired off after the sentry's sheer shock of discovering three Kriegies lying at the shaft head, and another one down a hole in the ground. As the German sentry was marching his captives back towards the German guardroom at gunpoint, the Kriegie officer controlling the flow of men at the tunnel entrance shaft, on hearing the single gunshot, had realised that the escape had been detected. He hurriedly recovered the last few escapers that had already entered the tunnel before the alarm was raised, and together they replaced the wood burning stove and its plinth over Harry's entrance shaft.

Following the initial confrontation with the German guard around the exit shaft, another hour and a half passed before the Germans, not knowing what they might face therein, were able to muster sufficient armed manpower to confidently enter the North Compound in force. By that time most of the potential escapers that had been queuing for their turn to enter the tunnel were able to escape the departure hut and return to their own quarters. Throughout the camp travel passes, maps, compasses, disguises, and various other contraband items were hurriedly hidden or destroyed.

On their arrival, the overall Stalag Luft III Commandant Lieutenant Colonel von Lindeiner and his ferrets of the security staff were visibly furious to learn of the escape attempt of the few men so far discovered outside the compound. But their simple rage was nothing when compared to their mood a couple of hours later. Then, following roll calls and a photo check of the whole camp population to compare the remaining Kriegies to their respective ID photos, as filed on each man's *Personalkarte* within camp records, the Commandant and his security staff became absolutely incandescent with rage. For they had finally realised that, after recovering four Kriegies from the tunnel head and those still queuing inside the tunnel, a total of seventy-six of their Kriegie charges had gone missing overnight.

Within the following hours, the German High Command ordered Lieutenant Colonel von Lindeiner to be removed from his post, and the Gestapo took temporary charge of Stalag Luft III. As the Gestapo investigation of the North Compound progressed, thorough searches uncovered the vast amount of stolen German property that had been incorporated into the overall escape scheme. As none of that stolen property appeared to have been reported as missing, the Gestapo immediately assumed that the German staff must have colluded with their charges to accept bribes in exchange for various items required by the Kriegies. Several of the German maintenance staff were then promptly removed from the camp pending court martial, before later being shot by the Gestapo.

Most of the smaller contraband items had simply been stolen by the Kriegies from under the noses of German tradesmen that carried out repairs. Other items had simply just been carried away when found lying unattended around the compound. On discovery of any loss, the various tradesmen had been too frightened to report the incident, as they knew that they would have been charged with negligence and shot anyway; only much sooner of course!

When the German Gestapo investigation finally called for a full inventory of the whole camp to be taken, they were astounded at the sheer amount of equipment and furniture that had gone missing. Literally thousands of items had disappeared, including nearly one hundred double tiered bunks, six hundred mattresses, two hundred bed sheets, fifty large tables and several thousand bed boards, all of which had been dismantled and stripped to gather the timber and fabric for alternative uses. Most of the timber was utilised to shore up tunnels and shafts, whilst mattresses, together with their covers and bed sheets had yielded the valuable fabrics that were used in the manufacture of the clothing required for the escapees' assorted civilian disguises.

Chapter 22

Unexpected Aftermath

In the following days, orders from the German High Command dictated the immediate destruction of tunnel Harry and "all things associated with it". However, recalling the extensive collateral damage caused when Tom was blown up, some immediate caution was urged by the ferrets before any further action was taken. The decision was finally made to fill Harry in with refuse and sewage to render it extremely repulsive to any future exploration, before then filling the shafts at either end with compressed sand beneath a thick reinforced concrete cap.

Regarding the seventy-six Kriegies who had managed to vacate Luft III via Harry, little was heard for nearly two weeks. Then over a few days fifteen Kriegies were returned direct to Luft III, and another three sent to a camp much further to the north.

Very soon after return of the fifteen escapees, the new Luft III Commandant, one Lieutenant Colonel Cordes, received orders to separately summon the senior British Officer from each compound respectively to then separately attend a one-to-one meeting with him. He had been ordered to read them the following prewritten statement that had been forwarded to him from a higher level of German command, as follows:

> "I have been instructed by higher authority to communicate to you this report:
>
> "The Senior British Officer is to be informed that as a result of a tunnel from which seventy-six officers escaped from Stalag Luft III, North Compound, forty-one of these officers have been shot whilst resisting arrest or attempting further escape after arrest."

The Commandant uncomfortably avoided any eye contact when he was then asked how many of the shot men might have been wounded. He would only state that he was not permitted to answer questions or volunteer any further information. However, when repeatedly pressed on this point he finally relented to mumble that he thought none had been merely wounded.

Eventually a list of those escapees that were known to have been shot was posted on the Compound notice board. By that time, the notice contained forty-seven names, and within a further couple of days the total rose to fifty, as three more names were added to it.

It was as if the German High Command really did intend to destroy tunnel Harry and "all things associated with it", for as far as the North Compound Kriegies were concerned, there was absolutely no doubt that the shooting of exactly fifty of their comrades were acts of premeditated and cold-blooded murder. They were sure that none of the unarmed escapees would have been silly enough to have defied a "Halt" challenge from an armed German. The circumstances of those shootings certainly left a worrying thought among some of the Kriegies that there might have been a sudden desperate change of German policy towards the status of PoWs at that stage, as the tide of war was very slowly starting to turn against Germany. Consequently, some Kriegies began doubting the wisdom of any future escape attempts, which of course might well have been exactly what the Germans were hoping for. The fatal command, although signed by Himmler, had actually been issued by Adolf Hitler himself who, it was later learned, had originally wanted to execute all of the escapees that were recaptured. Hitler was only persuaded to reduce his demands to fifty by Hermann Goering, who used his influence as Head of the German Luftwaffe to talk Hitler down.

Over the coming weeks, the remainder of the seventy-six escapees were accounted for when it was learned that there were eight more survivors. Of those survivors it was known that five had been sent to a concentration camp, whilst only three had successfully reached England by various routes.

Roger Bushell and his travelling companion, the sole French escapee, were caught together fairly soon after escaping. Following his previous escape earlier in the war, Bushell had already been warned by the Gestapo that he would be shot if he came to their attention again. Therefore, immediately following capture by the Germans, Bushell and his companion were separated out for some special treatment before being transported away by car. Mid-journey both men were unexpectedly shot in the back of the head whilst relieving themselves beside the road.

It eventually came to light that, to ensure consistency with the German statement that "all were shot whilst attempting to escape", the other forty-eight of those that were executed were also shot from behind, all in small groups at the roadside, and all whilst relieving themselves during travel breaks in various remote rural locations across Germany.

It is interesting to reiterate at this point that men from all over the world had volunteered to fight the Nazis by joining the Royal Air Force and, of those that were executed, less than half were home grown British, numbering just twenty-two. Of the balance, fifteen were drawn from the nations of the British Commonwealth, whilst the remaining thirteen were foreign nationals from the various countries of occupied Europe, who had each individually become British citizens specifically to enable them to join the Royal Air Force and thus directly continue their fight against the Nazis.

The group of European murder victims unfortunately included the talented caricaturist Henri Picard, who had of course drawn the earlier mentioned caricature of Flap to celebrate my own first birthday. He had since gone on to utilise his considerable artistic talents to assist the Escape Committee's forgery department with the production of finely forged German passes and travel documents.

In the aftermath of the escape, a simple percentage analysis of the final results showed that of the seventy-six escapees that got away:

- Only four per cent had made a home run to England.
- Thirty per cent had been recaptured but survived.
- Another sixty-six per cent had also been recaptured, before blatantly being murdered in cold blood by the Gestapo.

As a direct consequence of those shocking results, many of the surviving Kriegies of the North Compound became traumatised to some degree; whether they had been actively involved in the escape attempt, or not.

Of the six hundred men who had been directly involved with the overall escape plan:

- Three hundred and eighty of those men had initially been disappointed by what they considered to be an unlucky lottery result that had not even granted them the chance to join the escape queue. Those men were latterly very thankful that fate had fortunately favoured them better than they thought, by keeping them well away from the disastrous final outcome of the escape project.

- A further one hundred and forty-four men had ventured much closer to danger on that eventful night. For having secured a place in the escape queue, and as they were queuing for their turn to escape through the tunnel, they had cursed the continuously unforeseen delays being caused by the selfish minority of escapers that were struggling to drag their excessively large luggage through the tunnel. However, without those delays, many more of those men would have passed through the tunnel exit, long before the German guard's warning shot finally put paid to the venture. Many of those men were subsequently traumatised by their rising feelings of guilt. For they soon realised that it was only the delays caused by the selfishness of those that they had cursed ahead of them, that had probably saved each one of them from the sixty-six per cent chance of being shot in the back by the Gestapo; probably whilst their backs were turned as they piddled on the side of a remote German country roadside.
- Finally, the most traumatised men out of the whole escape operation were the twenty-three out of the seventy-six escapees who, having been recaptured and handed to the Gestapo for a lengthy process of interrogation, were then randomly returned safely alive to various camps. Those included the fifteen sent back to the North Compound of Luft III, before they had fully realised the fate of their fifty shot comrades.

Flap had already experienced suffering from feelings of guilt and trauma when he first arrived at Stalag Luft III, all as a result of his fortunate sole survival from the seven-man crew of Lancaster OF-K King as it was blown to pieces on hitting the ground. He appreciated that luck alone had ensured that he was catapulted clear of the blast, as the sole scorched survivor. Even a year after the event, it would have been difficult having to write the previously mentioned postcard to crew member Arthur Cox's mother in reply to her enquiry regarding the fate of her son.

For whatever reason, the Great Escape was not a good memory for Flap either. He had lost good friends, including the Belgian caricaturist

Henri Picard and others, whilst he had survived yet again. Post war he only ever volunteered very scant information concerning the Great Escape and, if the conversation persisted for too long on that theme, he would soon change the subject to the far happier outcome associated with the East Compound's Wooden Horse escape project. Especially relating to how he had been able to experience the thrill of jumping over the horse whilst the nearby easily entertained spectator Goons remained totally oblivious to the activity going on in the ground beneath the horse as they were looking on. By comparison, that escape had also produced three successful home runs to England, but with far less effort, and no loss of life at all.

As far as the depth of Flap's involvement in the Great Escape project, I cannot be sure of his part beyond the fact that he was most probably among the six hundred or so Kriegies that had registered an interest in assisting the big escape plan overall. His efforts were mainly involved with woodworking and the manufacture of various other items as required, including metal implements and tools made from Klim milk tins, and of course taking regular turns on the tunnelled sand disposal rota.

On the night of the Great Escape, Flap may or may not have been eligible to queue for a turn to pass through the tunnel. I will never know, because he never said! The only certainties were that he did not escape; and he was not shot by the Gestapo! However, he had definitely been shocked by the needlessly cold-blooded execution of fifty fellow Royal Air Force officers.

In the aftermath of the escape, John Nunn revealed to Flap certain regrets of his own that were adversely affecting his morale. For it would appear that when planning tunnel Harry, and due to the obvious lack of accessibility to the outside surroundings of the North Compound, it was proving impossible to blindly estimate the length of tunnel required to ensure that Harry would reach the obscured shelter of the surrounding woodland. To the tunnel planners, it seemed just as pointless to waste time, effort and energy by digging a longer tunnel than necessary, as it would have been to dig a tunnel that might turn out to be far too short. Therefore, as Nunn was known to be a mathematics graduate, Roger Bushell asked him if he would use his knowledge of trigonometric calculations to work out the exact length of tunnel required to reach the woodlands. Subsequently, when, on the night of the escape, tunnel

Harry's exit fell short, Nunn had immediately decided that he must have made a miscalculation which, in his mind, he then immediately assumed was in some way responsible for the resultant high death toll that had resulted from the overall project.

On hearing of Nunn's concerns, Flap was quick to reassure him with a quick contradiction of his assumptions. For surely, if the tunnel had been of the required length there would not then have been any delay in starting to pass men through it. Additionally, once they were moving along, the men could also have exited much faster by not having to wait for the optimum moments of darkness between searchlight passes before they could exit the tunnel. Therefore, the total number of escapees could potentially have been so much higher that an even greater German retribution might well have then followed.

Unfortunately, it appeared that Nunn was still determined to assume some blame, for he countered Flap's argument with a simple statement to the effect that, if he had simply not provided the requested calculation at all, then perhaps the escape would not have taken place. Then nobody would have died!

Roger Bushell's original concept of generating a mass escape was primarily to enable as many RAF aircrew as possible to make a home run to Great Britain by whatever means possible. A secondary purpose was to distract German manpower and home resources away from other work that might have been more beneficial to the Reich's war effort, simply by creating a sudden need to hunt down a tidal wave of fugitives scattering across the countryside. In many respects, and at such a high cost of life, the escape was not the roaring success that had been expected. Only three successful home runs were achieved, whilst the limited number of men that had escaped from Stalag Luft III hardly constituted a tidal wave. However, later reports did indicate that there had reputedly been some further success by causing Himmler to overreact to initial reports of the escape by deploying sixty thousand of his home guard and all their equipment countrywide; all having been placed on a full alert.

In the meantime, and despite all the talk of trauma, the overall effort put towards arranging the Great Escape had provided the Kriegies with some indirectly hidden benefits during much of their engrossing work towards the overall escape plan. Those benefits took the unintended form of occupational therapies that had engaged and distracted those

Kriegies' minds from the traumas that they would have suffered during the generally bloody business of being shot down, whilst often witnessing the horrific deaths of their fellow air crewmen. It also became an established fact that the sense of achievement associated with the various manufacturing activities prevented many Kriegies from suffering from a form of psychosis, usually referred to in PoW camps as barbed wire psychosis. That form of psychosis was usually directly associated with the inactive rut of non-achievement and hopelessness associated with any form of imprisonment and could prompt a condition that started to destroy memory and concentration to the point that the afflicted were unable to remain still for very long. The recommended counteractive therapies for such conditions in civilian life are usually in the active form of modelling and handicrafts, designed to keep both mind and body immersed in the project at hand, from planning to completion. Thus, the challenges of planning, manufacturing and problem solving associated with the escape plans, plus the extra incentive of getting one over on the Germans anyway, had for months been the sole motivation to encourage many of the Kriegies to keep their minds active, and bother to get out of bed each morning.

However, in the immediate aftermath of the disastrous Great Escape, there was no denying that all motivation had dissolved, and an aimless lethargy had then set in among the Kriegies of the North Compound of Stalag Luft III.

Chapter 23

Then Life Went On

LUFT LIFE – Towards the end of April 1944, the Germans delivered fifty labelled cremation urns to the North Compound; one each for every one of the Kriegie RAF officers that had been murdered by the German Gestapo.

That delivery of cremation urns alone was responsible for stirring up so much resentment among the Kriegies that their mood quickly turned from lethargy to a new-found mood of determined defiance. The remnants of the old Escape Committee immediately called an open meeting, during which it was unanimously decided to launch another tunnelled escape project. The new project consisted of a plan to build another deep tunnel to be codenamed George; this time to run from beneath the theatre for three hundred yards, to a patch of woodland beyond the Eastern boundary.

Flap, with his plans for Klim tin implements, ducting, and various other modelling and handicraft skills, was happy to join the carpenters and various other amateur craftsmen who were all relieved to be usefully occupied by the new project. Collectively, their mood was lifted, as they found a fresh purpose in life and immersed themselves in the manufacture of the equipment necessary to enable tunnelling to commence again during May 1944. Simplified sand disposal on the new project did not need any outside transport, for the sand was simply taken from the tunnel and packed into the cavity beneath the theatre floor. Tunnelling was even able to continue beneath the floor when the theatre was in use.

On 6 and 7 June, the mood of the whole compound was further raised when the compound radio picked up reports of the Allied D-Day seaborne landings on the Normandy coast of France. Also, Rome had been liberated two days previously, and the Russians appeared to be making large territorial gains as they pushed westward.

Possibly feeling the gradual turn of the tide against them, on 12 June the German authorities decided that they ought to report the taking of "special armed measures against a mass escape of Allied PoWs" that had occurred in March to the Swiss office responsible for policing compliance with the Geneva Convention. However, the neutral Swiss camp inspector had already interviewed those PoWs that had survived the aftermath of the escape and been able to give him evidence of what had occurred at Gestapo HQ during March and April, when small groups of PoWs were mysteriously disappearing from the building under Gestapo escort. Having received the more recent and differing version of events direct from the Germans themselves, the Swiss office immediately notified details of the murders to the relevant offices of the British Government.

Consequently, on 23 June 1944, receipt of the Swiss report was acknowledged in the British Houses of Parliament. Unfortunately, some misconstrued details prematurely found their way into the public domain. Unexpected newspaper and radio reports then caused some considerable alarm to the relatives of those known to be held at Luft III, including Bernice Sherwood, and all long before it was known if the reported events had actually involved their respective relatives or not.

Meanwhile, at Luft III North Compound, tunnelling activity continued steadily on towards the autumn of 1944, and the compound radio continued to bring encouraging news. On 25 July, the BBC announced the break-out of American forces from the confines of the Normandy beachhead, and a month later Paris was liberated.

By mid-September 1944, as news of American troops entering Germany for the first time combined with news of continued Russian progress westward, the Escape Committee began to doubt whether it was worth progressing any further with tunnel George. Some BBC radio reports had reported the Prime Minister's hope that the war in Europe might even be over before the year's end, and there were definite indications that the tunnelling effort might well be overtaken by fast moving events elsewhere. During October it was therefore decided to cease tunnelling, and then make use of the tunnel space that had so far been created as a hidden store to stockpile an emergency supply of food and equipment for use in any future crisis.

However, in the run up to Christmas 1944 sod's law stepped in to thwart the Kriegies' hopes of an early repatriation. First, the northern part of the Russian advance from the east disappointingly appeared to run out of steam. Then, on 16 December, the Germans launched a fierce counter-attack through Belgium against the Allied armies in France, with the intention of delaying the invasion of Germany by driving a wedge between the British and American armies that were pushing into Germany from the west. The Kriegies were therefore destined to spend yet another Christmas at Sagan.

HOME LIFE – At home in England, Bernice and I had moved out of our Lilac Cottage temporary home in Sonning. Flap received a newsy letter via Kriegie mail, revealing our new address to be a rented house called Thornleigh, in Eldorado Road, Cheltenham, which my mother and I were then to share with my maternal grandmother, whilst my maternal grandfather Naval Officer was on overseas duties with the Royal Navy in the far east, based in Colombo, Ceylon (now Sri Lanka).

Our new home was also conveniently in close proximity to my paternal grandmother, Flap's mother, who was living not far away, whilst engaged in Women's Royal Voluntary Service welfare work with nearby American Forces personnel.

Even now, my very earliest life memories are of the time spent at Thornleigh, for I was by then nearly three years old. One of the earliest memories there is that of Bernice and my grandmother taking it upon themselves to describe my missing father to me; for of course I had never knowingly met him before! According to them, this mystical figure had wings, his mates called him Flap, and he could fly! Maybe slightly confusing, but the flight business seemed quite logical to me at the time, as most living things capable of flight that I had so far encountered did flap. Furthermore, as none of the other children in the immediate neighbourhood appeared to have fathers at home either, I made the assumption that all the fathers must be off flying around somewhere else!

I only have vague memories of the Cheltenham house and its surroundings. I do recall that behind the house and its garden there was a footpath. The railway was not far away, and the sounds of the nearby trains fascinated me from a very early stage. Best of all, I discovered that the boy next door, instead of having a pedal car, had a ride-on pedal-powered model of a steam tank engine, painted in Great Western Railway green. To the dismay of my young neighbour, it became my sole purpose in life to borrow the green pedal-powered engine, retaining possession of it for as long as possible, and spending whole days pedalling the engine around the garden of Thornleigh.

I can also recall occasions when what seemed to me to be very large parcels arrived on a post van. Those parcels usually bore rows of double sized, vertically printed, red bordered stamps, depicting pictures of coconut laden palm trees. Arrival of those parcels caused great excitement, for they contained what I eventually realised was Ceylon tea; at that time valuable enough to be treated like a currency in its own right and sent home from Ceylon with the compliments of my naval officer grandfather. Those offerings being, apart from money, the best he could find to keep both Bernice and my grandmother happy from afar, during his long absence abroad.

I also have vague recollections of getting myself into trouble for causing a panic at Cheltenham. A black police car soon became involved, because as far as my mother was concerned, I had just simply disappeared off the face of the earth. However, for me the event was not that dramatic, for having simply been fascinated by the dustcart and the banter of the funny old men operating it, I had decided to follow the cart to continue enjoying the entertainment. The police soon found me at the farthest end of Eldorado Road, already heading home alone anyway.

At some time, and following his long absence abroad, I recall Flap's brother Tony paying us a visit at Thornleigh, when I must have been nearly three years old.

On leaving school, Flap's brother Tony had initially trained to be an aeronautical engineer. Consequently, he then found himself ensnared in a reserved occupation, being of great use to the war effort at home, but compulsorily exempting him from call up into the armed forces. However, later wishing that he had trained to be a pilot like his older brother, Tony had successfully fought to gain release from his reserved occupational status. That then enabled him to train as a pilot in the United States of America, at one of the RAF flying training schools that had been established there much earlier in the war under the Lease Lend Agreement between the UK and USA.

On hearing that my Uncle Tony could fly, I queried why I could not see his wings. He replied that I could not see them because he was simply not wearing them on that particular day and that logical explanation of course I had to simply accept.

Whilst visiting my mother and I, Tony took the opportunity of writing to Flap, via Bernice, as she was Flap's only permitted Kriegie correspondent registered with the Germans.

Early in the new year, Tony received a 'Kriegie Postkarte' from Flap that had been written on 19 December 1944, in reply to his earlier letter and sent once again via Bernice. In the script of that "Postkarte" Flap had commented *"tell them this Christmas was almost half rations & certainly no Booze!"* For the Luft III Kriegies, in the despondency of their dashed hopes of an early release by the advancing allies, soon realised that they had not even attempted to prepare their popular version of moonshine booze in preparation for the coming Kriegie Christmas of 1944.

A photo of the Kriegie Postkarte appears in the photo plate section of this book. It is interesting to ponder what Flap had written on the postcard that caused the German censor to delete a short passage of his handwriting thereon.

Chapter 24

The Long March

From mid-January, the northern part of the Russian thrust towards Germany from the east, through Poland and East Prussia, suddenly took on a new lease of life, and within a few days the Russian forces were once more on a roll towards Stalag Luft III, at Sagan.

On 21 January 1945, from the roof of the highest structure in the North Compound of Luft III and for as far as the eye could then see, streams of refugees were visible approaching Sagan on every possible route from the east. Rumours among the German guards were then suggesting that the Russians had already pushed to within fifty miles of Sagan.

The Kriegies were somewhat uneasy about what to expect if Luft III was overrun by the Russians. However, and possibly because of the many known atrocities that had been carried out in Russia by the German army of occupation, the guards appeared to have far more fear of the Russians than the Kriegies did. The guards were frequently asking their charges for updates of current events from the BBC news that they knew full well was being continuously monitored on the clandestine compound radios. The radios that the Germans did not find, and that everyone then pretended did not exist anyway, had suddenly become of equal benefit to both Kriegie and Captors alike. It became obvious from their behaviour around the compound, that several of the German camp staff officers were becoming greatly agitated at the lack of any information or firm order from their own higher command; not least because many of those officers had their immediate families quartered in and around the greater Sagan district.

The Kriegies on the other hand had received their very clear orders, direct from the Allied Supreme Commander in Europe, General Dwight Eisenhower, when, during a BBC broadcast, Eisenhower had ordered all PoWs to remain within their camp compounds until they were relieved by advancing Allied forces. Most of the Kriegies therefore felt quite comfortable with the idea of waiting where they were for the Russians to overrun Stalag Luft III, from where they confidently expected they would then be repatriated. That is to say that they were happy, until some of the German camp staff revealed that they had heard rumours, from higher up in their command. Those rumours were suggesting that Hitler might have ordered that the Kriegies from all German PoW camps should be mustered to a central collection point; then to act as hostage pawns during any peace negotiations, in an endeavour to ensure a peace settlement more favourable to the Germans than otherwise. Or worse still, the Kriegies might be used as human shields within German cities to deter the Allies from any further bombing of those German cities.

Over the coming days it was possible to hear the thunder of the Russian guns growing louder and louder and, as the battlefront came nearer, some apprehension and confusion reigned among the German guards of the North Compound. The bulk of the guards were suddenly issued with travelling ration packs, without further explanation from their superiors, and many therefore assumed that they were going to be sent towards the front line to fight the Russians.

Confusion also reigned as far as the Kriegies were concerned, for one minute they were being told that they would be left waiting in the camp for the Russians to relieve them. Then, later on the same day they were told that German High Command, somehow believing that they could still turn the war around in their favour or seek some sort of treaty with the Allies that did not involve total capitulation, wanted to retain the Kriegies as bargaining chips; or, at the very least, avoid the early release of so many skilled Allied aircrew that would be prepared to fight against Germany again.

The Kriegies finally decided of their own accord that wherever their current situation was going to lead them, travelling would inevitably be involved, whether under German or Russian command. The sensible Kriegies therefore decided to prepare themselves for any eventuality by commencing some physical training and feeding themselves up from the ample reserves of Red Cross food that they had stashed away for emergencies. All men then had to decide how they would pack their personal possessions and food supplies for travelling. The outside temperature was at freezing or below for most of the time, with snow and ice underfoot. Multiple items of camp furniture were therefore hurriedly disassembled, and the wood reassigned to new uses as many men made sledges to transport their spare rations and belongings. Others used blankets made up in sausage shaped bundles of belongings that could be carried over the shoulder or suspended around the neck. There was so much available from the stock of Red Cross parcels that the Kriegies pickings were finally limited by what they could physically carry or pull on a sledge, unopened Red Cross parcels being particularly suited to sledge travel.

Most men had possession of service issue great coats, the issue of which had been ensured for all PoWs by the Red Cross. Those were donned, and the pockets were then stuffed with universal currency in the form of Red Cross cigarettes and chocolate.

By 27 January, the Russian guns had grown steadily louder and louder, and the German camp personnel had steadily grown more and more agitated, harassed and confused. The guns were then so near that, in the absence of any orders to the contrary from their higher command, the Germans were making preparations to receive the Russians anyway.

In the meantime, and having assembled their luggage, most of the Kriegies of the North Compound had decided to carry on with their normal routines. Most men were relaxing as usual, whilst rehearsals for a forthcoming play were in full swing in the Compound theatre, almost as though nothing was about to change.

Then quite suddenly that evening, and probably to the relief of all the parties concerned, a German order came through to commence the urgent evacuation of Stalag Luft III. Immediately, a general shout went up to rouse the Kriegies to action and ensure that all their activities were interrupted.

Flap was eager to leave and, in the absence of any offer of mechanised transport from the Germans, he had made sure that his personal sledge was already packed with his food rations and generally larger possessions, whilst his photos, letters and small personal possessions were in his pockets and a small bundle designated to hang beneath his protective RAF great coat. However, it was past 3.00am on 28 January before the North Compound of Stalag Luft III finally got under way. Each man was handed an unopened Red Cross parcel as he left the compound, and each parcel was eagerly accepted whether the entirety of the contents were required, or not.

When all the compounds of Luft III and its surrounding satellite camps had departed the area, there was then a continuous column of approximately ten thousand men on the road, in straggled bunches, all heading west in a column many miles long that was emitting visible clouds of exhaled steam into the minus twelve degrees of the night air. Strange percussive sounds arose from the scuffing columns of men, as improvised sledges and feet grated on the ice, and a multitude of cooking utensils that were suspended around the necks and waists of the men generated off-tune musical notes within an overall eerie clanking sound.

Once under way, the Kriegies soon realised that they did not know where they were going. Nobody had told them! However, they were sure that they would never return to Luft III, for as they left the camp there were tall flames leaping from some of the wooden buildings that had apparently been torched by the Germans, all as part of some sort of vague scorched earth policy that was intended to deny any possible usage of the buildings to the fast approaching Russian invaders.

The night was dark and moonless, with frequent falls of snow and a still dropping temperature. Initially there was much rancour between Kriegies and grumpy guards about the infrequency of rest stops. However, the most fit and able bodied of the Germans that had guarded the Kriegies at Luft III had already been taken away on reassignment to fight the Russians, and as the remaining guards were mainly of sub-standard fitness or ability, it was not long before it was the guards who were first to beg for rest breaks and a general easing of the pace.

The first properly designated refreshment halt did not occur until the column had covered some ten and a half miles. By then it was daylight, and having reached a small town/village of unrecalled name, the chaotic state of German officialdom was laid bare. It appeared that the columns of Kriegies had not even been expected. It was only the generosity of the civilian population that rallied around to ensure the availability of liquid refreshment for Kriegies and guards alike, whilst many villagers were in turn rewarded with what were obviously regarded as luxury items in the form of cigarettes and chocolate taken from Red Cross parcels. Before departure, an announcement informed the Kriegies that their next overnight billet had been arranged at the village of Friedwaldau some further four and a half miles ahead.

On reaching Friedwaldau around midday, chaos reigned once more. The pre-arranged accommodation was grossly insufficient for the number of men involved, and the bulk of the Kriegies were left standing on the streets, immobile in freezing conditions, whilst the Germans in charge of the column sought out more shelter. It appeared that Friedwaldau was already short of accommodation because of the presence of many German refugees. However, whilst the Germans were attempting to seek out further accommodation, it turned out that many of the refugees were openly eager to assist the Kriegies by sheltering and feeding them. That was until the local mayor turned up to reveal himself as a fanatical Nazi who, protesting that the presence of the Kriegies was contaminating his village, enlisted the help of some nearby SS troops to evict the Kriegies. The whole column then had to march another four and a half miles to a village by the name of Leippa, where it was only rumoured that alternative shelter might be available.

The following hours were such that many Kriegies later described them as the worst period of the march. For during the previous long wait on the streets of Friedwaldau, and as the temperature had continued to drop, many men suffered various degrees of frostbite with no immediate medical assistance available to them. Then, when the column had finally reached Leippa at 5pm, it was again revealed that the allocated accommodation was far too small for the numbers of men involved. So, once again men had to wait on the road, getting frostbitten for another four hours, as the temperature continued to drop to minus twenty to produce the coldest night of that year.

It was then only the supreme efforts of the German ferret sergeant major that the Kriegies had nicknamed Dimwitz, that averted a tragedy. He immediately turned the village upside down to find sufficient living space to ensure that everyone found shelter. It was also the alertness of Dimwitz that soon realised that many of his charges and some of his own guards had gone missing. Local transport was commandeered, and search parties were promptly dispatched to search for those who had literally fallen by the wayside, suffering from the adverse hypothermic effects of frostbite and prolonged exposure to the elements.

Amazingly, and in spite of the continuing bitter cold, by 8am the following morning of 29 January, the men were assembled on the street and ready to resume their travels. By then the German guards had given up trying to count their charges and seemed to be relying entirely on the instincts of Dimwitz to decide if anyone was missing, or not. By midday a small town was reached, where the column paused. No rations or water were provided there, and once again it was the sympathetic civilians that rallied round to cater for the unexpected influx of men. A couple of the most severe frostbite cases from the previous day were left at the local hospital before the march then resumed less than an hour later. A briefing message verbally passed back through the column had informed the men that they needed to march a further twelve and a half miles to reach their overnight billets at the town of Muskau. That objective was reached by 6pm.

On arrival at Muskau, the first priority was to evacuate an elderly German guard to hospital. The old boy had been slow to recognise his own symptoms of an earlier frostbite, which had then slowly deteriorated to the point where it was going to cost him the loss of both of his legs.

To the amazement of the Kriegies and German guards alike, the column was met by the mayor of Muskau in his full mayoral regalia. The mayor informed the assembled company that most of the men would be billeted in and around a nearby local stately home, that was also being variously described by officials as a palace, or even a castle. The unknown number of Kriegies that exceeded the capacity of the stately home were allocated to a nearby recently vacated PoW camp.

Those lucky enough to be billeted in various accommodation around the "stately palatial castle" soon discovered that its grounds included stables, barns and agricultural buildings, all of which were warm, dry and weather tight. The owner of the stately home was in residence, and he seemed pleased to be able to show interested groups of Kriegies around his estate. Within a very short time Flap and his immediate associates had settled in and discovered that there was even the luxury of a limited amount of hot water available for bathing and showering.

Initially, the only downside of Muskau seemed to be the total lack of rations or self-catering facilities available to the Kriegies. However, with total absence of Nazism or any form of petty officialdom, the citizens of Muskau turned out to be a very civil lot of moderate political outlook. The local bakery was soon opened up to produce a huge amount of fresh warm bread, and local families seemed quite eager to invite Kriegies into their homes to share what food that they had, especially when rewarded with cigarettes and chocolate taken from the continuing ample supply of Red Cross parcels that remained in Kriegie hands.

The Kriegies made many friends with local families, amongst whom the main topic of conversation appeared to centre around how the Russians might behave when they arrived, and whether local German families should flee well ahead of the Russians; or not. Members of some families even expressed a wish to accompany the Kriegies, whenever they might leave. In that respect, whilst the Kriegies had expected to remain in Muskau for one day only, their stay was eventually extended into a very popular three day recuperative respite from the punishing marching conditions that they had recently experienced.

In the meantime, the Kriegies of the East Compound of Stalag Luft III, who had followed the same route as the North Compound, arrived at Muskau, having been deliberately scheduled to take a day longer than the North Compound to cover almost the same route. The East Compound column were immediately allocated sufficient billets in the local Muskau glass factory, which those Kriegies soon discovered was fortuitously still in full production in the capable hands of French PoWs being forced to labour there. Following their frozen march from Sagan, the Kriegies of the East Compound therefore found themselves in seventh heaven. The factory furnaces provided a sumptuous supply of continuous heat and hot water, and with a little assistance from the Kriegies the factory canteen was able to upgrade production to supply hot bread and soup for the entire column.

During the couple of days that the Kriegies of the North and the East Compounds were both sojourning in Muskau, and almost imperceptibly at first, the snow had begun to dissolve. After the harsh marching conditions that had so far been experienced, an unprecedented early thaw appeared to be setting in. However, much concern was immediately uttered, for without snow the Kriegies multitude of still well loaded home-made sledges would not run smoothly over the ground. After a short pause to consider the situation, Muskau suddenly became a thriving centre of commerce, as Kriegies bartered wildly with the local population to obtain wheels in whatever form they could secure; preferably attached to complete wheelbarrows, prams or handcarts, but failing that even loose wheels of any sort soon reached an unheard of premium value, as long as tools were then made available to quickly convert sledges into hand carts and trolleys.

On the morning of 1 February, there came an announcement that all the Kriegies of the North Compound and half of those from the East Compound were to march over the coming night to the town of Spremberg, from where they would be transported by train to the Bremen area. There was immediately much muttering at having to hit the road again. Not least because the Kriegies had been so agreeably received by the population of Muskau, but also through sheer disbelief that they were being asked to march in the bitter cold of that particular winter night.

It was already dark when the column of men were assembled on the streets of Muskau. The guards initially attempted a count of heads, but soon gave up in favour of an approximation only, for they were just as annoyed as the Kriegies at the thought of the probable trials of the night to come. As the men prepared to depart, they noticed that the general population of Muskau, who had made them so welcome throughout their stay, were then very conspicuous by their absence from the streets. It was rumoured that they had been ordered to stay indoors, just in case any of those citizens that had expressed a wish to march westward away from the Russians with the Kriegies had actually meant it, and possibly gone home to pack their bags.

Once over the hill and away from Muskau, any attempt at formality was abandoned. The men from the two compounds blended into one as some old acquaintances were revived, and the attitude of guards relaxed as they mingled with whoever was most free with the fags and the chocolate.

Although the snow had gone, it was still very cold, and the potential for a harsh dose of frostbite still remained a real possibility as the column trudged wearily on through the freezing night of the German countryside. Many of those who had not succeeded in obtaining wheels to convert their sledges had transferred their goods to self-made back packs instead, but they were soon beginning to reel under the strain of carrying so much weight on their shoulders. The truth then really began to sink in that after two or three years of Stalag rations, none of the Kriegies had been in the best of condition when they had left Luft III in the first place. They had already been weakened from the effects of prolonged under nourishment, without expending the sheer physical outlay since demanded of them in the appalling overall conditions so far encountered on the long march. Flap and his fellow physical training enthusiasts had probably been in a far better condition than most when they set out, but even they were soon beginning to wilt.

By six o'clock on the morning of 2 February, the head of the column reached the town of Grundstein where the column was able to rest awhile. In the meantime, the intuition of Dimwitz again persuaded him that some faces that he knew were missing. He therefore sent out a mechanised search party to retrace the night's route and bring in those that had as usual fallen by the wayside, which in this case included another frostbitten elderly guard.

The march was reluctantly resumed by 11am, and Spremberg railway yard was reached in the earlier part of the afternoon on the same day. Soon after the column's arrival, a train of filthy old cattle trucks trundled into the station to move the North Compound Kriegies onward towards Bremen.

The following slow rail journey towards Bremen turned out to be another absolute nightmare. The cattle trucks were draughty and cold as they moved through the winter air. They also lacked sufficient space for the men to lie down properly. It was only through sheer bloody exhaustion that men managed to sleep on the wagon floors, in semi-torpid crumpled huddles, whilst trying to keep warm.

There was a continual shortage of water, and no sanitation. Also, a lack of any proper food provision left the men reliant on what little food that had remained in their Red Cross parcels. Unfortunately, most Red Cross parcels had been repacked by the men at outset, and then designated to contain only the lightest to carry and the most highly valued items in the form of chocolate and cigarettes, both of which could later be bartered for food. However, whilst this strategy had served the men so well whilst marching from town to town among the general population of the German countryside, but now finding themselves stuck on the train in isolation from the populace, there simply was no-one to barter with.

Chapter 25

Train Terminus Tarmstedt

It was not until forty-eight hours after leaving Spremberg that the long and torturous train journey finally terminated in the late afternoon of 4 February at Tarmstedt, some fifteen miles north-east of Bremen, in North West Germany. By then many of the Kriegies were very ill. Many were suffering from the weakening effects of their exposure to the elements in the draughty cattle trucks, combined with a general lack of sustenance from proper food. Many others had picked up infections caused by the generally filthy and unsanitary conditions aboard the train.

As the train shuddered to a halt for the final time, it was not until the German guards were heard shouting out the order to disembark that there was a collective sigh of relief. However, that slightest of feeble celebrations was to prove somewhat premature. For having disembarked, it was then announced that the already disheartened, dishevelled, and diseased men would have to march for the last couple of miles to their new quarters.

The bulk of the Kriegies, who had marched away from Stalag Luft III some eight days previously in moderately good health, had been so debilitated by the effects of the fierce arctic weather suffered during the great march to Spremberg, and the shocking travelling conditions that they subsequently endured during the two-day rail journey to Tarmstedt, that what was supposed to be a march for the final two miles of their journey to their new quarters soon turned into a slow painful struggle. It became more of a shuffle than a march for many of their number, who were largely by then such seriously ill men that they were barely able to hold each other upright.

Then unbelievably, having managed to hobble the final two miles to the gates of Tarmstedt PoW camp to which they had been allocated, even more agony ensued for the Kriegies. First, the assembled company were promptly refused admission by the over officious camp Commandant, until such time as each man and his meagre belongings had been personally searched. Then secondly, it started to pour with freezing cold rain!

Additionally, no sooner had the huge, assembled company of men halted, than some started simply collapsing from the combined effects of frostbite and exposure, together with the effects of a virulent gastrointestinal illness that had taken hold during the grim overcrowded conditions experienced on their recent train journey, which had altogether soon debilitated the Kriegies and many of the guards alike. The terrible conditions quickly forced abandonment of any sense of modesty. The Kriegies were soon desperately trying to avoid getting in each other's way, for whilst some were spraying copious spumes of vomit onto the road, others were having to drop their trousers in utmost haste to violently eject streams of steaming diarrhoea on to the cold wet road. Some men were even suffering the double indignity of simultaneously spraying the road surface from both ends of their anatomy at once. The assembled company of men were generating so much liquid excrement and vomit on to the already stinking and streaming wet road that before long the German guards absolutely refused to continue any further searches under such disgusting conditions.

Eventually, the pointlessly farcical process of trying to search each of the disgustingly dishevelled and stinking individuals in such poor exposed conditions was abandoned.

Unfortunately, further immediate horrors soon followed, for when the Kriegies finally gained access to their new abode, they discovered that the previous occupants of the camp had thoroughly smashed the place up before their departure. Graffiti upon the walls indicated that British Naval officers were responsible for the damage, probably with the honourable intention of denying the Germans any further beneficial use of the facility as they vacated it. Little did the Navy men then know of the distress that they would cause to the filthy dishevelled ranks of RAF Kriegies that were to soon follow behind them.

Most of the camp's electrical system was out of order, and a large number of the cooking facilities were broken. There was a dire lack of furnishing overall, including a shortage of beds that had been compensated for by merely piling up straw and wood shavings, upon which many of the Kriegies immediately collapsed as they entered each barrack block, before then falling into fitful slumbers.

The 5 February was the Kriegies' first full day in their new surroundings at Tarmstedt. Although they did not really expect to be there for very long, most men had seemingly awoken determined to ensure their own survival as far as possible, by sorting out the broken shambles that was Tarmstedt. Accordingly, senior officers designated groups of willing Kriegies to various tasks that required immediate attention.

A sick parade was organised to enable representation to be made to the Germans demanding immediate hospital treatment for the most severely ill Kriegies, and immediate medication for the treatment of the less severely ill.

With the intention of improving the quality and quantity of food supplies, a small party of officers were also detailed to make contact with the local Black Market, via any of the individual German guards that might be susceptible to co-operating in exchange for bribes in the form of the usual currency of Red Cross cigarettes and chocolate.

A clandestine Kriegie work party was assigned to the construction of a soundproofed underground radio room to enable continuous BBC news bulletins to be beamed in for circulation around the camp. By bribing certain of the guards, contact was made with a neighbouring compound containing British Merchant Navy officers in order to secure additional radio sets to compensate for those that had been lost on the march from Luft III.

Due to the lack of fuel for cooking or heating, representations were made to the Germans to allow guarded working parties of Kriegies out into the nearby countryside for the purpose of foraging for firewood.

With the foregoing projects all well in hand or completed, life at Tarmstedt eventually began to settle down into a steady routine. For many Kriegies, and for Flap in particular, being a bit of an amateur naturalist, enlistment onto the foregoing guarded foraging parties into the German countryside soon became the most favoured form of Kriegie relaxation. The previous camp at Luft III had been deprived of any view of the outside world, having been deliberately isolated in the all surrounding and boringly bleak angular scenery of a fir forest. By contrast at Tarmstedt, the more relaxing view of open countryside was apparent. The ground was carpeted with grassland and dotted with irregular shaped deciduous trees that actually moved back and forth when the wind blew.

Foraging enabled unhindered conversations with the seemingly very relaxed German guards, who at this uncertain time were very quick to state their disapproval of how the war was being unnecessarily prolonged by pointless continued German resistance against the Allies, that by then were advancing relentlessly into Germany from all directions, leaving only a shrinking area towards the north of Germany available to move the Kriegies around in.

Whilst foraging in fine weather conditions, heavy gunfire could be clearly heard emanating from the British Army that had been gradually advancing towards Tarmstedt from the south-west since before the Kriegies had arrived there. There was of course much consolation that it was British forces then approaching, as opposed to the threat from advancing Russian forces as they had left Sagan.

As the skies cleared a little more, the sun produced enough warmth around midday for the RAF Kriegies to partake in a bit of combined sunbathing and plane spotting from sheltered positions.

When compared to the low numbers of heavy bomber aircraft that had been available before Flap was knocked out of the game, there were now unbelievably huge numbers of both British and American bomber aircraft passing relentlessly overhead; some in formation, but many in loose gaggles, and sometimes what could only be described as swarms, but now all flying in broad daylight with impunity as they endeavoured to bomb Germany into a final submission.

From BBC radio reports received during the latter part of February, the Kriegies learnt that the massive allied air activity that they had observed overhead was an all-out effort to soften up the Germans ahead of the Russian advance that appeared to have been slowed down. Massive raids fell on Chemnitz, Leipzig, and Berlin. The Kriegies would soon learn more of one massive raid that fell on the city of Dresden, where recriminations over the size of the all-consuming firestorm that was created there soon brought into question the very policy of relentlessly bombing further German cities at that late stage of the war. But the Germans would not throw the towel in!

The BBC kept the Kriegies well informed throughout, as the advance of the British Army from the south-west continued relentlessly on through March to reach nearby Bremen before the end of that month. At this point in time, the Kriegies dared to believe that their release from captivity was imminent. Even the German camp staff were preparing to desert their positions and flee ahead of the British advance. However, the excitement was short lived for, as inexplicable as it may have seemed to the Kriegies at that time, the British advance seemed to halt, just short of nearby Bremen!

During the first week of April, Kriegie life at Tarmstedt Camp then became unbearably fraught with rumour and counter rumour, some Kriegies believing that the Germans were only hanging on to the Kriegies in preparation for using them as pawns in any peace negotiations that might take place with the advancing allies. Life for the camp Commandant and his staff had also become just as fraught, with rumours, orders and counter orders arising from the less and less dependable German chain of command.

The latest rumours suggested that the German High Command had proposed marching the Kriegies and their guards on to the moorland wilderness of nearby Luneburg Heath, to the east of Tarmstedt. There it was proposed to turn the Kriegies loose to camp out, whilst fending for themselves and awaiting the eventual arrival of the British Army. However, it appeared that this untrue rumour had simply arisen from the misunderstanding of an overheard German conversation.

It was not until 6 April that heavy gunfire announced the revival of the British advance but, due to receipt of so many contradictory reports from various sources, it became impossible to judge the true speed or exact direction of the British advance during the following two days. Then, unexpectedly on 8 April, the Germans advised the Kriegies that whilst one German officer and forty guards were to remain at Tarmstedt to guard the Kriegies, the bulk of the German staff would be leaving imminently ahead of the expected arrival of the British advance. However, that order was then countermanded the following morning, before the Kriegies were later made aware of a new German High Command order to evacuate the whole camp by 6pm of that same day.

In the meantime, as the sound of the British Army's guns were still growing louder and louder, there seemed to be a good chance that the camp would be imminently overrun by the British Army. An urgently held meeting of the most senior Kriegie officers therefore decided to issue an order encouraging the Kriegies to cause as much resistance and obstruction as possible towards delaying any departure from the camp.

However, the Kriegies' delaying tactics only managed to delay their departure from Tarmstedt until the following morning of 10 April. Then, a German command ordered the camp guards to enter the Kriegie barracks and forcibly drive the occupants and their belongings out on to the road at gun point.

Chapter 26

To the End of the Road

As the next stage of the Long March commenced, it was soon apparent that there were insufficient Germans available to guard the marching column of Kriegies as they set off once more for an unknown destination. Kriegie enquiries, when directed to the most cooperative of the guards, revealed that the most able bodied of guards had been called away to arms, probably in order to bolster actively retreating German forces in defence of the Fatherland.

As the Kriegie columns marched along, the spring weather gradually began to turn fair and sunny. It therefore became easy for the Kriegies to encourage and distract their mainly elderly guards into dawdling along in the warm sunshine and frustrate any German commands to hurry the Kriegie marchers away from any chance of being overtaken by the advancing British forces. The slower pace suited the remaining mostly elderly German guards anyway, as they made it quite clear that they would prefer to be overrun by the British, rather than by the rapidly advancing Russians that they were once more then walking towards.

By mid-afternoon, the German Commandant had grown tired of trying to force the pace of the column. For what had set out with the intention of being a march had gradually turned into a gentle stroll through the sunny countryside. Therefore, a German order was issued to halt the column, and the strollers were directed off the road into nearby fields for the night.

Immediate protests from the Kriegies about the lack of proper accommodation being provided for the night were met by a German response that simply blamed the Kriegies for not marching fast enough to reach their scheduled overnight stop. However, whilst those discussions were taking place, the bulk of the Kriegies had decided to make the most of their rural circumstances anyway.

Kriegie foragers, all well armed with Red Cross goodies to trade, were sent out to successfully barter for food, fuel and straw bedding from the nearby villages and farms. By the time darkness fell over the extensive area of fields occupied by the masses of Kriegies, there were hundreds of campfires blazing away, and a tantalising smell of cooking and wood smoke was then billowing over the spring countryside.

The following day, 11 April, dawned fine and dry. The march was resumed around nine a.m. No particular destination was specified. The weather continued fine with the temperature steadily rising as the day went on. Horses and carts were commandeered from somewhere nearby, to assist with the carrying of luggage, red cross parcels and rations. In the meantime, the relationship between the guards and the Kriegies continued to mellow, and there was a rising atmosphere of mutual support and personal preservation. By early afternoon, this casual atmosphere had apparently reduced the column's pace to even less than a stroll, and more akin to an amble. Then, with no clear order apparently being given, the march seemed to just peter out as those at the head of the column simply turned off the road and ambled off into the nearby fields. On this respite, even the German guards keenly joined in with the Kriegies on their foraging expeditions for fresh water, firewood and fresh produce from the local farms and villages, all in anticipation of being able to sample the sort of food that the guards had smelt the Kriegies cooking the previous evening. Copious amounts of fresh eggs and potatoes were secured to supplement tinned Red Cross rations. Even a limited amount of beer was made available from a nearby village in exchange for luxurious Red Cross barter!

That night the Kriegies and the German guards dined as one to share the culinary delicacies created from the jointly acquired offerings that had been carried from nearby German villages. During conversations over their meals, the German guards were of the opinion that the marching column had been directed to head in a direction that would enable them to cross the river Elbe at a point just north of Hamburg, being that part of the country that German High Command had possibly assumed would be the last to be overrun by the allied armies that were then approaching from all directions; except the north, where only Denmark and the Baltic sea lay anyway.

The improving relationships that the Kriegies and their guards had by then established with one another continued into the days ahead. In the mutual expectation that the British advance might yet overtake the marchers, both prisoners and guards were united in a mutual conspiracy to do their utmost to delay the progress of the column.

Friday, 13 April, was a cloudless day under a brilliant blue sky. Having camped where running streams of clear water were available, an agreement for a day of rest was negotiated to enable Kriegies and guards to catch up with their washing. Whilst later lounging in the spring sunshine, as he waited for his laundry to dry, Flap realised that his skin was actually tanning quite fast, as the strong spring sunlight shone down through the crystal-clear country air.

During this sunny sojourn, Dimwitz, of his own initiative, carried out an escorted impromptu social tour around the various groups of relaxing ex-Luft III Kriegies. On espying Flap's group and their little encampment, he made a beeline for Flap to crack a little joke. It was with a broad smile on his face, that he then made the following announcement:

> "The official German quest to interpret the meaning of sparrow fart, together with some other unsolved mysteries, has been abandoned in favour of the more pressing matters currently causing concern to the German Intelligence Services."

Having raised a laugh amongst the group, Dimwitz then continued to speak further:

> "However, I wish you to know that I personally always understood the meaning of sparrow fart, ever since the First War between our two countries when I heard British Tommies using the same expression for the first light of day. It has therefore amused me greatly that, whether by accident or design, my current information is that our Gestapo led Intelligence Services still have the matter filed as outstanding."

After Dimwitz, officially Lagerfeldwebel (Compound Officer) Sergeant Major Glemnitz, had moved on to another group of Kriegie campers, some discussion continued amongst the Kriegies. Those involved decided that Dimwitz, who had previously declared himself as a German patriot who had served as a pilot during the First World War, was most definitely not a Nazi. Although his main duties had been to prevent escapes from

Stalag Luft III, he had proved himself to be a genuine humanist who had managed to carry out his duties fairly, and with a good sense of respect and good humour at all times.

The following day, the march finished early in an area where the nature of the countryside began to change from level to hilly, enabling occasional distant views of the Hamburg area. That day, when foraging for bartered supplies in the nearby villages, the Kriegies and their guards unfortunately found themselves drawn into conflict with retreating German troops. The German troops were in the villages just simply scavenging for food in order to survive. However, they had soon discovered that supplies were being withheld from them by the local citizens, for the simple reason that the German troops did not have any of the sought-after Red Cross goodies to offer the villagers in exchange for food supplies.

Orders received for 15 April stated that the march must reach the banks of the river Elbe on that same day. To speed up the pace of the marchers and ensure compliance with his orders, the German Commandant had managed to secure the services of several more horse drawn carts and fresh horses to carry the Kriegies' luggage. His theory was that the lightened Kriegies would thus be able to march much faster and, as a further incentive to hurry, might lose touch with their respective belongings if they did not keep pace with the relevant horse drawn carts.

The German Commandant's incentives had the desired effect, and the banks of the river Elbe were reached early enough that day to enable many Kriegies to bathe from the beaches of the Elbe estuary, before setting out to forage and trade with the locals as usual.

The following day, 16 April, the entire Kriegie column, horses, carts, and all their belongings, were all ferried across the river Elbe without incident, before marching a further distance into the verdant farmlands beyond, there to select a suitable site to pitch camp for the night.

On 17 April, exactly three years after Flap's arrival in Germany, the column moved further into the farming belt beyond the Elbe. However, it then turned out that many of the locals were ardent brown shirted Nazis who, it seemed, had not at that time quite appreciated how nearly their war was lost. It was therefore impossible for the Kriegies to forage and trade as usual and, for those that had attempted to make contact with the locals, several were arrested and threatened by swastika emblazoned

Nazi officials, who referred to the Kriegies as Luft gangsters and terror fliers before eventually marching them back to the camping grounds.

It was subsequently realised that the general hardening of attitude towards the RAF Kriegies, particularly from local German officials, was solely due to the recent massive allied bombing campaigns that were falling on the east German cities directly ahead of the Russians' advance from the east, all of which had resulted from the huge armadas of British and American bombers that the Kriegies had witnessed passing overhead in broad daylight during the previous few weeks. During mid-February, the German city of Dresden had received such massive attention from the bombers that a huge fire storm was created that had turned that city into a desolate wasteland with a massive loss of German lives.

In preceding weeks, the Kriegies had also marvelled at witnessing a few German jet aircraft of some sort overhead, probably being desperately operated against the Allied bomber fleets that they were continuously observing overhead.

Flap and his party could only gaze in awe at the mixed sights that were passing overhead; and, of course, wonder if they themselves might eventually have the opportunity to fly a jet-propelled aircraft.

From 18 to 25 April the Kriegies were accommodated in scattered groups throughout various villages in the same area. During that period there was pressure from German High Command ordering that the whole column should be marched further north-east to the town of Lubeck. However, a German speaking Red Cross doctor immediately blocked any order to enter Lubeck, on the basis of a rumoured outbreak of typhus that had broken out due to the overcrowded refugee conditions already prevailing in that town. During the same week, the German Air Force guards who had been with the ex-Stalag Luft III Kriegies throughout their whole period of capture were rounded up and marched off to form a fighting unit in support of the German Army front.

For their part, the Kriegies were content to stay exactly where they were. They had access to ample food supplies from local sources, and from sparrow fart to bedtime they were able to soak up the spring sunshine, whilst just lounging around, bathing, or even fishing in the local waterways for welcome alternative food sources.

During the following week, a nearby local German landowner with considerable country estates under his ownership had conceived a brilliant idea for protecting his estates from the possibility of becoming a destructive battlefield. He quite simply visited the local Red Cross officials and issued an invitation to move approximately sixteen hundred RAF Kriegie officers on to his land, where giant upward facing letters reading "RAF PoW" were soon made up from all sorts of light-coloured materials laid out flat on the ground in order to be visible to any passing reconnaissance flights from either side of the nearby front lines.

The Red Cross then ensured delivery of hundreds of Red Cross parcels to the new sites. However, having moved on to the estates on 27 April, the Kriegies barely had time to organise themselves and establish a routine when, on 2 May, some British tanks and light armour unexpectedly arrived on the scene.

Albeit that the manpower of the British armoured force was only minute, the presence of the Brits, with little or no persuasion, was sufficient for all the guards and neighbourhood German personnel to take the opportunity of surrendering their arms to the Senior British Officer present. News of the opportunity to surrender then spread so fast through the German forces beyond the estates that the ex-Kriegies themselves had to set up guarded safe storage for the multitudinous collections of weapons that were then being handed in by, and taken from, the growing numbers of surrendering German forces personnel.

On the morning of the following day, the main British advance, consisting of armour with infantry following close behind, swept past the Kriegie occupied estates. Later, a party of officers from the advancing British force attended the estate camps to request all PoWs to remain where they were for a few days, until such time as officers from a separate unit responsible for the repatriation of British PoWs could make some logistical arrangements for the urgent evacuation of all the ex-Kriegies back towards the UK.

In the meantime, and with time to kill whilst awaiting their repatriation, many Kriegies were jubilantly indulging in all sorts of mischief. Deals were struck with local residents to enable the borrowing of cars in exchange for tanks full of fuel that would later be scrounged from British Army vehicles, before the cars were eventually returned to their owners. The availability of such transport enabled the bartering for essential supplies to take place over a much wider area of countryside. During one such expedition, Flap was able to drive an early and rather basic version of a Volkswagen Beetle. The novelty of that car's all-round independent suspension, flat four cylinder air cooled engine, and generally solid construction, together made such an impression on Flap that he vowed that, if ever given the chance, he would buy a VW Beetle for himself. He really had been impressed!

Chapter 27

Kriegie Exodus

Within the following two or three days, the first column of Army lorries arrived at the Kriegie occupied estates to transport the RAF towards home, via various transit camps on the road journey to safe airfields in the north-west of Germany, Belgium, France, or Holland. From there it was planned that they would all be flown home by fleets of such various types of RAF aircraft as might be available at any one time.

The total road journey time to the airfields was scheduled to take four or five days, and the luckiest of the PoWs overall were the RAF ex-Kriegies who were then flown home by Lancasters similar to those that had brought many of them to Germany in the first place. In order to carry the maximum possible number of passengers, the Lancaster crews were reduced from the customary seven to five only. Each Lancaster was then able to carry an additional twenty-five passengers, all carefully placed and spaced out as loaded, to preserve the overall trim of the aircraft when flying. The operation to bring the Prisoners of War home as quickly as possible from all theatres of the war was promptly named "Operation Exodus". Before it was over, Operation Exodus would involve approximately two thousand nine hundred return flights, to repatriate upwards of seventy-two thousand five hundred ex-PoWs from across all branches of the British forces.

Flap's service record shows that he must have been amongst the first to depart from the estate camps, for he was back in the UK by 9 May 1945, just four days after the first ex-Kriegie transport had left the estate camps in Germany. During Flap's passage home, Field Marshal Montgomery had, upon Luneburg Heath, Germany, on 7 May, accepted Germany's signed surrender of all the German forces within north-west Germany, Holland and Denmark. Officially, hostilities ceased on 8 May, which was then promptly declared Victory in Europe Day, although the last of the fighting in Europe did not actually cease until the very first day after VE day, just as Flap landed back on English soil, and just over three years since his original departure on Lancaster L7573 OF-K from Woodhall Spa.

There does not appear to be a record of where Flap's flight home had departed from, but he always stated he had been landed back at RAF Little Rissington on 9 May 1945.

So pleased to place his feet on English soil, Flap was in the jovial company of other like-minded ex-PoW officers as he was immediately bussed to the doors of 106 Personnel Reception Centre, at RAF Cosford, Shropshire.

On arrival at Cosford, there was a very warm and sympathetic welcome for all new arrivals, all of whom were promptly checked to ensure that they had been chemically sprayed as a precaution against parasitic infestations before leaving Little Rissington. They were then invited to take a very hot shower or bath, before being subjected to a full medical check to ensure that they did not bring any unwelcome infections or untreated conditions home with them.

Flap noticed with satisfaction that, unlike the first RAF medical that he was subjected to when he had first joined the RAF in 1936, the amiable doctor conducting the current medical had been properly trained. He only used his pencil correctly: the thin end to write with, and the thick end to chew. At no time did he use the thick end of the pencil to lift, prod or poke the body parts of his patients before having a chew. The doctor completed his examination by congratulating Flap on the very healthy glow from his recently acquired suntan.

Following issue of a clean set of battledress uniform and a standard kit bag to place his belongings in, Flap was handed a signed welcome message from the King, together with a postage-paid postcard to be forwarded home to Eldorado Road, to announce his arrival in the country, if required.

There was a short debriefing session, before Flap was provided with a brand-new ID card, ration book, clothing coupons and a pay advance. In common with all repatriated PoWs, he was then handed written confirmation of his period of recuperative leave, and a travel warrant to cover his transport to Cheltenham. All having been prepared for him whilst he attended the debriefing session.

In the meantime, there had been an absolute hive of activity at Eldorado Road, Cheltenham. Some of Flap's RAF associates, who had heard that he was on his way home in a Lancaster, had set out to meet him at Little Rissington where he was expected to arrive. However, having somehow missed Flap at Little Rissington, they had phoned Bernice to tell her the good news before repatriation officialdom had swung into action to delay Flap's appearance at home.

From my own recollections of the time, as a three-and-a-half-year-old at home, and following the phone call, I had immediately noticed that the demeanour of Bernice and my grandmother had changed dramatically. Both of them were humming and singing, and they started to rush around the house excitedly as they tidied the place up.

During their mid-morning Ceylon tea break, they both sat me down to explain that, believe it or not, they had just been informed that Flap, my father, had flown back from Germany. Now apparently, the thing they called "the War" had ended and, as I then understood it, all the Dads were flying home.

I was a bit disappointed that Flap did not fly right to the front door. However, he turned up alright. The very next day, he phoned us from Cheltenham station to announce his arrival and told us that he would walk the short distance to our home. The home that he had never seen. I immediately rushed out into the front garden and draped myself over the front gate to wait. There I had a good view down the road and, before I knew it, there he was, my Dad Flap, striding up the road with a long round bag over his shoulder! He looked exactly the same in life as he did in the photograph by my mother's bed. He was even dressed the same, wearing RAF battledress over a white roll neck pullover. Without stopping, he adjusted the bag on his shoulder, before scooping me up under his other arm, and heading for the front door as Bernice appeared. The bag was immediately dumped on the floor, and his other arm went out around Bernice.

My grandmother soon appeared with a large pot of the good old Ceylon tea, on a tray with biscuits. Both the ladies agreed that Flap, with his magnificently tanned skin, looked as though he had just returned from a blooming good holiday.

There was so much news to catch up on that the conversation flowed freely, with a fair amount of laughter. Especially when I demanded to see

Flap's wings and enquired whether they might be in the long round bag that he had been carrying. Then they just laughed even more. Of course, I was really disappointed when Flap simply pointed to the little winged "RAF" pilot's flying badge displayed on the breast of his RAF battle dress. Then they just laughed even more. But those paltry little wings were most definitely not the type or size of the wings that I had envisaged for so long.

I really did suffer a massive disappointment over the size of Flap's wings. However, he did bring me a long overdue present. You may recall that my first birthday present was created in Stalag Luft III, on 16 January 1943, in the form of a hand drawn and hand coloured caricature of Flap, as shown on an earlier page. This picture had survived intact throughout Flap's travels, carefully concealed beneath his greatcoat. However, you will also recall that the artist, Flight Lieutenant Henri Picard of the Belgian Squadron, RAF, PoW No: 685, unfortunately did not survive. He was executed on 29 March 1944, at the side of a German country road; unexpectedly shot in the back by a member of the German Gestapo soon after his recapture and following his exit from Stalag Luft III during the Great Escape.

After allowing a few days for the excitement to settle down, I recall Flap managing to acquire the use of a car. There then followed a period of what I can only describe as an extended family holiday. During that time I got used to having a father as well as mother, whilst Flap and Bernice had to get used to being with each other all over again. As a family, we travelled here and there to visit some of Flap and Bernice's old friends in various haunts familiar to them around the country. We travelled for what to me seemed like weeks that summer, as Flap used up his permitted entitlement to a period of resettlement leave that had been granted to him.

One of the very first places we visited was Woodhall Spa, my birthplace, to call on neighbours and friends from Tor-o-moor Road and the immediate area. Then, as we moved around from one place to another, I was introduced to relatives and pre-war friends of Flap and Bernice, some of whom had also been detained in Germany. They could all talk for hours about their experiences over the last few years, whilst remembering long lost absent friends and memories from earlier in the war, or before.

Whilst the extensive talking went on, I met and enjoyed playing with countless other children, and still have recollection of a farm that we visited, where there was a whole flock of goats eating the lilac leaves in the garden.

According to Flap's service record, he enjoyed an extended period of recuperative leave from arriving home on 10 May 1945, right through until 26 July 1945. A total of some seventy-seven days leave respectively, before he was then enrolled on an RAF Personnel Refresher (general update) Course for two months.

There then followed a month's flight refresher course at No. 7 Flying Instruction School, at RAF Cottesmore from the end of September 1945, which boosted Flap's expectation that he would soon be able to return to flying duties.

In the meantime, the war with Japan had ended, leading to expectations that my maternal grandfather, Bernice's father, Lieutenant Commander Kenneth Gain would soon be able to return home from his naval duties in the far east.

Chapter 28

Making a Family Home

By October 1945, Flap had been granted a promotion to the rank of Wing Commander. Initially, he regarded the promotion as a fair reward for his past services to the Crown. However, he was soon disappointed at the lack of any offer to resume flying duties. Consequently, he was gradually beginning to regard his promotion as some sort of compensation for the increasingly dull duties that he was then being asked to perform. On the other hand, might the Air Ministry have been deliberately attempting to rest weary war veterans, following their often traumatic and harrowing experiences during the war? Either way, Flap was not overly impressed to be kept away from the flying duties that he had joined the RAF to experience.

There were other disappointing matters that were also disturbing Flap's mood. He was extremely puzzled by the very obvious lack of any demonstrable post war gratitude being shown by Winston Churchill and his Government for the wartime sacrifices made by RAF Bomber Command aircrews, especially when compared with the very obvious appreciation then being shown for many other branches of the armed services.

However, for Flap life in the Royal Air Force had to go on, for that was the only life he knew. Consequently, on 22 October 1945, at his newly appointed rank of Wing Commander, Flap was posted to an administrative position controlling the activities of three RAF Recruitment Centres situated in and around RAF Wilmslow, Cheshire. Then, on expiry of that appointment, he was posted to nearby RAF Handforth, where right through to April 1950, his dual role would involve the administration of an RAF Maintenance Unit, whilst also acting as Officer Commanding a staff numbering one thousand plus RAF Senior NCOs and Aircraftsmen.

Initially, whilst Flap was organising himself at RAF Wilmslow, Bernice, my grandmother, and I had remained at Cheltenham, with Flap returning at weekends only. At Cheltenham it soon became apparent that Bernice was expecting another baby.

Luckily, during the latter part of 1945, the Americans, who had been occupying my maternal grandparents' home at Turpins, Sonning, had packed up and vacated that accommodation. Accordingly, by January's end of 1946, we had all been able to leave Cheltenham and move to the Sonning house. At weekends, Flap would come home, where he and Bernice could again enjoy the Thames, whilst introducing me to the sights and sounds of Sonning and the river.

The house named Turpins, at Sonning, actually comprising of four cottages knocked into one, was reputedly the home of the highwayman Dick Turpin's aunt. It was said that after robbing travellers on the nearby Bath Road at pistol point, the legendary Dick Turpin would ride his horse furiously back to the stables at Turpins and leave it there. He would then run down the lane beside the house, through the churchyard, to immediately cross the river Thames and the county border into Oxfordshire, thus leaving the pursuing hue and cry behind him in Berkshire.

To keep me busy during the week, I was encouraged to search the property and its garden for Dick Turpin's hidden treasures. That usually involved me digging little holes around the garden that revealed little of any real value. My finds consisted mostly of the broken discards of previous occupiers of the property. However, the area around the back door did provide many items of interest, and I do still have in my possession an East India Company coin, and a brass-coloured gaming token/coin dated 1752, both having been found there.

On 14 May 1946, a baby brother, Graham, arrived for me, born at Reading. Bernice and my grandmother tried on their old nonsense again, by telling me that my brother had flown in. I quickly pointed out that he most definitely did not have any wings at all, not even tiny little ones on his chest like Flap. However, they just carried on with their nonsense, by insisting that my brother did not need his own wings as he had apparently been delivered by a big bird that did have the necessary wings!

Whilst waiting for my brother to arrive, Flap had located available family accommodation within a large house share at 109, Manchester Road, Wilmslow, just south of where the railway passes below that road. Within a few weeks we had moved in as a family unit, not far from Flap's RAF responsibilities, then also remaining near Wilmslow.

When Flap had first joined the RAF in 1936, he had initially signed on for a four-year short service commission only. During the war in 1940, his commission had then been extended to ten years, with the guaranteed availability of a lump sum gratuity payment in lieu of pension rights on conclusion of that ten years of service. Accordingly, it was later in 1946 that the ten-year short service commission expired. However, by some crafty manoeuvring by higher up collaborators elsewhere, possibly the Air Ministry, Flap discovered that it would be possible to accept payment of the gratuity at the end of his initial ten years' service, before then immediately re-applying for a further ten-year RAF commission. Furthermore, although acceptance of the new commission would automatically mean that the already paid gratuity would then have to be re-paid towards Flap's future pension rights, instead of repaying that gratuity as lump sum, Flap could elect to make such repayment by small regular instalments from his future pay; thus effectively generating an interest free loan over five years.

Flap therefore decided that he would accept the lump sum gratuity under the above instalment terms, and with the help of a small mortgage, placed the total sum produced towards the purchase of a family home in the Wilmslow area.

On receipt of gratuity funds, the house hunt began immediately. Initially, there was little progress, and the new year of 1947 produced further delays by turning into one of the coldest English winters that had been experienced for several years. The severe conditions reminded Flap of the first part of the January 1945 march from Luft III. Even I, as a five-year-old then, can still remember sheets of ice on the inside of the leaded sitting room windows of our Wilmslow house share in 1947. There was not any central heating then, and the ice was there on the windows every morning until well after the living room fire was lit.

Eventually, a suitably priced four-bedroom house was located at The Moorings, Thoresway Road, Wilmslow, the fourth bedroom being required because Bernice was, by then, expecting yet another new arrival.

A £400 mortgage, plus the gratuity payment, produced sufficient funds to secure "The Moorings". A small cash balance, left over on completion of the purchase, was used to purchase beds and the most necessary of furniture, plus a second-hand Riley Kestrel motor car. As far as Bernice and her memories of a Thames boating childhood were concerned, the

Wilmslow property had for some unknown reason already been most suitably named by a previous owner.

The move into The Moorings came fairly soon after Flap was posted to nearby 61 Maintenance Unit, at RAF Handforth just north of Wilmslow. RAF Handforth was an RAF equipment store, surplus store and recycling unit, handling anything from smashed up aircraft to furniture, building materials, general equipment and supplies; all of which encouraged Flap to revert to Luft III do it yourself improvisation mode in and around his new home. All manner of objects and raw materials travelled home to The Moorings in, or strapped on to, the recently acquired Riley Kestrel.

The Riley Kestrel also enabled Flap to take his soon to be extended family down to the Sussex coast to visit his mother and father at Mayfield, Wells Farm, West Wittering, that summer. In retirement, Flap's sea captain father had turned into a superb gardener, and all manner of fresh garden fruit and vegetable produce was available from Mayfield's huge garden during that holiday, all to supplement the expense of catering for a suddenly expanded family at Mayfield.

During that summer, and to Flap's satisfaction, news reports made mention of the trial of eighteen members of the German Gestapo, of various ranks, who having been arrested for implication in the murders of fifty of the recaptured Stalag Luft III Great Escapers, were all set to face trial at the British Military War Crimes Court, Hamburg.

On return from West Wittering, Flap's new neighbours at The Moorings looked on in amazement as the frameworks for a three-piece suite were one at a time manufactured in the garage of The Moorings. The frames were made out of already once used surplus timber, together with plywood obtained from tea chests and discarded RAF packing cases. Once completed, the frames were then covered in a kapok type wadding to form cushioning. Finally, the suite was upholstered, using thick government surplus curtain material. Curtains were then made up from that same material, to match.

Next out of the garage there came a very light, geometrically shaped coffee table, the upright side panels of which Flap swore were made out of pieces of a special plywood and balsa wood laminated sandwich that had been salvaged from the remains of a wrecked de Havilland Mosquito aircraft.

Then from the garage, there followed a double fronted toy cupboard, with drawers above. That unfortunately had an asbestos sheet back in it! But then, in 1947, nobody knew of the dangers of asbestos.

Finally, two compact wardrobes appeared for the junior bedrooms.

As the year of 1947 approached its end, 61 Maintenance Unit of the RAF provided all sorts of surplus materials to enable Flap to produce some definitely rather interesting family Christmas presents.

By the time that the New Year of 1948 arrived, Bernice, my expectant again mother was looking huge. A week later I was bundled off with my unopened birthday presents to stay with my paternal grandparents, Flap's Mum and Dad, at West Wittering, Sussex, again. Then, on my own birthday of 16 January 1948, the phone rang at West Wittering with a call from Flap, just to tell me that I had received another unexpected birthday present. It was the birth of a second brother for me; bang on my very own birthday!

Further on into to the New Year, it appeared that everything at The Moorings was satisfactory, apart from the fact that Bernice was then finding it hard going with three boys to look after – not only whilst Flap was at work, but also whilst he still appeared to be obsessively consumed with Luft III style do it yourself projects. Even the Riley Kestrel had received some special treatment, when it became the first vehicle in the neighbourhood to have an interior warm air heater fitted to it. The basic car heater was made out of powdered milk tins, with further bottomless milk tins soldered together to form the ducting that brought hot air in from the engine compartment, all fabricated as per Stalag Luft III tunnel ventilation ducting. Red Cross Klim tins were not available, but those from my new brother's powdered baby milk supplies were ideal!

There was soon further satisfactory news of interest to Flap that was receiving prominence in the BBC radio news bulletins and national newspapers: the final outcome of the trial of the German Gestapo operatives that had been responsible for the murder of fifty PoWs following the Great Escape was being announced. Those news reports confirmed that, of the eighteen defendants tried, fourteen were to be hanged for their crimes. Further offenders received long-term jail sentences of various lengths, depending on the degree of their involvement. In some cases, those sentences included life imprisonment.

It had also been revealed during the trial of one Gottlob Berger, the general in overall charge of German PoW camps in 1944, that Hitler had indeed intended to use threats against the PoWs in his hands to bargain with the allies for a peace treaty on more favourable terms to the Germans than otherwise. Hitler's plan was to order the transportation of massed PoWs to his fortified Alpine retreat, where they would have been destined to be held as hostages. However, at the trial, it was revealed that Hitler's plans had been thwarted by the more humane members of his very own staff who, during a pre-arranged distraction, managed to substitute the relevant order papers for something else that Hitler had then signed. They had therefore deliberately tricked Hitler into thinking that he had signed the necessary orders to commence the transportation of hostage PoWs.

With the coming of the spring weather at Wilmslow, which slowly led into a moderately pleasant summer, the home atmosphere appeared to be calm. Kids outside in the garden during daylight hours; Flap too, sorting out the garden when at home.

Then disaster! Without any prior warning, the gas cooker fell right through the kitchen floor!

That was enough for Bernice. She was distraught when she rang Flap at work to tell him. He, of course, was not too pleased either!

It would appear that the surveyor who had previously checked the house over for mortgage purposes had omitted to pay enough attention to various features of the house. One of which being the fact that a previous owner had built a massive coal bunker across the rear of the house, thus covering the vents to the under-floor cavity beneath the kitchen. This had resulted in a lack of ventilation, which in turn had encouraged dry rot to take hold and weaken the wooden floor and its timber supports; all damage unseen beneath the linoleum floor covering, until part of the floor collapsed!

The kitchen floor was immediately condemned as dangerous, and this necessitated Bernice and her three sons moving out whilst repairs were carried out.

In the meantime, since Bernice's father, my maternal grandfather, had returned from his naval duties in Ceylon, and following ample warnings in correspondence from those that had been left in charge of his business interests during his absence, it had been confirmed that the family's multiple outlet butchers business in London had deteriorated severely during the war. The deterioration had been to such an extent that it was no longer a viable proposition to pursue. He had therefore disposed of all property assets, including the family home Turpins, and then used the resultant funds, together with such compensation that had been received for the loss of the motor yacht *Matoya*, that had never been returned to him after its war service, to set up a holiday business on the north coast of Kent, at Allhallows on Sea. It was therefore at Allhallows on Sea that our family sought shelter for the duration of repairs to the collapsed flooring at The Moorings. Meanwhile, Flap remained at his Wilmslow RAF duties, and able to supervise repairs to The Moorings, nearby.

Flap's home insurers were not liable for repairs to The Moorings, on the basis that the damage was not caused by an insured peril; and of course, Flap was not allowed to use government surplus materials to repair the damage. He therefore had to raise a further loan that he could ill afford to service, and it was nearly Christmas once again, before we were all able to move back home to The Moorings.

By 1949, an easy-going family routine had been established, and that summer turned out to be one of the hottest summers for years. We did not have a fridge, and I recall having to dig out hollows beneath large, shaded paving slabs, under which we had to keep our butter and milk cool. The hosepipe was permanently out in the garden to keep the kids cool, and a fortnight of summer holiday was spent at Allhallows on Sea, again.

Chapter 29

Into the Air Again

Flap and Bernice did not really have a chance together to enjoy their own house at Wilmslow for very long. It was always inevitable that Flap might receive notification of an onward posting to a position in another area. And so it was, in April 1950, that Flap was advised that he would soon be posted to the RAF's Central Navigation and Control School (CNCS) at RAF Shawbury, where it was decided that his navigational instruction experiences, as gained with the RAF's wartime operational training units, would be useful to the school in their role of navigational trainers and researchers.

However, before posting to Shawbury, Flap was required to embark on a two-month twin engine flying refresher course, much to Bernice's disapproval. Bernice had developed a dread fear of Flap flying long distances again and had hoped that his flying days might have been over. The course itself was required to enable Flap to familiarise himself with the twin engine Vickers Wellington bombers that had been retained from war service for use by CNCS, particularly on account of that aircraft's long-range capabilities.

It was therefore early June of 1950 before Flap was able to take up his new position as Commanding Officer of No. 1 Squadron at CNCS at Shawbury, and at the reduced rank of Squadron Leader. In the meantime, "The Moorings" was put on the market, and arrangements were made for Flap and the Riley Kestrel to commute back and forth between the Wilmslow family home and Shawbury, weekly.

During the second half of 1950, the family had settled down to the new routine. Flap avoided any mention of his RAF activities, and all was peaceful. That was until the morning of 6 December 1950, when our morning newspaper was delivered through the front door. As Bernice picked up the newspaper and caught sight of the bold front-page headline, she let out a horrible wailing noise that we kids had not heard before. The colour had completely drained from her cheeks, for the headline read

"RAF Wellington Crashes into Spanish Mountain, Seven Crew Lost", whilst also making mention of the aircraft's home base of Shawbury. At that time, it was instantly obvious that Bernice was receiving very different vibes than those she had felt on 18 April 1942. For back then, when David Penman had knocked on her door to tell her that he was convinced Flap had been consumed by fire at Augsburg, Germany, Bernice had quickly contradicted him, with the absolute assertion that she would have known if Flap was dead.

In December 1950, Bernice must have experienced very different feelings, for at that time she was thrown into a state of total panic. However, the panic was thankfully quelled within the hour, and Bernice's composure was completely restored by lunchtime. For whilst she had been trying to contact CNCS, RAF Shawbury, Flap had been trying to contact her, to forewarn her to ignore the newspaper reports that he had himself already seen and heard of. However, he had found the home phone was continuously engaged, probably by Bernice trying to ring him at Shawbury, of course!

It soon transpired that the crashed Wellington was indeed CNCS RAF Shawbury based and had been on a navigational training flight to Khartoum, via Gibraltar and Cyprus. On the scheduled return trip, when off course, flying too low, and lost in the bad visibility of a raging thunderstorm, the Wellington had flown straight into Montgo Mountain, near Javea, Spain.

"The Moorings" eventually sold. Then the family, with the exception of me, moved to a very fine, on station, four-bedroom officers' married quarter at Shawbury. However, for me, it was decided that I would be sent to live with my grandmother and grandfather, Flap's parents, during school term times, thus ensuring continuity of education at one school for all of the time. From then onwards, I only went home for school holidays.

On one such school holiday, Flap announced that at least one Lancaster bomber was imminently expected to be present on the Shawbury base, and that he would like to show me over that example of the plane he had flown to Augsburg. A Lancaster did duly arrive, and I was taken to visit it on a fine sunny day, when the parked Lancaster sat glinting in the sunlight. I was suitably impressed by the sheer size of the Lancaster, when compared to the size of the other aircraft based at Shawbury. My other memory is of the onboard Lancaster smell that I had immediately associated with early Bakelite type plastics, electric wiring insulations, oil and grease.

The following day the Lancaster was airborne, and for some reason performing circuits and bumps around the airfield. For a while, as I stood with a gaggle of other RAF kids outside the perimeter fence at the end of the runway, we were amazed at the sheer racket made by the Lancaster's four Rolls-Royce Merlin engines, as the aircraft, then under full throttle, climbed away over our heads from take-off. I already knew quite a lot about the Augsburg raid from the various documents and news cutting in my possession, and the overhead racket caused me to wonder what the combined racket of six fully laden Lancasters must have sounded like to the citizens of Augsburg, as they had roared low over that town on 17 April 1942.

By July 1952, Flap had been posted again. This time appointed Chief Ground Instructor at No.1 Flying Training School, then based at RAF Moreton in Marsh, Gloucester. Initially, there were no married quarters available on station at Moreton in Marsh. Therefore, the temporary family home became a country cottage that had been secured as an RAF rental hiring in the village of Ilmington, situated some miles due north of Moreton in Marsh, and midway between there and Stratford upon Avon.

Ilmington, supporting very few residents, was inconveniently distant from any shopping centre. However, a married quarter did become available at Moreton in Marsh itself, soon afterwards.

It was at Moreton in Marsh that I learned to distinguish and remember which was port (left) and starboard (right). For the Riley Kestrel family car had long since been replaced by an old sit-up and beg, square bodied, Standard Saloon that, in the absence of any necessity for MOT certificates at that time, was allowed to be on the road with soggy suspension and weak shock absorbers, amongst other faults! The defects meant that the car was prone to leaning over on bends and corners, away from the direction of such bend or turning. The defects did not seem to matter when driving solo, or front loaded only; but when fully loaded with family and a boot full of clutter, then the rear wheels would rub on their respective wheel arches as the car leaned over, this way and that with the corners. The resultant effect was a nuisance. It generated a lot of rude noises, as well as producing an unwanted braking effect on the car. Flap's simple solution to this problem was to shout port or starboard (left or right), depending on the expected change of direction required for any imminent change of course ahead. At the critical moment, rear seat passengers were required to then hurl themselves over to the same side of the rear seat as the direction being called out; thus preventing the opposite rear wheel from dropping down on to its respective wheel arch during the turn.

By the new year of 1955, Flap was becoming due for another posting. Following conversations with contemporary RAF officers of his acquaintance, who had managed to secure semi-exotic overseas postings, Flap decided to make a nuisance of himself at the Air Ministry in an endeavour to secure a similar exotic posting to a sunnier clime.

The outcome was that, following successful interviews at the Air Ministry, during which Flap had agreed to accept any type of duties in order to achieve his objective of an overseas posting, even if his new duties had no connection with flying, he managed to secure a posting to Air Head Quarters (AHQ), Nicosia, Cyprus, effective from Easter 1955.

Flap and Bernice were really excited by the prospect of the new position in a warmer and sunnier climate. Furthermore, the job was to come with some fine accommodation included, being a married quarter consisting of a fully furnished semi-detached balconied bungalow on the Nicosia RAF base, with views of the Kyrenia mountains. There was also an added bonus, for they discovered that two of their previously neighbouring RAF Moreton in Marsh families were also moving to Nicosia with them. The only downside was for Flap, as he was not quite so keen to get involved with the administrative duties that he had agreed to be appointed to, within what he referred to as "the RAF works and bricks department". However, that is what it took to achieve the much desired overseas appointment!

When Flap and Bernice moved to Cyprus in 1955, it was decided that my oldest brother would join me living full time with Flap's mother only, his father having died in 1953. We were both promised that we would then be able to spend our summer holidays in sunny Cyprus. However, the first experience of Cyprus for my brother and I was not until the summer school holidays of 1956, when we both flew to Cyprus on board a four engine RAF Handley Page Hermes transport, in company with a plane load of other noisy forces juniors going out to join their families in Cyprus for the summer. There was certainly a lot of very noisy illegal drinking and smoking on that flight. However, the RAF cabin crew, who were probably used to far more boisterous behaviour when transporting slightly older national service personnel, seemed to have made the decision to just let the kids get on with it!

Unfortunately, there was a downside to Cyprus in the nineteen fifties, in the form of the Greek Cypriot terrorist organisation EOKA. That organisation was using terrorism to promote their cause for the freedom of Cyprus from British rule, with the intention of then seeking a union with Greece. Consequently, the RAF base, Nicosia airport, and the RAF living quarters, all shared the same space within a barricaded, wired, and guarded perimeter. For activities outside the perimeter, the threat of terrorism had the effect of restricting family outside trips towards those safer areas of Cyprus dominated by the Turkish Cypriots. Consequently, much family time was spent on the beaches of predominantly Turkish Northern Cyprus, where the swimming, snorkelling and spear fishing in warm clear water was superb. Because of the EOKA threat, all forces personnel carried side arms when away from the compound. Beach parties usually involved several families travelling to, and spending time on, the same beach for the collective protection of the several armed parents then present, and all known to each other.

During that Cyprus holiday, Flap confessed to fulfilling another long-standing ambition. For having earlier in the year described to an associate how he had enviously watched the German fighter jets operating from a German autobahn towards the end of the war, he was surprised to be offered the opportunity to fly a Gloster Meteor twin engine jet himself. He explained that he had needed to submit to a high altitude decompression test before being allowed to fly, but he did not mention whether he was allowed to fly the Meteor solo, or whether he flew dual with another. The Gloster Meteor was the only Allied jet fighter that had seen active service towards the end of the last war.

Our second visit to Cyprus, in 1957, saw the addition of anti-aircraft guns dotted around the Nicosia base, together with a greater Army presence, all the new activity being on account of the Suez Canal crisis when Egypt's President Nasser nationalised the Canal.

When Flap collected us from the airport terminal that year, it was obvious that he had achieved another long-standing ambition. For following his vow made in the German countryside in 1945, he turned up in the first new car that he had ever owned, a brand-new Volkswagen Beetle. He had discovered that, as a member of the UK forces abroad, he could purchase the new car of his dreams exempt from UK Purchase Tax, as it then was before the advent of VAT. Then, after a certain period of time he was able to ship the car home as a pre-used vehicle, exempt from any tax on its entry into the UK. Even after paying carriage charges to ship the VW home to the UK, he stood to achieve a massive saving over the UK tax inclusive retail price.

The eventual expiry of Flap's period of service in Cyprus happened to coincide with a period of UK Government cutbacks, which included proposals for a reduction in the number of personnel across all the armed forces. To assist the proposed reduction of services personnel, various tempting incentives of monetary value were being offered to encourage early retirements. Flap, bored with the lack of excitement or further prospects of RAF promotion, therefore decided to put his name forward under a Government White Paper Scheme that offered compensation for "Voluntary Premature Retirement".

Following some discourse with the relevant Air Ministry Department, Flap received an offer of a retirement package dated 14 October 1957, as follows:

- Fifty-six days paid terminal leave, with effect from 18 January 1958 and terminating on the 15 March 1958 retirement date.
- The rank of Wing Commander during retirement.
- A pension of £650 per annum.
- A terminal grant of £1,950.
- The granting of an additional special capital payment under the Government White Paper Scheme, of an amount to be notified at a later date.

In order to put the retirement offer into some perspective with 1958 values, the UK overall average annual salary in 1958 was about £400 per year, and the cost of an average house less than £2,000.

Flap and Bernice did not hesitate to agree that Flap would accept the retirement terms then offered.

As the calendar tipped into the new year of 1958, Flap and Bernice had the first half of January to pack all family possessions for shipping back to the UK. That included arranging for one VW Beetle to be separately shipped home, whenever a cheap seaborne shipping space might become available.

Flap, with Bernice and my youngest brother, each with their personal luggage, were then flown home courtesy of the RAF by the middle of January 1958.

In the meantime, my grandmother, Flap's mother, had died. My brother and I had therefore been placed into boarding school facilities in order to continue our English home education.

Chapter 30

Off to Civvy Street

Halfway through completing the RAF retirement application, Flap and Bernice had realised that on arrival in the UK they would not immediately have a home of their own. Fortunately, Bernice's sister, who already had a husband and three children of her own at home, let herself be persuaded to shelter the Sherwoods for a while; "just to give them time to find a home of their own", her sister had said.

Flap had never had to apply for a job before, and still did not intend to. Instead, he had some vaguely romantic notion of buying a countryside home with accommodation for five persons, and enough land to create a small holding. The intention being to then grow enough of something or other that could be sold to supplement his pension income. However, during the family's absence from the UK, such property prices had escalated to the point that suitable properties were not that favourably priced to suit Flap and his available funds.

Eventually, having overstayed their welcome with Bernice's sister, the family moved on to stay with Bernice's parents at Allhallows on Sea, on the north coast of Kent. Here the search for a suitable property did not fare any better either. However, and fortuitously coincidental for Flap, whilst staying at Allhallows the lease on the buildings and land that my grandparents were using for their holiday business came up for renewal. Then, following failure to negotiate a satisfactory agreement for a new lease on their business premises, my grandparents decided that they too would also be looking for a new business proposition. It was therefore decided that the two families would pool their resources and continue to search elsewhere for a new joint business opportunity.

The business search soon turned towards the West Country, which then appeared to be the up and coming holiday destination of the day. So, towards the end of 1958 the joint households rented a large house in Fowey, Cornwall, for six months; just to enable them to be in the middle of their favoured search area.

By Easter of 1959, an established restaurant business had been secured as a going concern at nearby St. Austell, Cornwall. Both families moved into the ample living accommodation above the premises over a single weekend, and business carried on uninterrupted from the following Monday.

My grandfather was the person with the real business acumen, having presided over the chain of London butchers shops before the war; and latterly, run his seaside holiday business for ten years on the site of what was advertised as the nearest beach to London. Accordingly, it was he who compiled the restaurant menus, and chose the meat and produce required. Flap concentrated on sourcing the meat and produce as instructed, whilst running the bar and acquiring the bar stock required. In the meantime, my two brothers and I were also living at home above the restaurant. For that first summer, I was temporarily the restaurant dogsbody, peeling spuds, cutting chips, making ice cream etc. The restaurant's first year takings were amazing for the size of the premises, mainly because the kitchens and dining rooms of a nearby holiday camp burned down mid-season, leaving hundreds of unfed holiday makers to find their own daily lunches and dinners. An emergency voucher system ensured that all businesses providing meals to the holiday camp guests were then reimbursed directly by the holiday camp.

During the second year, I was encouraged to find work in a seasonal hotel in order to gain ideas and experience for eventual expansion of the business. However, on returning home after the summer season, I was offered a more satisfactory alternative employment in the Civil Service that I was pleased to accept, leaving only occasional evenings that I was able to assist in and around the restaurant when required.

The third year of the restaurant project proved to be disastrous, for my grandfather, master butcher and chief caterer, quite simply died in his sleep one night. That left Flap to work out a hurried redeployment of staff, and a hurried meat grilling and catering course for himself, as he endeavoured to fill my grandfather's shoes.

By working all God's hours Flap took control of the business. However, the restaurant project only survived from then, on a gentle decline, until 1963. Flap then threw in the towel, declared the business insolvent, and sold up. The family were soon re-housed locally, and Flap secured a job as a sales representative, selling speciality meats to local retail and catering establishments.

More relaxed, without the restaurant to run and with a straightforward daytime job, Flap found some spare time on his hands that allowed him to pursue other interests.

One evening, whilst talking to some of my brothers' young friends, Flap related how, during his childhood, he and his brother had copied the local children of Cape Town, South Africa, by making canoes out of bent corrugated roof sheets. When the youngsters laughed at the possibility of such a vessel floating, Flap took it as a challenge to prove the theory in practice. By the 1960s, corrugated plastic roof sheets had become freely available, and for lightness Flap decided to use those to demonstrate the construction method of a corrugated canoe. Such a vessel was duly produced, with some extra framework to stiffen the flexibility of the light plastic material. Young friends were then invited en masse to a local beach for a summer's evening trial and demonstration of the canoe.

There was much merriment and speculation about the canoe's chances as it was carried down the beach, and not a few strange looks! A cheer went up when Flap climbed aboard the canoe and paddled away from the beach without sinking. Then everyone else wanted a turn at paddling! Some of the youngsters speculated whether an outboard motor could be fitted to the canoe. So, after some slight modification to the canoe's stern, the assembled company returned to the beach next evening for an outboard powered demonstration. This second trial was not quite so successful, as the outboard motor was far too powerful for the shape of the canoe's slight frame, and considerable merriment ensued as the canoe attempted to turn itself into a diving submarine.

A further suggestion to try adding a sail was the next modification project, and over the following couple of weeks, Flap added a centre board, plus mast and rigging to the canoe. He then painted it red, before cobbling together some sails made of discarded material from someone's shed. The sailing trial was a triumph and stimulated much interest from some of the youngsters about the how, and the why, of the general techniques of sailing, such that they all wanted to try and sail the canoe themselves.

Such was the interest in sailing generated by the cobbled together canoe and sails, that several of the youngsters, including one of my own brothers, soon made enquiries about joining the nearby sailing club at Carlyon Bay, St. Austell. When Flap heard what was going on, he ventured to make enquiries of the sailing club as well. The net outcome was that the membership of the sailing club suddenly increased quite dramatically.

Initially, when Flap and the youngsters had joined the Carlyon Bay Sailing Club, they gained sailing experience by crewing for other boat owners. However, it was not long before Flap and my youngest brother decided that they would like to own their own sailing boat. Flap had developed a liking for sailing catamarans in particular, probably because of the speed that they could attain whilst very nearly "flying" over the surface of the water. They soon came across an advert for a dilapidated Dart Catamaran, advertised as suitable for renovation, and being offered for sale at Falmouth, Cornwall. Flap drove down to Falmouth to inspect the Dart and found that it did not have a serviceable road trailer. Also, and whilst having some rigging in place, it did not have any serviceable sails. Having negotiated a suitably low price for what was not far short of being a wreck, and not being able to tow the wreck home for lack of a trailer, Flap decided that he would borrow a couple of outboard motors. Then, with the help of my youngest brother, they would power the wreck back along the coast to St. Austell. On the appointed day, a friend drove Flap, my brother, two outboard motors, a supply of fuel and a couple of life jackets down to Falmouth. Family and friends then spent most of that day on the St. Austell beach awaiting their first sighting of the wreck. It was late afternoon, when my mother and some of the friends were beginning to get jittery about the enterprise, before the dilapidated Catamaran finally appeared in St. Austell Bay. Once hauled up the beach on a borrowed trailer, the catamaran was chained and padlocked to a stout fir tree. As if anyone would have wanted to steal such a wreck anyway! Flap was soon able to locate a trailer that he suitably modified to fit the catamaran, which was then towed home to enable Kriegie style renovation works to commence in the back yard.

Whilst Flap, together with my brothers and friends, were off sailing, I had preferred to put my efforts towards funding renovation and extension of an old wreck of a cottage, with a view to turning it into a home in preparation for getting married in 1964. Then, in early 1965, I had the opportunity to change employment, and I became a local representative for an insurance company.

Eventually, another vacancy occurred with the same insurance company and, with my encouragement, Flap was able to secure that position for himself. In the meantime, I had managed to achieve a slightly senior position in that company, which then enabled Flap and I to spend some time with each other whilst achieving a mutually beneficial working relationship for the same company.

Flap's appointment with the same company as myself suited me well, for during the years that I had spent living with my paternal grandmother, I had met great uncles, great aunts, cousins and family friends who, whilst making glowing references to Flap's wartime exploits, had collectively over time left me in possession of quantities of well-preserved wartime newspaper cuttings, photographs, magazine clippings, official booklets and books, all relevant to Flap's life and wartime exploits. Those papers were all carefully preserved by me, initially for my own immediate interest, but also in earlier times to feed the interest and curiosity of my young school friends. Most schoolboys in the late 1940s and early 1950s were crazy about anything concerning aeroplanes, and all avidly read war comics depicting slickly named flying heroes and air aces. My contemporaries were therefore amused to know that my father was a real live pilot, who had flown a Lancaster, whilst also being endowed with the slick and well published nickname of "Flap".

It was very clear that my grandmother's family were collectively very proud of Flap and his achievements but, particularly in my grandmother's case, rather outspoken about the citations and awards made to the partaking aircrews following the Augsburg Raid. In particular, the strange circumstances under which Flap, her son, was initially recommended for the award of a Victoria Cross, which was later reduced to the award of a Distinguished Service Order, when it was later discovered that he was alive.

However, it was clear to me that some of my accumulated Flap related paper collection did need further explanation. Therefore, whilst working with Flap, and particularly when driving together between our homes and various mutual business calls, I was able to take advantage of some ideal opportunities to gently interrogate him for further information and explanations regarding some of his renown wartime experiences. He was often hard work to question, for he never wished to show any great pride in the achievements that other people felt that he should definitely be very proud of. He had never willingly volunteered information about the war years without being prompted, and twenty-five years after the war's end, he still seemed to be concealing a massive disappointment over the post war national failure to recognise the wartime sacrifices of Bomber Command crews on a par with other branches of the armed forces.

Post war, the British government and many people of this country had appeared to be ashamed of certain deeds that had been performed by Bomber Command, especially in respect of the severe blanket bombing of German cities towards the end of the war by the huge fleets of Allied aircraft that Flap and the Kriegies had observed overhead when crossing the German countryside on the Long March of the Kriegies. Those deeds had, after all, been performed at the behest of the British Government and the leaders of the other allied countries, and just as explicitly at the behest of its very own peoples declared wishes to hasten an end to the war.

However, in addition to the British people's simple wishes to end the war, there were additional more pressing needs for a hasty end to hostilities, for Allied intelligence had realised that Hitler was depending upon his German scientists and engineers to enable him to reverse the considerable territorial gains that the Allies had made by early 1945. Because, thinking that he was in with a chance, Hitler had already ordered development of several frightening new weapons; those included new ballistic missile styled successors to the successful V1 and V2 rockets, radar guided missiles, remotely guided bombs, rocket assisted artillery, and massive guns that were designed to reach London from the French coast; and all together with new fast jet bomber and fighter aircraft, of which some projects were already well under construction in expectation of an early delivery to Hitler's forces.

So, whilst Flap and thousands of Kriegies were being marched and transported across Germany in early 1945, Hitler was indeed considering the sinister option of, one way or another, using the thousands of Kriegies in Nazi hands as bargaining chips, to maybe delay the end of the war just sufficiently long enough to allow his engineers and scientists to catch up with his plans for a fight back.

The records of Flap's operational flying with 144 and 97 Squadron respectively, evidence that he was never dispatched on missions to specifically target enemy civilians. However, if he had been ordered so to do, then I am quite sure that he would have carried out those orders; for carrying out the orders of your commanders on behalf of the government of the country is what members of the armed forces are required to do.

In any case, it should be remembered that it was Germany that first ventured to bomb civilian targets during the First World War, when their Zeppelin airships and early Gotha bomber aircraft were sent to indiscriminately bomb the civilians of London and various coastal towns of eastern England. Consequentially therefore, the German Luftwaffe only hesitated briefly before again bombing British civilian targets in the build up to the Battle of Britain.

As a further thought, individual bombing raids carried out by neither side during the European Theatre of the Second World War bear any comparison to the immediate and consequentially huge loss of life resulting from the two atomic bombing attacks carried out by the United States against the Japanese cities of Hiroshima and Nagasaki respectively during August 1945. Those two raids, which, within two or three days, together caused approximately one hundred and twenty thousand immediate deaths, soon brought about a very prompt end to the Japanese war that must have saved a far greater total of lives on both sides overall, than if the Japanese war had continued to be slogged out in a conventional manner.

After the war's end, it was soon realised that, out of a total of 125,000 Bomber Command Aircrew, 55,573 were killed, 8,403 were wounded, and 9,838 were taken prisoner of war. By anybody's reckoning that was more than half of the aircrew that were killed or wounded, and it was totally beyond Flap's comprehension as to how that could be ignored.

By the late sixties, Flap had been elected as Commodore of the Carlyon Bay Sailing Club, St. Austell. Soon thereafter, the club fell into disfavour with its clubhouse landlords, and it became necessary to find alternative accommodation for the club. Members soon reported back that there were suitable buildings for their purposes beside the disused landlocked harbour at Pentewan, St. Austell, with suitable access direct to the sea and beach. Flap approached the landowner with a successful proposition for rental of the required space and was himself soon elected to be the founding Commodore of the new Pentewan Sands Sailing Club (PSSC), which remains on the same site at Pentewan to this day.

For Flap, his need for gainful employment gradually became secondary to his need to immerse himself in the pleasure of sailing and its associated social activities. Sailing became the very mainstay of his continued existence, whilst his insurance job, where he was well liked by all his clients, became only a tolerated necessity to supplement his RAF pension and the funding of his sailing hobby.

I was eventually very pleased that I had used my mutual working relationship with Flap to the utmost, in order to obtain so many opportunities to ply him for information on family history and his war service, for in the summer of 1972, Flap became unwell. An urgent medical investigation soon established that he had fallen victim to the big "C", with a terminal diagnosis. He died on 8 February 1973, just five weeks short of his fifty-fifth birthday.

Flap's insurance clients, who only knew him as a very mild-mannered man, and never as Flap, were amazed when his obituary made mention of his wartime exploits. For, as already established, Flap did not usually speak of his war service to other people. He had never mentioned it to any of his clients that I was aware of, and none of them would ever have noticed a single little clue that was right under their noses every winter. For during the exceptionally cold English winter of 1962/63 and having appreciated the way his RAF greatcoat had protected him so well during the Long March across Germany during the icy winter of 1945, Flap had arranged for an unused RAF blue-grey greatcoat, that was already in his possession, to be remodelled for him, all in the style of a very smart double-breasted mid-length car coat, with mid-brown real leather buttons replacing those of the RAF. That converted greatcoat had then lasted him for the rest of his life!

Following Flap's funeral and subsequent cremation, there was some considerable debate as to whether his ashes should be claimed by the air in respect of his past devotion to flying or claimed by the sea for his more recent devotion to sailing. Eventually, in the absence of any positive decision by Bernice, Flap's ashes were scattered to the four winds in anticipation of those winds then deciding the unknown resting places of those remains, in a similar fashion to the unknown resting places of the remains of so many of the RAF aircrews that Flap had been associated with during the war.

Bernice then survived Flap by just over a further ten years, until an unexpected heart attack claimed her on 12 March 1983. Her ashes were then scattered in the same fashion, and in the same place.

By some strange coincidence, the new insurance company employee appointed to replace Flap also turned out to be an ex-RAF Boston boy of similar age, and with a keen interest in Bomber Command history. He, whilst also reluctant to talk very freely of his own wartime experiences, was however, always pleased to engage with any interest in Flap's history. Often when I was working with Flap's successor, he would turn the conversation around to the subject of Flap's exploits. Even when Boston boy himself had in turn long retired and moved far away from my home area, he habitually forwarded any items of interest that he had discovered about Flap and his associates, or of wartime Bomber Command interest in general. Such welcome correspondence continued until, in turn, a relative of Boston boy eventually notified me of his death also.

THE END

Last Words

I sincerely hope that you are reading this page because Flap's story has managed to hold your attention to the very end, and possibly even left you with a thirst for more!

If you have enjoyed your read and you do have a thirst for more information, then I would suggest that you log on specifically to a Google on-line search bar and type in the words "U-Tube film of Augsburg Raid". That search should bring up a variable full screen list of items that should be of interest to you. In October 2019, that list was showing as follows:

- Jack Currie's 1989 BBC TV Documentary on the Augsburg Raid (30 min's). Currie himself having been a Second World War bomber pilot.
- Flight Lieutenant Patrick Dorehill's 2012 BBC TV Interview. Squadron Leader Dorehill was Squadron Leader John Nettleton's co-pilot during the Augsburg Raid. Patrick Dorehill describes how being off the designated course over France, on the way to Augsburg, led to 44 Squadron's encounter with German fighter aircraft (20 min's).
- Heroes of Augsburg – Pathe News, 1942 vintage newsreel (2 min's).
- Augsburg crew interviews – Movietone – 1942 newsreel (2 min's).
- The obituary of Wing Commander David Penman. (Circa 8 December 2004) who, on the morning after the Augsburg Raid, went to visit Flap's wife Bernice Sherwood, to inform her of Flap's loss over Augsburg.

Famous Raids

Within this book, I have made mention of the 17 April 1942 Augsburg Raid as being the first of what are generally accepted to be RAF Bomber Command's twelve most famous raids. For your interest, all of those raids are listed herewith in chronological order, as follows:

- MAN Diesel Engine Works, Augsburg, 17 April 1942.
- The first thousand bomber raid from 30 to 31 May 1942.
- Le Creusot, 17 October 1942.
- Dambusters, 21 March 1943.
- Hamburg, 28 July 1943.
- Peenemunde, 17/18 August 1943.
- Amiens Prison, 18 February 1944.
- Saumur Tunnel, 9 June 1944.
- Precision attack on Gestapo HQ Aarhus, Denmark, 31 October 1944.
- Tirpitz, 12 November 1944.
- Dresden, February 1945.
- Grand Slam Raids, March 1945 onwards.

If you are keen to seek out information on any of the above raids, an on-line search naming any of the above titles in association with RAF Bomber Command should produce a useful result to read.

Bibliography

The Augsburg Raid – Jack Currie.
Avro Manchester – Robert Kirby.
Lancaster at War – Mike Garbett & Brian Goulding.
The Hardest Victory – Denis Richards.
No.5 Bomber Group RAF – W.J. Lawrence.
Stalag Luft III – Arthur Durand.
Escape from Germany – Aidan Crawley.

Operation Margin, Order 143 – AIR 16/757 National Archives.
106 Sq. Operational Record Book – AIR 27/831 National Archives.
144 Sq. Operational Record Book – AIR 27/980 National Archives.
97 Sq. Operational Record Book – AIR 27/766 National Archives.
97 Sq. General Record Book – AIR 27/769 National Archives.
Bomber Command Continues – HM Stationery Office – 1942.

Errors And Omissions

Whilst carrying out research, both before and during the writing of this book, I have endeavoured to the best of my ability to interpret all of the information received into my hands as accurately as possible. To assist me, information has arisen from various multiple sources, sometimes second or third hand, some written, some printed, some spoken, and of course some from technological media sources. Wherever possible I have then sought to corroborate each item of information from more than one source before accepting it as a hard fact.

If you do happen across any glaring errors that I may have made, then you would be welcome to notify them to the following dedicated email address: Flapsherwood@aol.com. However, at my own fast advancing age, I am afraid that I cannot undertake to guarantee you the courtesy of a reply at any particular time.

Index

Accelerated aircrew expansion, 65
Aircraft:
  Anson, Avro, multi-use & trainer, 20
  Battle, Fairey, light bomber, 22, 28
  Blenheim, Bristol, light bomber, 20, 23, 41
  Boston, Douglas USA, Fighter/bomber, 86
  Defiant, Boulton Paul, night fighter, 61
  Dragon Rapide, De Havilland, flying Classroom, 17
  Fury, Hawker, bi-plane fighter, 8
  Halifax, Handley Page, heavy bomber, 49–50, 69–72, 74
  Hampden, Handley Page, medium bomber, 19, 20–4, 27, 31–3, 36–40, 43–6, 49, 63–4, 68
  Hart, Hawker, bi-plane light bomber/trainer, 8
  Hermes, Handley Page, passenger transport, 199
  Hind, Hawker, bi-plane light bomber, 8
  Lancaster, Avro, heavy bomber, 76–8
    Faults, 80
    Improvements, 81
  Manchester, Avro, heavy bomber, 46, 48, 76
    Faults & problems, 50–1
  Manchester Mark 3, Avro, heavy Bomber, 76
  Messerschmitt (ME) 109, Luftwaffe fighter aircraft, 90
  Meteor, Gloster, jet fighter, 200
  Mosquito, De Havilland, 192
  Stirling, Short, heavy bomber and glider tug, 70
  Supermarine Spitfire, Vickers, fighter, 16
  Wellesley, Vickers Armstrong, medium bomber, 12
  Wellington, Vickers Armstrong, medium bomber, 16, 20, 24, 196
  Whitley, Armstrong Whitworth, medium bomber, 20
Aircraft engines:
  Bristol Hercules, 48
  Rolls-Royce Merlin, 48
  Rolls-Royce Peregrine, 48
  Rolls-Royce Vulture, 47–9, 51, 56, 59–60, 81
Airfields and RAF Stations:
  Coningsby, 52–7, 60, 73, 76, 78–80
  Cosford, 185
  Cottesmore, 188
  Finningley, 12, 14–15, 18–19, 31–2
  Handforth, 189, 192
  Hemswell, 23, 33, 36
  Little Rissington, 185–6
  Moreton-in-Marsh, 198–9
  Nicosia, Cyprus, 199–200
  North Coates, 9–10, 15, 26
  Shawbury, 196–7
  Swinderby, 63
  Upper Heyford, 26–7
  Waddington, 49–52, 57, 76, 88, 96, 99, 103
  West Raynham, 40
  Wilmslow, 189–92, 194–6
Air Force Squadrons:
  44: 76, 80–2, 85–6, 88–93, 102–103, 131
  61: 38
  76b: 11–13, 15–20, 26
  97: 51–60, 63–5, 69, 71–6, 78–82, 86, 88–93, 96–7, 103, 113
  106: 31–2, 64
  144: 2, 23, 32–3, 39, 45, 52, 208

207: 45, 48–52, 57–8
455: 63
Air Head Quarters, Nicosia, 199
Air Ministry, 6–7, 47–50, 99–101, 115, 199, 201
Air Observation (Navigational) School, 20–1, 23
Air Services Training Ltd (AST), Ansty, 6–7
Allhallows on Sea, Kent, 195, 203
America, 67, 82–3, 138, 158–160
  see also USA and United States
American Forces Administrative Unit, 116
Augsburg, Germany, 87, 89, 91–104, 116, 118, 130–2
Augsburg Raid, 80–104
Australia, 18, 63

Balsdon, Wing Commander D.F., 69, 71–3, 75
Barbed Wire Psychosis, 156
Barge fleet accumulations, 42
Barnes Wallace, 12
Battle of Britain, 39, 42–3, 209
Beam Approach Training, 57
Beaumont le Roger, France, 103
Berger, Lieutenant General Gottlob, 194
Berlin, 39, 40, 43–4, 57–9, 65, 107, 174
Bernice, Motor Cruiser, 13
Black market, 173
Blakeman, Flying Officer H.S., 65
Bomber Command HQ, High Wycombe, 85
Bordeaux, 42, 45
Borrowed Hampdens, 97 Sqd, 64
Boulogne, France, 42, 60, 62
Bremen, Germany, 169–71, 174–5
Bremen, Shipyards, 57
Brest, 39, 45, 51, 67, 69–70, 74–5, 77–9
British Commonwealth, 152
British Commonwealth Air Training Plan, 25
British Empire Air Training Agreement, 25
British Expeditionary Force, 21, 28–9
British Military War Crimes Court, 192
British Vice Consulate, 1

Buckley, Lieutenant Commander James, 120–1
Bushell, Sqduadron Leader Roger, 120–1, 127, 137, 151, 154–5
Butt Report, 65

Calais, 42, 84
Cambria (CS), Eastern Telegraph Cable Ship, 1
Cape Town, South Africa, 2–3
Carlyon Bay Sailing Club, 206, 209
Central Navigation and Control School (CNCS), 196–7
Centre compound, 108
Ceylon Tea, 160, 186
Cheltenham, 159–60, 185–6, 189–90
Chemnitz, 174
Chief ground instructor, 198
Churchill, Winston, 28, 54, 79, 83, 189
Circus Raids, 68–9
Civil Flying School, Ansty, Coventry, 7
Civil Service, 204
Coastal Command, 42–3, 79
Codner, Second Lieutenant Michael, 139
Collier, Wing Commander John, 80, 82, 85, 100
Cologne, 113
Commonwealth Air Training Plan, 25
Continental Channel Ports, 41
Corrugated canoes, 3, 205
Cox, Sergeant Arthur, 130
Currie, Sgt H., 110
Cyprus, 197, 199–201
  see also Nicosia, Cyprus

D-Day, 157
Dambusters Raid, 12
Dart Catamaran, 206
Daylight raid on German cruisers, 97 Sqd, 67–75
Debut raid on Kiel docks, 97 Sqd, 58
Declaration of war on Germany, 20
Deverill, Flying Officer, 89, 95
Dick Turpin, 190
Dimwitz, 111–12, 142–3, 166–7, 170, 179
Directive to destroy the German cruisers, 54

Index 217

Distinguished Flying Cross (DFC), 52, 75, 77, 110, 113
Distinguished Service Order (DSO), 101, 116, 207
Dives sur Mer, 86, 103
Dortmund-Emms Canal, Germany, 38–9
Dresden, Germany, 174, 181, 213
Dugdale, Squadron Leader J., 76
Dunkirk, 29–30, 66

Early bombing raids, 23–4
East compound, 108–12, 118–27, 134–9,168–9
Eastern Telegraph Co., 1
Egypt, *see also* Port Tawfik, 1–2, 18, 33, 200
Eisenhower, General Dwight, 162
Elbe, River, 178, 180
EOKA, 200
Escape Committee, 120, 127–8, 134, 137–9, 142–6, 157–8
Evereux, France, 103
Expectant parents, 60

Ferrets, 111–12, 120–1, 127–9, 133, 135–8, 142–3, 148–50
First thousand bomber RAF raid, 112–13
First tour of operations, 144 Sqd, 33–46
First World War, 1–2, 6, 15, 107, 111, 179, 209
Flap, origin of name, 26
Flight Magazine, 15–16
Flying Instruction School No.7, 188
Flying Training School No11, 7–8, 22
Formation Flying Skills, 81
Fowey, Cornwall, UK, 203
France, 20–3, 28–31, 84, 86, 91–2, 102–103
    see also Boulogne & Normandy
French, Flight Lieutenant D.J., 63
Friedrichshafen, 91
Friedwaldau, Germany, 165–6
Friesian Islands, 79

Gain, Lieutenant Commander Kenneth E., RNVR, 5
Garwell, Flying Officer A.J., 90–2

Gas Defence Course, 15
Gefangennummer, 385
German-French Armistice, 31
German Reich, 105
German U-boat, 54, 67, 83
Gestapo, 121, 148–9, 151–4, 157–8, 179, 187, 192–3
Gibraltar, 197
Glemnitz, Sgt Major Hermann, 111–12, 142–3, 166–7, 170, 179
Gneisenau, German cruiser, 55, 67, 69, 77–9
Goon Boxes, 108, 138
Government White Paper Scheme, 201
Great Escape, 146, 153–5, 187, 193
Grundstein, Germany, 170

Haines, Group Captain H.A., 100
Hallows, Flight Lieutenant B.R.W., 89, 93–4, 101
Hamburg, 43, 178, 180, 192, 213
Hampden crash, 37–8
Handforth, 189
Harris, Air Marshall A.T., 100
Harrison, Warrant Officer, 88
Heligoland Bight, Germany, 23
Hepburn, Flying Officer Donald, 89
Himmler, Heinrich, 151, 155
Hiroshima & Nagasaki, 209
Hitler, Adolf, 151

International Red Cross, 106, 115–16, 119

Kiel, Germany, 54–5
Kingston, Jamaica, 4
Kingston upon Thames, Greater London, 3–5, 13–14
Kriegie, 109
Kriegie Exodus, 184
Kriegies prepare to travel, 163
Kynock, Wing Commander J.H., 74

Lady Denison Pender, Cable Ship, 4
Lake Ammersee, 86
Lake Constance, 86
Lease Lend Agreement, 160
Le Havre, 42

Leippa, Germany, 166
Leipzig, 39, 74
Lilac Cottage, Sonning, 116, 118, 159
Lincolnshire, UK, 9–11, 82, 87, 107
Lindeiner, Colonel Friedrich-Wilhelm Von, 148
London Gazette, 7, 15, 18, 77, 116
Long March Home, The, 162–83
Lorenz, 35
Lubeck, 121, 181
Ludwigshafen, 104
Luft gangsters, 181
Lundy Island rendezvous, 69
Luneburg Heath, 175, 184

Mackid, Flight Lieutenant J.G., 69, 71, 75, 77–8, 113
Maginot Line, France, 21–2
Maintenance Unit 61, 192–3
MAN, Diesel Engine Works, Augsburg, 83
Manchester Road, Wilmslow, 190
Martin's School of Navigation, Shoreham, 17
Matoya, Motor Yacht, 13, 17, 29, 195
Merlin Engines, 48–50, 76, 81, 88, 91, 95, 198
Middle East Royal Air Force, 20
Mini armada over Brest, 70
Montgo Mountain, Spain, 197
Montgomery, Field Marshal, 184
Morant Cay, Jamaica, 4
Muskau, Germany, 167–9
Mycock, Warrant Officer T.J., 89, 95, 101, 118

Navigational Aids, 17, 23, 25
Nettleton, Squadron Leader John, 84, 90–2, 96, 99, 131
Newborough, British steamship, 3–4
Nickels, 34
Nicosia, Cyprus, 199–200
Normandy, France, 157
Norseman, Cable Ship, 3–4
North Compound, 120–39, 141, 146, 148, 150–8, 162–4, 168–70
see also Escape Committee
see also Great Escape
see also Tunnels Tom, Dick and Harry
Nunn, Flight Lieutenant J.L., 109–11, 154

Officer Training Corps (OTC), 6
Oflag XX1B, 120
Operation Exodus, 184
Operation Margin to Augsburg, Order No.143, 83
see also Augsburg raid
Operational Training Unit No.16, 19
Operational Training Units (OTUs), 25
Ostend, 42

Penman, Flight Lieutenant D.J., 82, 84–5, 99, 101, 118
Pentewan Sands Sailing Club (PSSC), 209
Personnel Reception Centre, 185
Pertwee, Captain Roger Edward, Suez Pilot, 1
Petwood Hotel, 79
Philpot, Flight Lieutenant Oliver, 139
Phoney War, 21–2, 24, 34
Picard, Flight Lieutenant Henri, 122–3, 152, 154, 187
Port Tawfik, Egypt, 2
Postal censors, Luft 3, 117
POW D.I.Y. skills, 121
Prinz Eugen, German cruiser, 69

Razzles, 35
Red Cross, 106, 111–12, 115–16, 119, 121–2, 129–30, 133, 135, 141–3, 163–4, 168, 170, 173, 177–8, 180–2, 193
Reconnaissance, 23, 39, 41–2, 69–70, 83–4, 182
Retirement package, 201
River Lech, Bavaria, 86
Rodley, Flying Officer E.E., (Rod), 82, 88, 94
Roosevelt, President, USA, 83
Royal Air Force, 6, 8, 10, 12, 30, 39, 42, 79, 86, 114, 152
Royal Australian Air Force, 63
Royal Navy, 5, 30–1, 79
Russian advance towards Luft III, 162

Index   219

St. Austell, Cornwall, UK, 204–206, 209
St. Elmo's Fire, 58
St. Eval, 79
St. Nazaire, 42, 45
Sagan, 107, 122, 139–40, 159, 162, 168, 174
Sandford, Flight Lieutenant R., 85
Scarlet Fever, 106
Scharnhorst, German cruiser, 55, 67, 69, 77–9
Selsey Bill, 82, 89
Sens, S.E. of Paris, 86, 91, 103–104
Shawbury, 196–7
Sherwood, Anthony D. (Tony), 160
Sherwood, Commodore Capt. Charles A., Master Mariner, 1, 4
Sherwood, Wing Commander John Seymour, 1, 99, 115
   Promotional history:
      1936, Pilot Officer (31.8.36), 7
      1939, Flying Officer (31.1.39), 8
      1940, Flight Lieutenant (3.9.40), 40
      1941, Squadron Leader (30.6.41), 63
      1945, Wing Commander (22.10.45), 189
      1950, Squadron Leader (15.3.50), 196
      1958, Wing Commander retired (15.3.58), 201
Sherwood, Mrs Violet Anna Rose, 1
Simba (the dog), 18, 32–3, 54, 115–17
Singapore, 4
Sonning on Thames, Berkshire, 17, 29, 43, 52–3, 116, 159, 190
South Africa, 25
   see also Cape Town
Spanish Civil War, 23
Sparrow Fart, 10–11, 27, 63, 107, 111, 179, 181
Spremberg, Germany, 169–71
Stalag Luft III, 107, 109, 111, 113, 115–21, 123, 125, 130, 140, 148, 150, 153, 155–6, 162–4, 168, 171, 180–1, 187, 192–3
   see also Stammlager Luft III
   Centre Compound, 108
   East Compound, 107–109, 111–12, 118–20, 122, 124–7 134–6, 139, 154, 168–9

   see also Wooden Horse Escape
   North Compound, 120–39, 141, 146, 148, 150–8, 162–4, 168–70
   see also Escape Committee, Great Escape, Tunnels Tom, Dick and Harry
Stammlager Luft III, main camp for aircrew, 107
Standard Nine Avon, 1932 Coupe, 13–14
Standard saloon car, 198
Stettin, Germany, 40
Stokes, Pilot Officer N.G., 72–4
Suez Canal, 1–2
Suez Canal crisis, 200

Tarmstedt, Germany, 171, 173–6
Tattershall Thorpe, 79
Temporary command of 97 Sqd, 74
Tom, Dick & Harry, 127–58
Treaty of Versailles, 2, 6, 21
Trenchard, Viscount Marshal of the Royal Air Force, Hugh, 102
Tunnels, Tom, Dick and Harry, 127–58
Turpins, Sonning on Thames, 17, 116, 190, 195

United States, 25, 82, 121, 160, 209
USA, 41, 67, 82, 93, 160
   see also America

Vegetables, 35, 38–9
Victoria Cross, 99–100, 116, 207
Victory in Europe Day, 184
Villers-sur-Mer, 103
Volkswagen Beetle, 183, 201–202

Wainfleet bombing range, 81
Webb, Pilot Officer A.T., 88
Wedding at Sonning, 52
Wellington crash, 197
West Wittering, 192–3
Williams, Flight Lieutenant Eric, 134, 139
Williams, Sergeant K., 71
Wilmslow, 190–6
Women's Royal Voluntary Service (WRVS), 159
Wooden Horse, 134–6, 139–40, 154